PRAISE FOR WHISPERING BACK

This was Adam Goodfellow and Nicole Golding's first book, and is available from www.whisperingback.co.uk.

'This book is the chronicle of a journey into knowledge…This is no wishy-washy idealistic sugar-food, but the strong story of two intelligent and committed young people. It kept me awake all night.'

British Dressage magazine

'Adam and Nicole remind us of the fundamental reason for being involved with horses…this journey is an inspiration. You may learn a lot about horses reading this book, but you will also learn about persistence and a clear intention, valuable lessons, whatever your life's journey may be.'

Tina Sederholm, author of *Words of a Horseman: The Life and Teachings of Lars Sederholm*

'Made me cry…a book to tie knots in many horse owners' heartstrings, as well as educating us with much-needed insight.'

Fiona Walker, author of *Kiss Chase* and *French Connection*

'Full of larger than life characters and eccentric tales. Great reading!'

Horse and Rider magazine

Your book is one of the most inspiring stories I have read in a long time. The sense of spiritual connection you engender with the horses you work with is awe-inspiring. The world is in great need of people who will follow their passion and dreams in the way you two have. Thank you for such a lovely ray of sunshine.

Merren McKay, New Zealand

I would just like to say how much I've enjoyed reading your book. I can say in all honesty that it's one of the best non-fiction books I've ever read. I've both laughed and cried on my way through it and I found myself 'there' with you and the horses.

Ma... tershire

Just wanted to let you know how much I enjoyed reading your book. I finished it in two days, just couldn't put it down. Your book has rekindled the spark.

Gillian Kalgoorlie, Western Australia

I have just finished your book "Whispering Back" and am left with tears in my eyes and a swelling in my heart. I just wish to say a huge "thank you" for your splendid work on horses and humans.

Hanne Bruun, Denmark

I just want to thank you for a lovely book. I have learned so much. Now I know that my horse was a teacher himself and I was many times the pupil !!!!

Ruline Greeff, South Africa

Thank you for allowing me an insight into the lives of these magnificent, magical beings by writing your book.

Kim Rudolph, Darwin, Australia

I laughed, cried (especially hard when Misty finally let you on her off-side) and clenched my teeth while reading it. I just couldn't put it down!

Amelia O'Connor, Western Cape, South Africa

It's been a long long time since I cried and laughed at the same time through reading a book - yours is just fantastic and so moving. Honestly, I really didn't want to put it down.

Raina Parker, Surrey, UK

I learnt so much from each page and found it hard to carry on with the mundane everyday stuff and just wanted to keep on reading about your amazing life and achievements. You made me laugh out loud with your wit and humour. It is a superb book.

Linda Martin, UK

Born to WHISPER

NICOLE GOLDING

ADAM GOODFELLOW

WP Whispering Publications

Born to
WHISPER
by
Nicole Golding and Adam Goodfellow

ISBN: 978-0-9564440-0-4

Published by Nicole Golding and Adam Goodfellow
in conjunction with Writersworld Ltd

Copy edited by Brian Stanton and Rosie Dickens

Cover Design by Charles Leveroni and Alistair Nash

Printed and bound by
www.printondemand-worldwide.com

www.writersworld.co.uk
WRITERSWORLD
2 Bear Close
Woodstock
Oxfordshire
OX20 1JX
England

This book is dedicated to our children.

YOU ARE NOT ALONE

(Hills/Goodfellow)

I've run all my life from things that I can't explain
The voice in my head is screaming at me again
Follow your heart cause you cannot steal the life
That you want. What is real?

You are not alone from this feeling of fear
You are not alone cause I got you right here

I'm turning to you for something that's almost clear
The dream of a dream of ghosts made of air
The dust's in my eyes I'm finding my way
With all the brand new the words I say

You are not alone from this feeling of fear
You are not alone cause I got you right here

Follow your heart cause you cannot steal the life
That you want. What is real?
We're searching for truth we're holding the darkness back
Not making the past the future

I watch you, I watch you, I'm watching over you

©2000 SCSI

Contents

Acknowledgements

There are many people who have made contributions to this book in one way or another, and to whom we owe thanks.

Without Jeannine Golding, who supports us immeasurably, we would not be able to teach our clinics, and therefore pay the rent. We would not be nearly so well nourished either. Jeannine, you are a most amazing person in so many ways, fully the equal of Monty Roberts in what you have overcome and achieved in your life. Thank you also for copy editing the text.

Lynn Goodfellow and Derek Partridge helped us establish ourselves as horse trainers, with vital financial, emotional and moral support, and continue to do so. We can't tell you what it means to know that we have you behind us.

We are grateful to our editor Brian Stanton, Charles Leveroni who designed the cover, and Graham Cook, at www.writersworld.co.uk. Rosie Dickens edited this book twice and her expertise has been instrumental in putting it in your hands. Matthew Parker gave useful advice, and prompted us to become authors in the first place. Tim Hills and Ian Stone encouraged us to take the plunge and publish it without the assistance of a publishing house. Alistair Nash very generously helped to design the cover, for nothing else but our thanks.

Jo and Derek Clark, Annabelle Harling, Chris Isaacs, Trevor Jones, Lindsay Cotterell, Maggie McDonnell, Venetia Kent, Neil Nimmo, Steve King, Kelly Marks, Claire Green, Chris Brandt, Craig Stevens, Mary Wanless, the anonymous owners of the King, Matt Savory, Donna and Dennis Hall reviewed and assisted in the writing and editing of various sections and provided photos. Susy Escuder wrote extensive notes to assist in writing about her horse, but *The Horse Who Thought He Was A Croc* is sadly not included, even though he would have been the perfect foil for *The Horse Who Thought He Was A Rock*. Dear friends, your help and support has been so important.

Over ten years we have had many working pupils and helpers. All have contributed to our sanity and enabled us both to work and to write. Jo Lindsey, Brian Mordensen, Tim Mullan, Rachael Bartlett, Kelly Brotherhood, Rebecah Cleblad-Earl and especially, Joana Rotland have been very important in creating this book. We owe you a great deal of thanks.

Tara Economakis, Liz Nightingale, Sarah Ifill and Meg Miskin-Garside, you know how important you have been to our story, and to the welfare of so many other big and little people.

Members of Adam's band SCSI, including Tim Hills, Matt Savory, Andy Hughes, Siom Messenger, Martin Van Dyke and also Dave Saunders, continue to work tirelessly to desensitise the horses to drums, guitars and other loud noises. The feedback keeps Adam less insane than he otherwise might be. Thanks also to our landlords, Henry and Susie Robinson and family, for having such poor hearing, thick walls in your house, or such a tolerant attitude to pounding beats. You have been so supportive, over more than a decade, of our efforts to make Moor Wood Stables a haven in this crazy world, both for horses and people. Thanks for the great photo too, Henry. How did you pick that moment when he was clean, dressed, and posing so perfectly?

Many thanks to Simon Palmer at www.into-the-lens.com for providing some wonderful photos, and touching up others. Thanks also to Paul Thompson for several photos We are so grateful to Louise Drummond, Kelly's PA, for always being ready to help with numerous unreasonable last-minute demands.

Without Meg Jackson and Tracy Morris, it's hard to imagine getting through a week, let alone writing a book. Having friends like you around is what makes life worth living.

Without Monty Roberts, or Kelly Marks, we would not have a story to tell. Your inspiration and guidance have left a permanent mark not only on us, but on horsemanship the world over.

Nicole Golding and Adam Goodfellow,
December 2009

xv

Note

Monty Roberts®, Join-Up® and Dually™ are service marks, trademarks, and/or trade dress of Monty and Pat Roberts, Inc.

All events described in this book are true, to the best of our recollection. Some names have been changed.

Foreword
BY KELLY MARKS

I first met Nicole in 1996 when I was teaching the second ever ten-week course in the concepts of Monty Roberts. An enthusiastic and conscientious student, Nicole made an impression from the very first day. I was fairly new to teaching at the time and Nicole helped me develop as a teacher and horseperson with her perceptive questions! Nicole was a major part of my horsemanship journey and I got to know her even better as she often stayed late in the evenings to put in extra work with a nervous Dartmoor pony.

When my sister bought a youngster for my niece, Nicole was an obvious choice to start "Nessie". She did a great job, with some help from her partner, Adam. As is well documented in their first book, *Whispering Back*, he also attended the course a couple of years later, having become involved with horses just a few years previously when he accidentally bought Nicole her first horse. By this time, Nicole was a teacher on that same course.

I couldn't have guessed even then how much Monty would change my life, let alone the lives of students like Nicole and Adam. I still look back on those early days with great sentiment. That's easy now it's all worked out so well! There were times in the beginning, though, when things were pretty scary. I felt a great responsibility not to let talented and generous students like Nicole and Adam down.

I am grateful they never let me face the challenges alone - through various crises, whether emotional, physical or financial, Nicole and Adam have supported me just as much as they claim I have supported them.

As the horse-loving population became aware of the effectiveness of Monty's methods, I found myself inundated with calls to help people with their horses. It was frustrating not to be able to help every owner and I was very happy when I thought of recommending one lady to seek help from Nicole. It made me consider the idea of putting people into the safe hands of certain former students and in this way, our network of Recommended Associates was created. There are now 43 "RAs" worldwide who have made an enormous difference to 'making the world a better

xvii

place for horses and people', which is Monty's mission. These RAs have become a supportive, open-minded community and my learning has continued to be enhanced by knowing them all.

In the pages that follow you'll read about Nicole and Adam's successes and challenges, the highs and lows of their life with horses, and also the adventure of starting a family. There's an honesty that pervades their writing, and I admire them for speaking out about the issues they are passionate about.

Sometimes, as Adam alludes to in this book, you look back on events and it's hard to imagine that they were not all planned in advance. At the time, of course, life seems just to present an infinite number of completely open choices. Back in October 1988, Nicole and Adam were thrown together by the sheer chance that they happened to be in the same college at Cambridge. At that time, I hadn't met or even heard of Monty, and neither had HM the Queen, nor almost anyone in the UK. He had no plans to write an autobiography, let alone to tour the world giving demonstrations, and I was enjoying my life as a jockey. All our stories were about to be changed by the Queen. Around that time - perhaps on that very day - she was browsing through a 'horsey' magazine when she came across his work. Her subsequent curiosity, and her dedication to the horse, brought Monty to Windsor Castle the following year, and the rest, as they say, is history.

It's been an amazing ride.

Kelly

INTRODUCTION

From The Horse's Mouth
(Sensi)

'A horse! A horse! My kingdom for a horse!'
William Shakespeare, Richard III, Act V, Sc IV

I first met Nicole in a field near Cambridge when I was just a youngster and she was not much more than a kid herself. She seemed a bit lost, and I don't just mean in a physical sense - although as I got to know her better, I realised that she almost never knows exactly where she is. It seemed as if something was missing in her life, and she kept looking at me wistfully; I think she might even have wept a little. I felt sorry for her, which is why I hung around and let her pick some grass and "tidy" up my mane. You could tell she thought she knew a thing or two about horses, though. When she brought the Hippy along to meet me, later that same day, she had the audacity to discuss my conformation with him - and even to find fault with it! I have to say they weren't what I would call perfect specimens themselves - she's very much back at the knee, and he's clearly a very poor doer. A certain pallor showed they didn't spend much time outside. I detected a real lack of good grass in their diet, although I'm a bit suspicious about the Hippy on that score.

But they were nice enough, and both kindly picked me some grass and herbs - the lovely sweet stuff from the other side of the gate that I'd been trying to work out a way to get to. As they walked off, I heard some talk of buying me! I had no idea it worked that way around. Surely I should choose who pays my bills? And these people looked poor. I mean, they were students, and they were driving a battered old mini, which it turns out was borrowed anyway. I'd seen far posher cars go by my field. But I guess money isn't everything, and they did come to see me every day, and seemed quite keen. They always brought a treat of some kind, and the girl in particular looked at me with such devotion in her eyes that I thought it boded well for her future dedication to my comfort.

There was some sort of delay, which they seemed very tense about, and then an insultingly small sum of money changed hands, and suddenly Nicole seemed extremely happy. She used to sit in my field for hours at a time, just staring at me, although I'm sure she was meant to be doing some sort of work for her degree.

To be honest, I had a few worries at the start. My first major concern arose when Nicole turned up at the field with a large white holey sheet, which she proceeded to try and put on my back without so much as a "by your leave". Fortunately, by spinning around in a very tight circle, I was able to get her to trip over the lead rope, or her own feet, and she gave up muttering, "It's only a sweat-sheet." What alarmed me was the suggestion that I'd be doing anything that would cause me to sweat. Then there was the trailer journey to Milton Keynes, where she used to live. It just didn't seem sensible to be in such an unstable, small space. I did eventually agree to go in, but only out of the goodness of my heart (well, I think there was some Pasture Mix at stake, too). Nicole travelled in the back with me, though, and I think she was anxious too because she didn't even touch the hay.

But the early days proceeded quite well. I let them both ride me, although the Hippy, whose name transpired to be Adam, frequently used to dismount, very inelegantly and for no apparent reason, whilst we were on the move. He did this without warning, and with no regard for his safety, as he would generally land on his head or something. It usually happened when I saw something scary, so I wonder if he got a bit frightened too, although why he would want to dismount when it was time to run away made no sense to me, as he can hardly move at trotting speed for more than a few yards. I was never sure that it was a sensible strategy, but he used to do it quite a lot. He must have realised that it wasn't a good ploy, because he did it less as time went on.

It would have been alright, except that as I got older Nicole began to develop some strange expectations, such as the random one that she should hold my nose in when I was being ridden. Why this was so important I've no idea. It just made it harder for me to

xx

move and balance, let alone admire the view, but she seemed to think it made me look better and was more advanced, or something. The approach was to put lots of pressure on my mouth, and when I slowed down in response to this, to kick me forwards with her legs. It didn't make much sense to me, and was rather irritating, and I was dismayed when she started insisting that Adam do the same thing. He was even worse at it and would probably have been better off just trying to stay on. I fought it all the way, and we had a heated discussion about it on every "schooling" session, but they proved remarkably hard to school. Luckily they weren't too bothered when we hacked out, or jumped, which we did quite a lot. And the rest of the time I got to eat grass.

It all changed when Nicole went on a course in Witney. There was a guest lecturer there who described my resistance to contorting my body in an unnatural way as "integrity". From then on, the whole riding experience became a lot more comfortable - at least for me. And by the way, I can now do what she calls "posh neck" no problem at all, and with no pressure on my mouth, either. I just wish she'd known how to explain it before.

Then there was this chap called Monty, who seemed to really know how horses think and want to be treated. This "join-up" thing makes a lot of sense, although when Nicole tried it with me I had to put a quick stop to it. She had just rigged up a small pen with a bit of electric tape, and then tried to "send me away". This seemed to me a pointless exercise which could only end in a loss of valuable calories, so I did my best to encourage her to see sense - by the time I had cleared the tape for the third time, she gave up disheartened. It's good for other horses, though. In fact, I frequently employ this technique myself to keep them in their place.

It wasn't long after this that we moved out of the pastures where I had been living with a small herd they had begun to accumulate. This included a very fearful, but more or less harmless Welsh mountain pony called Misty and a bothersome Exmoor pony with a massively overblown ego, who simply doesn't know how not to be annoying. He's called Finn, which is ironic because he's decidedly fat, clearly indicating that he's been eating too much of my grass. We spent a few months in a thoroughly unsuitable location where it seemed to rain almost continually, before we were all put into a lorry (unfortunately they neglected to leave the pesky pony behind), and taken off to pastures new, which were in a much more upmarket area known as the Cotswolds. I can't say it rained much less, but at least the ramshackle surroundings of the rainy place were replaced by the lovely scenery of a glorious old yard surrounded by many interesting trees, some of which are quite tasty. Instead of manky trough water tasting of chlorine, we now had a clear, fast-flowing stream which never needs cleaning out. Best of all, there were many fewer horses and a lot more grass for me and my gang, which gradually grew in number to about ten, sadly including the Exmoor, who still doesn't get the message that he is not wanted. I was introduced to a charming stallion who provided me with a lovely foal to whom I have taught everything I know about spooking.

Meantime Nicole and Adam spent a lot of time working on their riding, to the point where he could even stay on me when I pointed out something dangerous. They would go off every once in a while for a few days and come back rather better, even seeming to think they had something to teach other riders, because people began to come to my home, sometimes with horses, sometimes without (when they would often have the effrontery to ride me!), and try to pick up some of the skills Nicole and Adam had, pitifully slowly, begun to accumulate. On these "clinics", Adam and Nicole would also focus a lot on behavioural issues - at least, having been shown the errors of their old ways, they now understand that it's the humans rather than the horses who really need the help. Time and again, bargy, bolshy, disrespectful, confused and confusing humans are transformed into competent, leader-like individuals who are a pleasure to be around. One feels all 'horsey people' should be obliged to attend at least once.

I've owned Nicole and Adam for nearly 20 years now, and eleven of those years have been spent here at Moor Wood. A lot has changed in that time, and it looks like things have gone from strength to strength. I certainly hope so, as I'd be perfectly happy to live out my days here. They still drive a battered old car, but they have more important things to spend their money on, such as me. They continue to spend a lot of time studying different aspects of horsemanship and trying to refine their skills. They spend endless hours discussing their findings, sometimes quite heatedly. It's not just riding - the technicalities, art and ethics - or teaching and ground-handling that they go on about, they also seem obsessed by feet, saddles, bits, and something they call equine biomechanics, which seems to have something to do with how we move, and how it can be compromised by riders and tack and so on. I don't know why it requires so much study. I've been a horse all my life, and it doesn't seem that complicated to me. I wish they would spend more time studying pasture management, and I myself would gladly volunteer for some field trials. They also seem to have an unhealthy interest in muck - they collect it almost compulsively, from the field, the stables, the yard, even the school. I'm guessing it must be very valuable. Just as well, as we produce a lot of it. We would have an even more impressive output if we were allowed more to eat!

At one point, they took on a lot of liveries, which was very concerning to me, as it meant there was less grass. Also, it meant more staff for me to train, and it really is so hard to find good help these days. For years, I have been trying to tell them to take down all the fences and let me choose were I would like to graze, but they simply don't listen. Nor would they pay any attention to my suggestion that they take the Exmoor pony a very long way away and let him go. In my experience, humans really are extremely hard to train, and sometimes I even get the impression that they understand what I want and are simply being disobedient or just 'taking the Mickey'. Luckily, in light of the additional livery horses, they took on another 15-acre field, which we use in the winter. It's very sheltered, and it rests for most of the year, so it's pretty desres. Better yet, they decided to scale down the liveries, but we still have the field. This means there's an abundance of lovely grass, but they still won't listen to my fencing suggestions. In fact, they've implemented a very irritating practise called "strip-grazing", which means that the grass really is always greener on the other side of the fence.

Judging by the number of horseboxes that turn up on an alarmingly frequent basis, the clinics are getting more and more popular. I still have to do some work on them, and I do my bit to attempt to educate these poor souls. The worst tend to be the ones who think they know what they are doing and try that old trick of kicking and pulling at the same time. These days, I simply turn and nudge their foot, sigh and stand there while Nicole or Adam explains why it's best not to do it that way. If I do say so myself, I also teach a very good lesson on steering. The Hippy also goes out a lot to help people and their horses at their own yards, which I must admit I much prefer.

Anyway, there's a lot more I could say, maybe I'll write my own book, "Munching Back" or perhaps, "Perfect Dinners". I just wanted to mention that I hope this book sells really well, because although I now enjoy plenty of grass all through the year, I still don't live in total luxury. I could really do with a 'fly-wallah'- someone stationed on each flank through the summer months to swat flies for me, for example. Then, and I don't wish to go on about it, there's still that fencing work to be done. Perhaps these and other management failings will be put right with the proceeds from this book. For, although they still have many lamentable shortcomings, I do think that Adam and Nicole are doing their best to make the world a better place for us horses.

ONE

We're Not Worthy
(Adam)

'Follow your heart, cause you cannot steal
The life that you want.'
Tim Hills / Adam Goodfellow, You Are Not Alone

Standing there at the Intelligent Horsemanship stall at the Equus trade fair, I was feeling pretty good about myself, and to be honest, I had reason to be. I had finally found something I really loved in life, something fulfilling and worthwhile to me, something valuable to others. It can be a real struggle to find something to do with your life, at least it was for me. I spent many years seeking happiness, trying to find what I wanted to do with my talents, driving my parents to distraction, because I refused to get onto any career ladder. The limbo of unemployment, unjustifiable as it was even in the depths of the recession of the early nineties, seemed preferable to beginning to drift up a ladder I felt sure I would jump off later. Then, through no fault of my own, I discovered horses when I bought one for my girlfriend, completely by mistake. I had no idea what I was getting myself into. Not only did I not know the first thing about horses, I also had no idea how much they cost, or that eventually we would find a way to earn it all back and more. But most of all, I had no idea just how much they were going to teach me about myself, or how much they were ultimately going to help me.

So, as a result of a random, throwaway comment, which led to the purchase of a horse I hadn't even got enough money to buy, let

1

alone pamper, at the age of twenty I became the world's most amateur horseman. This implausible occurrence led to a string of lucky coincidences that centred around a man who doesn't believe there is such a thing as luck - Monty Roberts. Not every amateur horseman, or even their horse-mad girlfriend gets a chance to meet Monty properly. But to have the great good fortune to be at a pair of fairly loose ends at precisely the moment that his revolutionary methods began to take the horse world by storm, that's more than even a very lucky guy could ask for. To become part of the team that helped make this happen, and be among the first people in the world to learn and practise these methods, thereby setting up a business in what is possibly the loveliest stable yard in the prettiest part of that beautiful country called England, all adds up to me being the luckiest man who has ever walked the earth. Of course, the romance of horse whispering can wear off when mucking out late at night in a filthy gale, but in general it's the most amazing life anyone could hope to lead. In our case, one more lucky coincidence led to a good friend of mine (who just happened to work for a publishing house), suggesting we should write it all down and make a fortune. Unfortunately, he forgot to mention that most of that "fortune" would go to the publishing house, not ourselves, but you can't ask for everything.

Anyhow, that's how I found myself at 'Equus', a massive equine trade fair, inside a vast exhibition complex in London, and I was feeling really good about it, because on the table next to me at the Intelligent Horsemanship stall, alongside several best-sellers by Monty Roberts and Kelly Marks, were copies of our brand new book, *Whispering Back*. Being so soon after publication, it had seemed a good idea to tear myself away from the gorgeous surroundings of home, and get down to London, where as well as elaborately signing copies for anyone who could be badgered into buying one, I could also see a few demonstrations by other horse trainers. In horsemanship there is always so much to be learned but, in all honesty, I was not anticipating seeing anything to match the quality of work I had seen from Monty and Kelly. Little did I expect that I was about to meet someone I admire perhaps more than any horseman in all the world, and he didn't even do a demonstration.

In fact, I was doing my best to avoid this date with destiny. After several hours the supposed glamour of authorship had begun to rub off, and my painfully incompetent salesmanship was strongly in evidence. I had been trying to get away for more than an hour, but had repeatedly been distracted, not least by the arrival of my friend and soon-to-be working pupil, Annabelle, who had immediately engaged me in one of her typically engrossing conversations. So it was hardly what you would think of as work, standing there proud as punch, chatting to people. I suppose I was working, though, and I guess I had always expected that any horseman I would greatly admire would appear not when I was at work, but rather when I was studying. I would obviously read their book, see them at a demonstration or on a DVD.

So, I had literally bidden Annabelle another last farewell, when a woman approached, vaguely followed by a scruffy teenage boy. Dressed in black and with lank dark hair, he carried an awkwardness in his very presence as if he were totally out of place in these surroundings, but also as if he would have been equally out of place anywhere. I immediately felt a strong sense of kinship, because he seemed such a manifestation of my former self. I smiled at the woman and agreed when she enthused about Monty, whom she had seen in demonstrations.

We got chatting and I began a typically inept attempt to steer her towards the purchase of a copy of a certain book which, although it wasn't actually by Monty Roberts, had an introduction by him, as indicated by the appearance of his name on the cover in very large type. In fact, his name was so much more prominent than ours, that with the judicial use of my thumb and a plastic bag, I was sure I could sell it to her before she realised that he had only written the introduction.

Meanwhile, Annabelle had got talking to the Dark Teen, who had been charmed almost out of his shell by her graceful, quiet attention. Naturally, he pretended not to know the person he was with, since she was his mother. While Annabelle continued to chat to the Dark One, his mother began to tell me how much he enjoyed horses, or specifically, the new horsemanship typified by Monty. It meant a great deal to him, to be able to communicate with them. "You see," she said, and glancing over to check that he was still occupied, she mouthed inaudibly, "He's autistic."

At the time I knew almost nothing about autism, in fact, about all I knew was that autistic is not the same as artistic, and that autism is a mental condition which makes it harder for people to understand others and express themselves, often leading to anger

3

and frustration. Looking over at the kid, he looked like he was doing just fine, but I guess anyone could talk to Annabelle. I continued to try to steer the conversation back in the Whispering direction, not least because I was sure that she and in particular he, would enjoy reading our book. It's a privilege to have the chance to influence young people, especially towards non-violence, although I soon found I had no work to do on that score. For, as we bemoaned that breed of professionals whose methods depend and revolve around violence, our conversation caught his ear and he turned and began to speak.

As soon as he got started I knew that the story he was telling involved him losing his temper, for I could sense his adrenaline beginning to build. I immediately felt a strong emotional connection with him, as I could tell he had been through the same journey I had, of learning from traditional authority about "showing the horse who's boss" by means of violence. I wanted to interrupt and say, "It's OK, we all make mistakes. I used to be a disaster around horses, and I often resorted to violence, but now I'm well known for being able to help horses get over major. I'm sure if you got angry with your horse, that he will forgive you if you learn and find a new way. After all, nobody's perfect..." But that wasn't where his story was going.

He'd gone to a riding school he hadn't ridden at before, he explained, and had a lesson on a school horse. The horse was very unenthusiastic and he felt really sorry for it, as it obviously didn't want to have anything to do with being worked, and wouldn't do what it was being asked - to canter. I could tell we were reaching the climax of his story and I felt dreadful for him. If an instructor had told him that he should hit the horse, I didn't think he should be angry with himself for listening, nor continue to blame himself so harshly.

To my astonishment, that wasn't it at all. Still seething with resentment at the memory, the emphasis in his words was intense. "She told me I had to hit the horse, hard, so I picked the whip up," he almost shouted, "And I chucked it on the ground, told her what I thought of her and her riding lesson, got off and left - and I didn't give her any money."

I looked across at Annabelle, who like me, was absolutely dumbstruck by the moral courage shown by this scrawny kid whose heavy metal t-shirt and need of a hair cut would probably not have made a good impression on Monty. But in his utter conviction, and willingness to rebel in the face of a brutalising authority, Monty would certainly have seen a kindred spirit. For my part, I felt deeply humbled, indeed a tinge of shame. Here I was, sound of body and mind (at least in the opinion of the medical profession, if not my friends and family), and educated at some of the supposedly best institutions in the world, yet I had once thought it acceptable to beat horses with a whip, and I mean beat them, not just tap or touch them with it. On one notable occasion, which we related at the start of the book I was trying to sell them, and which I suddenly felt completely unworthy to write, I had done just that, simply to get my horse across a puddle. Here was this kid, whose mental condition made it particularly difficult for him to express himself or relate his feelings, and yet, unlike me (or Nicole, who'd told me to hit my horse harder), he'd worked out what was right and wrong without any help from anyone. Moreover, he had the courage to stand up for his principles in the face of an adult professional. I, at the age of twenty-five, had needed Mr Roberts to show me the blindingly obvious - that horses are flight animals whose adrenaline goes up if you deliver them pain.

They presently left, leaving me several pegs lower, but all the better for it. I stayed a while with Annabelle, now more engrossed in conversation than ever, except that we could hardly find the words to express our admiration for this guy. All I could think of was the scene from Wayne's World, where the kids drop to their knees and worship their rock star idol, grovelling, "We're not worthy, we're not worthy". I did manage to retain some dignity, refraining from copying this abject obeisance, but it was one of those moments when you get jolted back to reality. It's funny how horses seem to do that to you, give you a good jolt, helping you to stay grounded, and not always because you've just fallen off.

Funny also what a small world it is, and funny how events unfold. Horses led me to the beautiful place where I live, and through horses I've been fortunate enough not only to live a dream I never had (to be a horse whisperer), but also to fulfil one I had when I was exactly the age of my hero, the Dark Teen, because I know he also dreams of rock and roll, and shares my passion for playing in a hard rock band. This I know, not because I had the sense to get his name and autograph when I met him (I was too busy trying to give him mine), but because when I tried, with my usual technological incompetence, to find my own band's page on an Internet networking site, I resorted to searching for my own name and up came his web page, where you can listen to music he's composed with his own rock band. Evidently to some extent, I've been an inspiration to him, because I featured on his web site. Hopefully when he reads this, he'll realise what an inspiration he's been to me. What goes around surely comes around, with horses and with life.

It's a privilege, as well as a responsibility, to be in a position to give some advice or relate some stories that might help someone like this wonderful teenager and his horse not to go down some of the blind alleys we've been down. I know how much horses mean to people, and how much people love them, and I believe that at heart most humans are fundamentally good-natured. I can't think of one person I've worked for whom I would not say that of. Sadly, though, I've seen far too many miserable, misunderstood, and mistreated horses whose owners care about them as much as anyone could, but whose practice is not what I think the horses consider to be optimal. Professional advice - from vets, farriers, and saddlers as well as instructors - is sometimes seen as sacrosanct, even when it appears illogical and leads to great unhappiness for all concerned. If working as a professional horseman and problem-solver has shown me anything, it is that having an open mind - that first piece of advice I hope I learned from Monty - is essential at all times. It isn't easy, not least because it means you might sometimes have to admit that you may be wrong, and even that your horse has suffered as a result. However, along with that open, questioning attitude, limitless funds, and the willingness to pick ourselves up after every jolt, the only other thing we really need to be good horsemen is a moral compass even a fraction as strong as the one possessed by that young man.

I don't believe in fate, but I also don't know what to believe about uncanny coincidences. There seem to be a lot of them around. My meeting with the Dark Teen would never have happened without horses, and so much else in my life has come to me through them. Yet, for almost as long ago as I can remember, I've had another thread. As well as loving animals and nature, I've always played music. Beginning with the recorder, then singing and the violin - I seemed to spend years playing 'Twinkle, twinkle, little star' in a variety of ways, but it didn't matter. It was always magic. Not, however, on the scale of the Beatles tapes I got hold of around the age of ten. The one good thing that came out of John Lennon's tragic death was that the radio was full of Beatles music for months afterwards, and for years I was such a purist that I would not entertain the possibility of putting anything else on my tape deck. The UK was in the grip of punk but I was at boarding school in my pink blazer and shorts, and in the grip of the Beatles. I knew the lyrics, the melodies, and who sang or wrote every one of their songs. I just wanted more than anything to sing and play like that.

Eventually, of course, other musicians got a look in, notably the Rolling Stones, Pink Floyd, the Doors, Led Zeppelin, Queen, Dylan, Marley and Bowie. By the time I was in my teens, their music and the ethos and lifestyle they represented seemed to be the only things in my life that meant anything, the only things I could relate to. But the one who really pushed it to the edge for me was Hendrix. He played it straight from the soul.

Finally I persuaded my mum to buy me a guitar. Immediately, before I had even played a note, I was in a band and although I never had lessons, I learned loads of tunes. I will never forget that first time we played, with bass, drums and an electric guitar, and it sounded just like the Stones - unbelievable. I think I was in five different acts before I finished school, and one of them was good enough to cause a proper riot in the school hall, one of the finest moments of my life.

Ten years later though, here I was living in the Cotswolds doing horse whispering. It's all very well but it isn't exactly rock and roll. A man has got to have some loud rock, especially if he's going to spend the whole of the rest of his time trying to calm everybody down. I'd been in some passably good bands at University, and afterwards, and done lots of recordings as well. It was good to be able to belt out covers, and by then I could play pretty well, but when we moved to the Cotswolds it all seemed destined to stop, not least because we didn't know anybody except the odd local client.

Except that when we came to Moor Wood, which seemed so perfect it made me question whether fate might really play a part - we were shown around and there was an amazing yard of six stone boxes for rent, 10 acres of land, and a miniscule one-up-one-down part of a cottage. We lived in a tiny flat in Milton Keynes at the time, but now we faced the prospect of moving into something considerably smaller. It would have been "bijou" for one, but then our prospective landlords looked at each other and said there was a room in their barn which was pretty basic but they could let us have it for an extra 'peppercorn', although it turned out to be pretty expensive pepper.

The moment I walked in I knew where the drums would go, I could picture mikes and amps and guitars. I had a bit of recording equipment and I knew it was a perfect place for a studio. Never mind the fact that half of the roof leaked badly. Swallows were flying in and out through large holes in it, leaving further deposits of guano to add to the thick layer on the floor, but I could see a different picture in my mind. And it's come true. For 10 years I've played and recorded with a series of friends that I began to meet through another one of those freak coincidences, those little moments when a word changes everything.

Tim's girlfriend Gemma was a livery client of our new landlords, so I had met her in passing, but I hadn't seen him before. I happened to step outside when they arrived one time and we spoke a few words. When Tim mentioned music I thought about it for a second, and decided to take the chance that he wasn't a bad 'un and invited him up to the studio. By then I had a table in there, my guitars and amp, and my 8-track and mixing desk were set up. It was swept and a bit more civilised, but I could only use the dry half of the room. There was no heating and it could be very interesting when the swallows were feeling assertive.

I was just coming to the end of my 10-week course learning about Monty Roberts's work, and Kelly had asked me to do something rather unusual. She wanted me to compose a song which would help everyone remember all the things they would have to check when they were on the phone dealing with clients. So, I'd been messing about with a couple of bass and drum samples alongside which I had lain two good beefy guitar riffs, and added a marathon beast of a solo throughout. It came together like magic. For the vocal I spoke items from the list in alternate sections, and three of the other students came and did voice-overs as if they were clients calling up with their problems.

I played it to Tim, and he loved it. We got together and had a jam with a drummer, a vocalist, Tim on bass and me on guitar.

There was a second guitarist there - I'd actually met him before because he worked as a cashier in the bank we used in Cirencester, and it was hard not to notice him because of his huge affro - but I wasn't very keen on the idea. In my last band I'd been the sole guitar player and you'll appreciate that it can easily get uncontrollably loud, even without two guitarists competing amplificatorally.

From that initial manifestation of SCSI - the greatest rock 'n' roll band in Woodmancote - who first played that night, it turns out that only the other guitarist still plays with me, ten years later. It's weird and a bit chilling to think that he could have been nothing more to me than a guy with bad hair who cashed cheques in the bank, instead of the indispensable inspiration with whom I would write some of my best songs (including 'You Are Not Alone', some lyrics of which are printed at the front of this book). I must confess that we have finally given up practising three nights a week and our plans for world conquest have been shelved. In the meantime, we invented a new sound: the barn beat. Not quite the Beatles, but if only the world had ever realised it, we were the UK's answer to the Foo Fighters. Writing those words I realise where we came unstuck. We needed to get a big thing going between SCSI and the Foos, the way Blur and Oasis did. Instead we haven't got much further than Cheltenham and the World Wide Web. You can check us out on http://www.worldofscsi.com/.

As unimaginable as it would have been to the people who built the granary barn to store hay in, that room has seen and heard rock music that has had bats reeling around the place in confusion. It's also been used to teach hundreds of people the finer points of horse whispering and riding theory. Fate or not, it has all seemed to fit in perfectly. Without the horses I'd never have met my band. And without the music I wouldn't have found the Dark Teen on the web, now would I? Eventually a horse called Amber would come into my life, whose owner is the daughter of a member of one of the great bands I mentioned earlier. The very first thing I ever learned to play on the guitar was a classic bass line written by him. Fifteen years later, I would meet him, and save his daughter's horse from the train wreck she had become. And it makes me wonder… maybe we are acting out a pre-recorded track, and the song was right all along. Maybe, after all, life is a roller coaster - you've just got to ride it.

TWO

The Luckiest Girl In The World
(Nicole)

When people visit our wonderful yard in the Cotswolds and say "WOW, this place is stunning", they usually follow it with, "But you must be bored of hearing that all the time." The fact is that we never tire of being reminded how lucky we are. To be paid to ride and help people with their horses would have been my dream from the very earliest years of my life. Back then, of course, I had never heard of Monty Roberts and there was no such thing as 'horse whispering', but had I known then what I would be doing now, I would have considered myself the luckiest girl in the world. It would be churlish to point out that living here isn't always as relaxing for us as it is for the people who visit. We're sometimes surprised when visitors say, "The atmosphere is so calm and peaceful here", but then they usually haven't witnessed the occasionally frustrating process of collecting in all the horses, some of whom have an interesting sense of humour at times ("Let's be good and all go into the yard together, but then let's all run back out into the field again - to the opposite end - before they have a chance to catch up and shut the gate! Hee hee, follow me!"), nor what a rush it was to get out the door and away from the telephone in time for their arrival. And of course, when people sip tea on the lawn and watch the dog playing, it isn't usually the sort of dark and stormy weather that often accompanies emergency late night fencing repairs. If truth be known, in the early days, we were so head-down and frantically working, that we barely looked up and saw the changing seasons. Occasionally, we would be momentarily blown away by the light catching the huge cedar tree, turning the bark to burnished gold, or we would pause for a moment whilst doing the night stables and look up at the vast expanse of stars in a crystal clear sky, and time would stop while we contemplated the infinite vastness of it all, and reminded ourselves that we needed stillness and peace to be able to work.

In fact, I think that this is what made the otherwise gruelling hours and pressure of working with difficult horses sustainable. On all but a few occasions, starting work with a horse transported us into another zone, one where time had no meaning, and we would get lost in the process of connecting with the horse. Seeing a horse's true nature emerge from underneath layers of baggage and trauma was miraculous every time. And instead of draining our energy, we would feel renewed.

But in spite of living in such beautiful surroundings, working with wonderful people, feeling inspired and encouraged by working with my very best friend and lover, and having daily 'Misty hugs' with the loveliest Welsh mountain pony in the world, there was something missing. Sensi, the horse that had started it all, leading us down this path and being such a daily feature of my life, had now taken second place, and I missed the interaction terribly. Looking back, it's a little hard to pinpoint why exactly I ended up doing so much less with her than I would have wanted. On the one hand, it's easy to make up plausible sounding excuses. On the other, it's easy to chastise oneself for lack of effort, when a closer look at the situation reveals that really what I was asking of myself was highly unrealistic. It was only when we were writing *Whispering Back* and looked at the diary for details of events leading up to our move from Milton Keynes to Moor Wood, for example, that I stopped feeling guilty about our complete failure to pack up the flat. Seeing that in fact there were only two days available in which to do so made it clearer that what we'd done was actually a fairly remarkable achievement. And so with Sensi. I probably took her out for a reasonable number of hacks when we first moved in, given that we had a pretty hectic schedule and were desperately trying to make ends meet. All the guilt I laid on myself subsequently for not doing more with her completely failed to take into account that she was actually very lame after she had Karma, her foal.

She experienced a catalogue of disasters during her pregnancy, from breaking her nose in twenty five places shortly after conception, to laminitis in the tenth month, which led to a nasty fall off a wall as she tried to escape to better grazing. The resultant hole in her stifle made her unable to put any weight on that

12

leg, and with all her ligaments softening for the birth, her pelvis was severely damaged by the process. Although the birth itself was non traumatic, and she was perfectly capable of getting around the field and feeding Karma without evident discomfort, her muscles and ligaments were so compromised by the process that she could only walk in a straight line by a process of strange distortions and compensations. The vet suggested that I could quite legitimately claim loss of use for her. But I never did, simply because in spite of all the evidence before my eyes, I just couldn't countenance that what he was saying could possibly be true.

So she needed time to recover, and for the first 18 months or so she did just that. We would take her and Karma out for the occasional walk, but otherwise she just meandered around the field. She had a few treatments to help encourage her body back to functionality, but she just didn't seem to have the strength to embark on a proper training and rehabilitation programme.

Jo, our trusty groom, should have been my inspiration. She had worked for us for a few years, and had skillfully overseen a succession of working pupils keen to improve their horsemanship with the "new" techniques we could teach them. Her arrival - following a cold call that she made to us before we even realised we needed a groom - had certainly made our lives easier, and she kept the yard and stables immaculate. But I used to watch her ride out for long hacks on the weekend, whilst I was doing the jobs she would do during the week, and think, "something's wrong here." Not that I objected to doing mundane tasks - on the contrary, I've always enjoyed stable work, and still feel that if I could just find someone to pay me my teaching rate for mucking out the field, I'd be very happy. But I just thought, "how has she managed to organise her life such that she can afford 2 horses, a trailer and a 4 x 4, a house, and has time to ride every day, finish work by 4:30pm, and have a social life, all on what can only be described as a fairly minimal wage, whilst we seem to work 7 days a week, for 12 hours a day, are always worrying about meeting the rent, and hardly ever have time to ride our own horses?" I'm still not sure about how she managed to make the money stretch so far, but I came to realise that there was more than a touch of wisdom about this young person.

She felt she had an entitlement to ride. It was what she worked for, and it was what she intended to do. She'd even managed to negotiate with us that on dark, winter mornings, she should be able to ride her own horses first, before she started work for us, on the basis that some of the stable jobs could be done in artificial light in the evening. It did in fact mean that some of the horses who were in for training would end up working in the dark, but we never questioned it, probably because her conviction that it was the right thing to do was so strong. I came to realise that what I was struggling with was a sense of non-entitlement. I didn't feel it was appropriate for me to have fun with my pony unless everything else that needed to be done was done. As we never reached this state, I never felt free to ride. But I'd put myself in a no-win situation. I felt guilty if I rode, and guilty if I didn't, and in the end I would distract myself with more muck clearing, or sorting out the admin. This was all in spite of reading countless personal development and self-help books, and being very clear that we are all the architects of our own lives, make our own choices day-by-day, and that we really cannot blame any other person or circumstance for where we are in our lives.

But what I've come to realise is that change can take time. And whilst horses can often make changes in their behaviour astonishingly quickly, it can also take years rather than hours for problems to resolve. And even the most dedicated owner will usually take longer than their horse to initiate changes in their lives. So fretting over the timescale is rarely very useful, and I started to think that maybe I should treat myself with the same patience and consideration that I would a horse, and recognise that change doesn't have to happen overnight.

Bringing Sensi back into health was a good start in reclaiming some time for myself. Of course, there was the unselfish motive of making her more comfortable and hopefully even prolonging her life, but the fact remained that it was something I was doing purely because I wanted to, for which no-one was paying me any money, and through which the business was not profiting in any way.

The first thing to do was to get Pennie Hooper, our trusted equine massage therapist, to have a look at her. Never one for sugar-coating, I nevertheless couldn't escape the feeling that Pennie was trying to be gentle with me. "Oh, Nicole, she's very weak, you know. These ligaments have taken a real battering. There's a tear here in the muscle around her tail - can you feel? There's a real stiffness in all the joints on her offside, but this nearside stifle - and hock and fetlock - has a severely restricted range of movement.

She's got no topline at all, everything's sagged from the birth. This is really quite a challenge....."

"Well, what can I do to help her?" I asked, determined to find something to do. Pennie looked at Sensi thoughtfully.

"Well, obviously no riding, probably for at least a year. No work in the school. No turns or circles. I guess you could lead her out, or long-line her. But try to avoid hills in the beginning."

I looked out at the steep slopes and banks of the fields Sensi lived in, up the drive that's impassable in snow or ice, and wondered how I was going to manage the last directive. I quickly worked out that there were a few short routes where the hills were more gradual. I'd just have to stick to those.

Sensi, then aged thirteen, seemed quite happy to bimble around the field, receive regular massage, and consider herself retired. It was hard to take, given how she had always been so forward, and even at the end of a long distance ride of several days would still be keen to canter. She certainly wasn't fretting to get back to work, and consented to accompanying me on the walks with a slightly bemused air. She seemed to feel there was more point when we brought Karma, as she was then able to teach her daughter more advanced spooking techniques than she could in the field.

The walks gradually got a little bit longer, and I started adding in bits of suppling groundwork, a little long-lining in the school and out-and-about, stretches, and slightly steeper hills. She started to feel a little better in herself, to have a bit more energy, and appeared more enthusiastic about doing the work. Every time Pennie saw her, about once a month or so, she would cautiously mention a slight improvement. After about a year, I allowed myself the occasional sit on her. Just bareback while she mowed the lawn. And simply looking at her black-tinged ears, her delicate forelock falling down over her bumpy nose as she neatly cropped the sweet grass, I'd feel so happy that I had to force myself to get off quickly, before my weight began to compromise her muscles and undo the work which had been so painstakingly built up.

More months passed, and I added a saddle to her carefully padded back, filling in the gaps where her muscle should have been. I'd ride her for a circuit or two after carefully warming her up on long-lines, trying not to be too alarmed by the fact that she couldn't walk in anything vaguely resembling a straight line, especially in the school. Out and about she was better, I later discovered - her

15

body would be crooked, but we could go more or less straight down the road. In the school, she seemed to be doing her best to keep her body straight, and as a result seemed to have to do minuscule circles on the right rein, and fall out widely on the left.

Having had a reasonable amount of "Ride with your Mind" input from riding coach Mary Wanless on other horses during this time, I now had a more acute sense of what was going on underneath me. I could clearly feel that whilst there was a bulge of reasonable muscle under my left seat bone, there was virtually nothing under my right, making it feel like I was sitting on a cliff edge. This was a fairly alarming feeling, but what should have probably worried me more was the fact that I basically had no control over Sensi at all.

Throughout her early years, Sensi had been of the opinion that she should have at least some say in the speed and direction at which she travelled, but she was always open to negotiation. However, since becoming a mother, and landing the position of lead mare within the herd, she seemed to have developed an ideological objection to the whole concept of being controlled, particularly under saddle. She was polite on the ground, easy to lead and handle, but under saddle and to a lesser extent on the long-lines, she was just not prepared to be directed. Something as simple as a walk-halt transition could take two circuits of the school to execute, and even then that was often only after I'd managed to arrange enough directional control to steer her into the corner. She never did anything outrageous, like rearing or bucking or bolting off, but I had to admit that a complete lack of steering and brakes hardly constituted a safe ride. And all this was before she was even properly fit and strong!

In spite of having had her teeth frequently seen to and not seeming to have any problems, she became keen on snatching the reins out of my hands, regardless of whichever bit I used, even when she was already being ridden pretty much on the buckle end, or if I was riding her bitless in a dually halter. Again, it seemed to be even the suggestion of constraint she was objecting to. Another interesting development in her character was a significant sense of anxiety when being ridden out on her own. I think because she was lead mare she worried about leaving the others on their own. Whatever the reason, on more than one occasion I found myself piaffing down a steep escarpment, worrying about her back, and my neck. I had enough going for my riding to be able to hold her together and not let her take off without hanging on her mouth, but I couldn't stop the prancing. I found the coiled energy quite exhilarating but I was always worried that she would damage herself, even though by then we had done eighteen months of careful rehabilitation.

The reports from Pennie, and also from a cranio-sacral osteopath, kept coming back with the same message. She's getting there, you're doing well, but don't push her - minimal amounts of trot, and absolutely no cantering. It was difficult to be self-controlled, because the report from Sensi was that she was up for whatever I wanted to try. But she's always been stoic and uncomplaining, and I knew that to push it could set us back. Patience prevailed.

The day I could start having short lessons on her was a real breakthrough. By then, I really felt that the long-lining and massage had done as much as it could to straighten her out. To help her move her body in a different way, it would need to be done under saddle, and I'd need help. I began having lessons with one of Mary Wanless' students.

By sorting out what I was doing with my body, I was able to initiate changes in Sensi. Through a heightened awareness of my muscle use, particularly those between my knees and my armpits, I could see how Sensi's crookedness was affecting my body. If I could somehow ride as though the horse underneath me was symmetrical, I could encourage her actually to be so.

I don't know if that will strike the reader as sounding very simple or rather difficult. I certainly found it challenging, but once I'd got an angle on it, it was immensely powerful. Although I possibly developed a certain over-stiffness in the body, a result of trying too hard to get the muscles to do what I wanted them to, Sensi clearly found it a huge support. And although perhaps I restricted her freedom of movement to a degree, her problem was to do with being much too loose rather than too tight. It was like all her elasticity had gone over-soggy, and needed firming up, not further loosening. As time went on, I was able to feel a real connection with her back muscles, and on a good day could turn her, stop her, control her speed, and encourage her to lift up her back and work in a connected way in a straight line, in walk, and eventually in trot.

The time I spent assisting Sensi back to physical health provided me with a wonderful opportunity to develop our relationship. As time went on, I realised she was beginning to look at me in a different way. I hadn't been working with Monty's methods for very long when she became pregnant, and I have to say she was sceptical about the sudden change in approach. She had avoided join-up by simply jumping out of the electric fence enclosure I was trying to use in our fields in Milton Keynes. I think she sensed my inexperience, and I may not have noticed things I was doing wrong. However, as I became more competent, she began to view me with more respect, and I realised how tolerant she had always been of my inexperience and lack of expertise. She was immensely good natured about it, but I think she knew that some of the stuff I was trying to do with her was flawed. The whole "kicking the horse forward from the leg into a restraining hand" philosophy - at least the way I was attempting to apply it - struck her as nonsensical long before I realised how ineffective, counter-productive, crude and illogical it was.

Now, at age twenty two, Sensi is still improving. I'm able to use her on clinics here, and she gives concise and immediate feedback if people ride inappropriately (by kicking, for example), or if they're unclear how to steer. She's still not perfectly straight, and people sometimes notice she's a little stiff behind, but she's as keen as ever and I still have many exciting rides when her blood gets up. And if I find myself unable to ride her as often as I like, I don't give myself a hard time. Just knowing that my wise old friend is out with her gang, enjoying prime Cotswold grazing, is enough. And when she finally lets me know that her riding days are over, I hope I'm able to let her live out her days with as much peace and freedom as she deserves. Not everyone is lucky enough to meet their Master Teacher, or to have the privilege to live with and learn from them for such a long time.

THREE

The King
(Adam)

Someone once wrote, after having been to a demo by Kelly Marks, that she was disappointed with what she'd seen. It had only been common sense, mixed with kindness, competence, and horse psychology. Kelly, of course, was delighted to be complimented, even if unintentionally. Who wouldn't be pleased to be associated with such noble qualities? But, although her work might be based on common sense, it isn't common practice. Too often, it isn't even common advice. If it were, there wouldn't be so many horses around suffering from so many unnecessary problems - or people suffering too. And it wouldn't be possible for someone with as little experience as I had, when I qualified in 1998, to succeed with a horse that an experienced professional had spectacularly failed with.

As a corporate member of the British Horse Society, the Intelligent Horsemanship Association, founded by Kelly, aims to spread the best training methods as widely as possible. Kelly and Monty certainly don't see themselves as being outside the establishment, and indeed Monty feels that the acceptance of his work by the Queen is the single most valuable endorsement that he could have. You can't get more 'establishment' than that! Nevertheless, I still find it a surprise that so few people put their hands up, even in an audience of a thousand or more, when asked how many professionals are present at his demonstrations. Monty is one of the most successful trainers of competitive horses in the US in the Twentieth Century. People generally think of him as the "starting expert" or as a problem-solver. But, as well as training and breeding world class thoroughbred racehorses such as Alleged, Monty has been a nine times 'world' champion in national competitions in the US in cutting, roping, reining, Western pleasure

19

horse and working cow horse divisions and has won many trophies in rodeo, in intensely competitive disciplines. He has also trained at least one Grand Prix show jumper. From the first moment I saw him work I was mesmerised and immediately convinced of the efficacy and impact of what he was doing, as well as how wrong I had been to use violence to force a horse to do what I wanted. I couldn't understand why professionals were not flocking to Kelly's courses. Of course, I wasn't having to admit to my clients and horses I had worked for that what I had been doing was at best, inefficient, and at worst, downright cruel. I had only myself and a couple of horses to answer to, and even then it wasn't easy.

Perhaps the most understandable reason why so many professionals have closed their minds to the possibility that Monty's methods might be an improvement on traditional ways, is that they have often managed to achieve good results using other techniques. If you're involved in competitive horsemanship and the person who wins uses traditional methods, why should you look at it another way? Unfortunately, but understandably, a lot of people end up trying alternatives only because they come up against a brick wall in training one particular horse. It takes a crisis for most people to start considering another approach.

It never made the headlines but one of the most prominent British team event riders found themselves in just such a crisis when their horse was in danger of being disqualified in the vet check at a major competition a few years ago. In a roundabout way I was the one who actually fixed his problem - through two of the most remarkable clients I have ever met.

Now Jenny and Toby could hardly be called inexperienced by anyone, but crisis point is exactly what they had reached when they rang me about their three year old, recently gelded colt. They had just about concluded that there was no way forward except to have this horse put down. He was dangerous. Anyone walking quietly past his door was liable to be viciously attacked. Simple tasks such as taking him in and out of the stable and to the field had become a major production requiring two men with leading poles to accomplish it. Breaking him in to be a reliable ridden horse looked like an impossible dream.

Like so many of the people whom we meet, they weren't to blame for this state of affairs. The plan had always been to sell the King as a weanling and having delivered him to his new home,

Jenny and Toby headed off immediately on a foreign holiday. They were unaware for a couple of weeks that the cheque had bounced and on their return they tried to find out what had happened. When the promised money did not materialize, and Jenny and Toby faced facts and finally went back and got him, they were shocked at what they saw.

In a miserable hovel at the back of the yard, their beloved weanling had been reduced to a sick, emaciated shadow of his former brilliance. He had lost a shocking amount of weight, and was riddled with a virus, which they later discovered had affected the development of his joints. Horrified at the fate that had befallen him, they got him in the lorry and took him back home, where they nursed him back to health. However, as he got better, and bigger and stronger, he became more and more vicious.

You couldn't hope to meet a more pleasant couple, but it was also clear, by their own admission, that they were at a loss as to what to do with him. Toby, who was originally supposed to own the King, had not handled him for almost two years since having a massive bust-up while leading him. In a lifetime he had never come closer to losing his temper with a horse. "Virtual warfare" was how they described it in a magazine article. Toby was a well-respected horseman, devoted to hunting and eventing, well known in the highest circles of the sport. Jenny was a BHS Instructor who had been teaching riding for about forty years or so, which is as long as I've been alive. They both had access to a range of the top trainers in this country. Yet despite, possibly in part because of, everything they had done with the King, things had got to the point where she couldn't handle him at all. Fortunately, despite her many years of experience, Jenny was always very open-minded, so after a friend had invited her to go to a Monty demonstration, which she was very impressed by, she thought it worth a try. She contacted me and called me out.

Even if their horse had not been such an extreme case, it was challenging enough to be visiting them. Toby and Jenny had bred one of the top horses in the field of eventing. King was the rebellious grandson from the same dam. Unfortunately, despite his impeccable breeding, it looked like he might not make the Olympic team, considering that at the age of three he could not be safely caught or led, have his feet picked up or be handled. His not-so-endearing trait of making bare-toothed lunges over the stable door also cast doubt on the suitability of his temperament.

Aggression is one of my favourite things to work on with horses. It's really about communicating with the horse and establishing and respecting boundaries, on both sides. Rather than marching straight up to his stable, I began by hanging around on the edge of his space, several yards away, finding out where I could stand without evoking a response from him. Once he had relaxed a little, and taking care to keep my body language very non-confrontational, I moved fractionally across this boundary, giving him time to adjust, and in this manner made my way slowly up to his stable door.

He seemed surprised by this approach (as were Toby and Jenny), and appeared to be both curious and irritated, torn between investigating this strange new human and wanting to take chunks out of me. All I would do when he opened his teeth to bite was make a quick opening movement with my hand and a sharp "Pssch!" noise, and he would move back sharply. Of course, I never made any attempt to strike or even stroke him. When he had moved away, I would invite him forward again, by stepping backwards, and moving my hand away. By this process of advance and retreat I established that we could communicate, won a degree of trust and created some important boundaries. Soon I could stroke and scratch his head and even touch around his mouth without being savaged. Essentially an engaging and inquisitive character, he certainly didn't seem quite such a mess as I'd expected. His intelligence was immediately visible. Don't get me wrong, though - he certainly knew how to bite. But something about him, in between his attempts to hurt you, was very endearing. He had real presence.

He wasn't frightened by the headcollar, and putting it on him was a case of taking it slowly, being tactful, and not giving him the impression of being forced into anything. Once it was on, I had a better chance to look at him. His face and head, when not thrusting forward like an alligator, were among the most charming and intelligent I had ever seen, dark bay and perfectly proportioned to his deep chest and strong neck. But the muscles along his neck were tight with tension. It was clear he was teething and generally very stressed, wanting to put everything in his mouth, which was frustrating for us both. He had such a need to bite that perhaps we should have provided him with an old shoe or stick on which he could take out his frustration - except that he probably would have turned out to have a virulent allergy to all the materials in a shoe, or to the plant. He was known to be allergic to almost everything under the sun, including metal and therefore most bits, several medicines and plants including, it was later discovered, one that grew outside his stable window. But despite this he was also a horse bursting with personality and ability. The power and energy he could muster was immense.

"You'll notice his foreleg," said Jenny. One of them was definitely wonky, noticeably from the knee down, a legacy of his previous illness. It was far too flawed to allow him to endure the rigours of big-time eventing, although probably not so much that he could never be ridden. At this particular moment, however, even that prospect didn't look likely. Nevertheless, to make him rideable was their ultimate goal, and I was to be both the first step and last resort in that process. If I couldn't make a big difference to his behaviour, it would be the end of the road for this young horse.

I got to work, in the round pen that they had recently constructed, edged with bales of haylage. Jenny had shown me a video of the first of about four join-ups she had done with the King which had made a little difference to his behaviour. She had not received any formal training and was attempting to replicate what she had seen at the Monty demo. Under the circumstances, she was doing a pretty reasonable job, but her inexperience showed. Not surprisingly, she was so busy making sure she got her aggressive body language right that she had almost forgotten that the purpose of join-up is to get the horse to want to be with you. As she sent him round and round the pen, it was as if she had lost track of the fact that the horse was there with her, with all his emotions, which were far more sensitive than she had supposed. It was clear he was ready to communicate, but was too anxious because her body language had still not softened after several minutes. When I began work, he had done barely a circuit before I offered a response to his attempts to "renegotiate the deal". I saved any sending away for moments when he made an aggressive gesture. In this way I was able to give him a very clear understanding of how he could behave differently and do a whole lot less work.

I believe he experienced a degree of frustration at times in this process, as he had undoubtedly done during his initial 'join-up' work with Jenny, but with a difference. Before, he had been frustrated with Jenny because he couldn't find a way to be allowed to stop running around. Now, his frustration was linked to his own behaviour. When he tried to bite or bully me and got sent away, this would be followed by much head-tossing as if to indicate he was frustrated with himself for doing something he knew was out of line, and that this was the cause of being put back to work.

This theme continued into leading work, for if he followed me politely without trying to barge, overtake or go off on his own, I made it completely comfortable for him. Rather than beginning with pressure on the rope to give him instructions, he was presented with the choice of following my body as I moved off, or, a second or two later, running sharply into pressure when he ran out of rope. Likewise, if he stopped politely outside my personal space when I stopped my feet, no negative consequences would occur - instead I would gently stroke his forehead. If he failed this simple task, he would find me doing whatever was necessary to back him smartly away from me. Very soon he was "leading" (i.e., not leading, but following) better than his stable mate who allegedly had no issues with leading. Toby and Jenny were very pleased with the results and we decided to put our new understanding to the test by leading him around the farm.

We went all over their property, which is exceptionally flat, and throughout the walk the King behaved sensibly if not exactly perfectly. I felt in no danger, although I never let my guard down. We went through a number of gates and back and forth across the area where Toby had such a massive battle leading him as a yearling, without a problem, even though it was early spring and there was no grass in his field and loads along the verges. It was as if he had never had an issue.

Almost as an afterthought I led him up the drive leading to their front door. This was really the only place on the property where there was a slope, as their door was at the top of a large bank of earth. The drive led there in a loop and he waltzed up it in perfect order. On the way back down, however, he planted his feet and when I asked him forward, he reared right up.

Before I met Monty Roberts, there is no question what would have happened to me in that position. Heading down a slope with a rearing horse would have been so dangerous - given that I would have been leading right next to the horse's shoulder in the traditional way - that I would have almost certainly been seriously injured by a flailing foreleg or worse still, been pulled under the horse as he came down, and crushed. My adrenaline would have been so high that I would have been unable to remain detached from the proceedings and look objectively at what had happened and why. Toby and Jenny both immediately pointed out that this was the kind of behaviour they were used to and I can imagine they were expecting me to discipline it appropriately - without anger, but very strictly all the same.

The starting point with any behavioural issue is always to attempt to eliminate all physical pain before training. This is often surprisingly very difficult to achieve. Despite spending any amount of money on equine specialists such as vets, dentists, saddlers, farriers, chiropractors and physiotherapists, one can end up missing physical issues. Jenny and Toby were as well aware as I that physical problems are often the cause of behavioural ones, but all the same when it came down to it, none of us immediately recognised that the King was not rearing to try and kill us and take over the farm for his own devious ends - he was trying to tell us his leg was killing him, and when he had to go down the slope it was much worse and he had now lost his sense of humour over it.

Up until then it had been bearable, but going down the slope was putting too much extra weight on his foreleg and the pain was much greater. When I asked him to move straight across the slope, across the softer lawn, which also reduced the concussion in his leg, he was perfectly happy to do so. Toby and Jenny were also surprisingly unperturbed about having several lines of deep hoof prints all over the grass, but then they are proper hunting folk, and to such people all grass exists primarily for its potential to be ridden across. We were all somewhat humbled by the realisation that even though we knew he had a wonky leg, in the heat of the moment we had not been far off blaming the King for expressing the fact that he was in pain.

That day was a major turning point for the King and also for Toby and Jenny. They were faced with irrefutable evidence that there might be better answers for certain questions, at least for dealing with aggression, biting, leading, lunging, catching, backing and picking up feet. The evidence was not just there in the marked change in their horse's behaviour as a result of a few hours' work, but as Jenny later wrote in a magazine article, "A bigger shock was to come. Once the horse had become so gentle he could be handled and led, I asked Adam how long he had been working with horses.

He scratched his head and said, 'At Easter it will be three years'."

Between them, Toby and Jenny had almost a century of working with horses under their belts. Clearly, if experience reliably determines your level of competence and ability to deal with an equestrian problem, I was very much less well equipped than them. The reason I could make such progress with their horse was simply because I was doing things differently, and using logical, ethical, and above all, learnable techniques.

To their credit, both Toby and Jenny were now completely open to change. But that didn't mean it would be easy. As we walked away from the King's stable, I knew my work was only just beginning. As people say, "If you always do what you always did, you always get what you always got" - it was time to work on changing how they interacted with the King in almost every way.

Turning to me, Jenny started before I'd even broached the subject. "I know you're going to want me to lead him like you just did but I don't want to have him behind me. I'll just feel so unsafe if I can't see him - is it ok for me just to keep him by my shoulder here?" she asked, indicating a spot where he would have actually been in the lead himself.

Any change tends to feel unusual and therefore can be worrying at first, so I began by pointing out that the way she had been leading had not been safe or easily understood by the King. Doing it like that, he was also easily able to bite and kick her, as well as use his considerable weight to shove her about. In addition, if he reared she was already under his feet. Besides all this, because she was holding the rope so close to his chin, if he decided to go AWOL he could pull her off balance in a flash before she could get herself into a better position. However, I pointed out that I also agreed with her, that he should not be behind her. I did not consider it safe to have him directly behind unless he was at least eight feet away. From there he would be completely unable to bite or kick her, and rearing would not be a danger, as her long rope would allow her to stay well out of the way. If something spooked him, he would have some time to avoid his leader, instead of being so close that he would have landed on you before he had even consciously realised there was something moving in the bushes. However, I advised her to keep him in her peripheral vision and be ready to take action to deal with whatever he might throw at her. She looked at me with distinct unease in her eye.

I took this as my cue to pass her a lunge line while I held on to the clip, falling silent. She gazed in blank astonishment, so I licked and chewed a bit and then wandered off to find some grass. For several minutes she got dragged around and generally taken advantage of, while I tried every trick the King knew and a few others he didn't. As we continued, with me coaching her extensively on how to react to each different scenario, she became more and more proficient. In learning an effective response to every one of the likely moves her horse might throw at her, Jenny also became far more confident about the new leading position she was now quite happy to adopt. When she later took him for a walk out to his field, the same walk she had been dreading twice a day for years, she was very capable of controlling him. It looked like his reign of terror was over.

The King developed in the following weeks into a very willing youngster who still retained all his original character and boldness. Jenny and Toby began the first of many efforts to make his leg more comfortable. On my second visit to them I put on his first saddle and long-lines, and about a month later, after more work, Nicole and I backed him when Jenny brought him and another horse to Moor Wood for a riding clinic. He was an easy and unremarkable horse to start.

I was lucky enough to be invited back by Jenny and Toby several times. They got the bug really badly, and couldn't get enough "Monty stuff". They've gone on to become even more formidable horsemen, already having been teachers with many years of experience, capable of jumping massive hedges and ditches which would have me running for cover. They have an insatiable thirst for knowledge that has led them to study a number of other "natural horsemanship" systems, and to develop their own hybrid methods. The King managed some eventing with Toby, after several treatments to help his leg and a change of farrier. He always suffered from being accident-prone and also had an infection of the dreaded strangles. He was a wonderful spirit and great teacher, but I never expected for all his courage and talent that he'd ever reach the Olympics. His soundness continued to deteriorate due to his feet. For years he had corrective shoeing but it didn't help. The decision to end his difficulties was made before he lost his dignity.

As for Toby and Jenny, like Monty, they have become more prominent and well-respected trainers with age. Through them, some of Monty's methods, and those of others they have studied, are being drip-fed to the top event trainers - in disguise, though, as Jenny put it, because she didn't feel ready to 'come out' to the eventing fraternity. That was in 2001, which in terms of my own professional development seems like a very long time ago, but little in the world of eventing seems to have changed. The work I did for them was a major departure in all sorts of ways from the manuals that form and inform that world. None of the staples of the industry they had such an intense knowledge of - voice commands, lunging, titbits, cavessons, and the chiffney, not to mention the whip - had any place in the work I introduced to them. They were the first ones to celebrate the extraordinary turn around in their horse's behaviour, and both Toby and Jenny learned with an unending enthusiasm. But for whatever reasons, they were not keen to be associated with Monty in public, nor with me. Eight years later, they still wished us not to use their real names in this account.

I think it's sad that this should be the case. Perhaps it doesn't give people at their level much kudos to say that they have been learning from someone as inexperienced as I was at the time, although to me, it's the most admirable quality anyone could have, to be as open minded as they were to new ideas. I only hope that when I've got fifty years experience under my belt I'll still be willing to look at new alternatives.

In any case, as I began to explain earlier, one of the world's most famous event riders unwittingly has both myself and Monty, as well as Jenny, to thank for not getting disqualified at a top event. This rider had a horse who was virtually impossible to handle at the vet check, and had been warned that they would be disqualified if the horse was not better behaved. Jenny, being nearby, offered to help, asking for just ten minutes to work on him round the back of the stables. Many people would have used that time to bash the horse around with a chiffney or a whip, but she just went through some of the same procedures I had shown her that very first day with the King. She caused the horse to walk when she walked, without overtaking or bashing into her; to halt when she halted, with the same respect for her space; and crucially, to back up when she moved into his space. Those few minutes of handling by a small middle aged lady made enough difference to the horse that he passed the vet test and went on to be placed in the competition.

At the present time, that's probably my biggest claim to

fame in the world of eventing, and I know it's not much. Still, I feel I have a lot to be proud of, for saving the King's life, and possibly someone else's life as well. But it was my clients who really showed that, as long as you have an open mind, it's never too late to change.

FOUR

A Very English Mustang
(Nicole)

If there's something special about working with a potential top-flight eventer, there's something even more wonderful about dealing with a 'wild' horse. Or more accurately, in this country, an unhandled or untouched feral one. Maybe it's just a romantic ideal - the notion of two such very different species as a human and horse coming together, the gradual conquering of their mutual fear, the fragile, growing trust. The sense of every time being like the first time, when man first saw the noble Equus and thought, "I wonder if I could sit on that thing?", I'm not sure. But I do know that to be asked to work with an unhandled horse, to make that first touch, is a huge privilege and responsibility, and one of the hardest tests of anyone's ability, tact and understanding. It's also the sort of highly specialised work that few professional horse trainers have any experience of.

Oddly, even in England you don't have to go too far to find wild horses. Not even to more remote regions such as Dartmoor or Exmoor. Counties such as Oxfordshire and Buckinghamshire have a surprising number lurking in their green fields. Sometimes people just breed large numbers of horses in fairly natural circumstances, and allow the herd to run. Then, unless something happens early on, a horse can reach a few years of age without having received any handling. It can happen when horses herded from the hills are rescued from the meat trade, and then turned away without any further contact, or when an unapproachable mare is bred from, and no-one can get near the foal either. Whatever the reason, touching the horse for the first time, putting on the first headcollar, taking those initial steps in leading, and going through the early stages of handling the feet, is a huge thrill. It's generally just as dangerous to

31

work with such a horse who lives just down the road as it is to go to Namibia, as Kelly famously did for TV a few years ago to work with horses that have hardly ever been within a mile of a human. At least those horses in Namibia have never had any contact with humans, and have no reason to fear them. Feral horses in the UK, such as those coming off Exmoor, often have very good reason to fear humans having had some extremely negative contact - being herded into a crush, branded, forcibly wormed and packed off to market in a lorry.

When I went on the second ever Monty Roberts course, back in 1996, the theory all took place in the classrooms of the West Oxfordshire College in Witney, and the practical side was run from the College's thoroughbred stud. Kelly had only just retired from racing at the height of her career, having won the Ladies' European Championship, and with Monty's background in racing, the association with the College made good sense. Thoroughbred youngsters being prepared for the track are perhaps not typical of the sort of horses we are asked to work with (although stressed, traumatised and damaged ex-racehorses form a significant portion of our work), and I remember that Kelly used to joke that their idea of a "raw" horse was a two year old with a pulled mane and shod feet, wearing a surcingle and a bridle! Although Kelly was able to procure a variety of horses for us to work with on the course, when the opportunity arose to relocate to another stud in the area, she jumped at the chance. Willow Farm couldn't have been more different from the thoroughbred stud. Home of a large-scale breeder, the approach there was fundamentally hands-off; the stallion ran out with the mares, the foals were born in the fields, and not interfered with for months unless some sort of medical problem arose.

It was a ten week long course, which might sound a lot, but every minute was so precious, and I was having so much fun that I couldn't believe how fast the time flew by. When my course finished, just before Christmas, it felt as if a part of my life had come to an end. I had relished every moment, and the void it left was palpable. Before I left, I impressed upon Kelly that I would be willing to help her in the future in whatever way I could. The hours at my new job as Communications Officer with Thames Valley Police in Milton Keynes were of the "unsociable" kind that mostly left my days free, so I would be able to travel to Witney at fairly short notice. If Kelly hadn't taken me up on this offer, our lives would be very different today. As it was, she asked me to come back the next term to speak to the new intake of students, and also told me that I would be welcome to come and watch Monty whenever he was visiting the courses. This continued contact not only meant that my education in these revolutionary techniques continued apace, but that I was able to drift easily into a teaching role. Watching Kelly take student after student through their join-ups in the round pen enabled me to feel confident when she casually suggested that I should coach the next person. As time went on, my role expanded, so that when Adam did his course just a year and a half after I completed mine, I was one of his official teachers. I tried not to take too much advantage of this position of authority.

Watching Monty work at Willow Farm was fascinating, and we came to understand what the term "untouched" could really mean. Monty's mouth started watering when he saw the wealth of potential learning to be had there. A veritable University, he used to say. To top it all, these were pure bred Hackneys, and Hackney-Welsh cob crosses, who make even the highest-strung Arabs and thoroughbreds look placid. If we hadn't moved to Willow Farm, we would never have had the grounding in handling untouched horses that has enabled us to help so many owners and their 'wild' horses. Certainly, none of my BHS training had prepared me in any way, nor had the tricks I knew for catching difficult horses. While using a titbit and hiding the headcollar behind your back may not make the situation any worse, it's unlikely to make any headway with a wild horse.

The horses at Willow Farm did at least have a reasonable amount of experience of being herded, however, and with one or two ridden horses in the herd, it was possible to gather them from their enormous field and "decant" them into small pens, and thus start work in a more manageable area. This is much more practical than trying to work in one hundred acres of boggy reclaimed marshland (it wasn't called Willow Farm for nothing!), but the smaller space that makes getting closer to the horse easier also means injury to the handler is more probable too. After all, if you can get close enough to touch the horse, it stands to reason that they are close enough to touch you, perhaps with a lightning-fast strike of a hoof. But working carefully, initially under Monty's direction, allowed Kelly and the students on the courses not only to touch, handle, and halter-break these youngsters, but also, in time, to introduce the first saddle, long-lines, bridle and rider. Being a part of this process was a real privilege for me.

So, after several months of working with these raw horses, we had become somewhat expert, which is why Kelly was asked to catch an untouched horse in another part of Oxfordshire. This horse had been part of a group running with a stallion, and none of them had been approachable for a long time. This mare had come to the owner's attention because she was hopping lame. In an overgrazed, marshy field, without a variety of terrain to roam over, and no hard ground or tarmac to file them down, her feet had become overgrown, cracked, and abscesses had developed, causing her excruciating pain. The owners had decided to round up all the horses, put them in a lorry, and sell them off, but in spite of the fact that all her field companions had complied, this mare refused to leave the field. It may have been something to do with the narrow concrete bridge she would have had to cross, or maybe she had an understandable suspicion of the lorry, but she remained elusive. Even when she was on her own, she had no wish for human company, and all the usual attempts to gain her trust, such as feeding her, had done nothing but teach her an ever-expanding repertoire of ways to avoid human contact. She looked likely to present a real challenge.

At the same time, the producers of a local TV news programme had decided they wanted to cover a story on 'horse whispering in the home counties', so Kelly suggested that we take them along, as well as the course students, and make a project out of catching her. I have to admit I thought it was a bit ambitious. I even jokingly suggested we bring a vet with a tranquilliser gun, like they use for big game in Africa. We later discovered that this method is sometimes used by welfare charities, but of course it carries its own risks, and is also extremely expensive. Monty, when consulted by phone, also warned Kelly about the dangers of the situation. The youngsters we had been working with were challenging enough, but they were immature, and essentially just "green". This horse was a mature mare, who had had foals, and was also in pain. She had never been enclosed before, and had already successfully evaded capture. If we were able to get her into a round pen, she could potentially be very dangerous. He really didn't want his most promising student to put herself in this kind of danger.

Kelly listened seriously to his advice, but decided to go ahead with the attempt anyway.

After the morning sessions on the course, we took a number of round pen panels, and all twelve students and four teachers, out to the field to assess the situation. The aim was to try to gently "haze" her into a smaller enclosure, so that Kelly could begin the work of gaining her trust. Hopefully, she would accept her first headcollar, learn to lead, and finally load into a trailer to be taken away for further handling and training. It had been several weeks since all the other horses had been removed, and luckily in that time the abscesses had burst out of the top of her hoof, so she was no longer in as much pain. The horse didn't have a name, so Kelly named her Martine, after the presenter of the television show.

One of the students on the course with a four wheel drive kindly volunteered to tow the steel mesh round-pen panels over, and the task of building a pen and getting the mare into it was successfully completed without any major traumas - I think she was so unfamiliar with artificial barriers that she didn't realise she was completely enclosed until it was too late for her to do anything about it. So now she had gone from a twenty acre field to a twenty foot round-pen - a good start, but what next? How should one go about touching a five-year-old horse for the first time? Any unnecessary running around was out of the question, as she didn't need any pressure on her damaged foot, so a conventional join-up wasn't possible. A small enclosure was a good start, but also quite an uncomfortable place to be in with such a wild animal. Closer inspection revealed that she was a formidable horse. Only about 15.2 hands high, but extremely well built, she looked more like caged tiger than a frightened flight animal. Her chestnut coat gleamed over rippling muscles, in spite of her lack of care and attention. I'd seen Kelly work with many unhandled weanlings and yearlings, but never such a mature, untouched, intimidating horse.

"Make it comfortable for the horse when he is doing what you want him to do, and uncomfortable for him when he is doing what you don't want him to do", was one of the sayings we had learned from Monty, but the problem was that almost anything we did was likely to make her feel threatened, and hence defensive, which was likely to come out as aggression. The students and I sat a little distance away as quietly as we could, trying not to make any movements which might set Martine off and endanger Kelly, who put on her helmet and gloves and went into the pen with only a long lead rope to protect herself if Martine decided to go for her. Talking to her quietly, mostly in order to ensure that she herself kept breathing, Kelly started working around the edge of Martine's comfort zone, occasionally stepping in closer, and rewarding tolerance by immediately moving further away. Initially, the mare was terrified by the presence of a human in her space, but as she began to realise that Kelly wasn't going to hurt her, she began to relax slightly. This didn't mean she was going to be at all happy about being touched, however, let alone having a head collar put on her.

Kelly continued to work patiently, gradually moving in closer. If the mare "made a break for it", Kelly would use a mildly aggressive movement to push her slightly away, and by degrees the mare came to understand that Kelly could actually control her movements, from a distance, and that it wasn't necessarily such a bad thing. This was reassuring to us watching, too, because it suggested that if the horse did come at Kelly, aggressive body language might well see her off.

Very often with an untouched horse the easiest place to get to is the shoulder. It's also the safest spot to work from, as you're comparatively clear of both front and back legs, although the emphasis here is on comparatively, because in the blink of an eye a horse can wheel round and kick, or strike with its front feet, or indeed bite. Martine had strong opinions about this approach, however. Any attempt to get near her shoulder resulted in some kind of violent eruption - either a lightning fast foreleg strike, a rear, or a quick race around the pen. With her adrenaline up to the point where she no longer felt the pain from her feet, she managed to appear completely sound, as if to say "I'm alright, really, you can let me back in my field now." At one point, she even tried climbing out of the pen. The breakthrough came when her nose accidentally brushed Kelly's hand, and Kelly immediately moved away. A second attempt confirmed the mare's suspicions - that she could train the human to move away from her, just by allowing her nose to be touched. A few more times, and she began to quite like sniffing Kelly's hand. So, the first contact had been made. Now what?

Famously, in order to demonstrate his methods for the TV programme 'QED', Monty trained a registered wild mustang on an open range in Nevada. The horse in question, named Shy Boy, was separated from his herd by several riders before Monty followed him for over twenty-four hours, riding several different mounts, before going through the movements he uses in a round pen while performing join-up. After Monty achieved join-up with Shy Boy in the wild, he put on a rope halter from the back of his very well trained mount. Usually, it is easier to tie one of these on than it is to introduce a head collar. It's a very mild form of halter that can be used to introduce the horse to the concept of yielding to pressure. The first step is to get the rope over the horse's neck, and then to tie a bowline knot. A loop in the rope can then be passed over the horse's nose. Sounds easy? Convincing a wild mare to have a rope attached to her is quite a challenge, and a lot more dangerous when you aren't above her, on board another horse.

Having discovered what the mare found comfortable - that is, having her nose touched, Kelly was gradually able to move into other areas. A brief touch on the side of Martine's face, and then she would move back to the comfort zone of her nose. This process was repeated at least ten times. Kelly knew if she moved too quickly or too far, she'd pay the price of having the horse rush away, or perhaps strike at her. If this happened, time would need to be spent to re-establish trust again. Kelly worked on patiently, while the students ate their lunch in the sun. Five minutes or so of impeccable timing and Kelly was able to touch Martine on the shoulder, for a moment, with her hand.

The next stage was to introduce the rope - touching the same places again, but this time with the rope in her hand. Presumably, unlike Shy Boy and the horses Kelly later worked with in Namibia, Martine had never seen a snake, and after a few moments she began to accept the rope on her shoulder. The trick was to get it over her neck and tie the knot before she realised quite what was happening. Everyone watching held their breath, but it was vital that Kelly didn't give the game away by doing the same, or raising her pulse rate. Working at a pace that was steady and careful without resembling stalking, she seemed to be the calmest person there as she slipped the rope over Martine's neck and, unavoidably entering the most dangerous part of a horse's kick zone - under its neck - she leaned down to pick up the loose end, while Martine stood like a rock, ready to strike at the slightest wrong move. With the knot complete, Kelly again rewarded her by moving away. A big step had been achieved. She had a rope around Martine's neck.

The next step of placing the loop over the horse's nose was comparatively easy, as she was by now quite happy with her nose being touched. With this makeshift halter on, things were looking relatively under control - until Martine suddenly erupted.

A horse's instinctive reaction to any sort of pressure on their head is to fight against it - and this wild chestnut mare was no exception. Her response to the gentlest tension on the line was to throw herself across the pen, generally dragging Kelly with her. Somehow, in the maelstrom, Kelly kept her head. Making sure to stay out of the way and also keep the rope from getting tangled around Martine's neck or flailing legs, Kelly immediately released the pressure on the rope as soon as the mare took even the slightest move in the right direction. Gradually, as she began to calm down a bit, Martine began to learn what was required of her. Within five minutes, she was taking one small tentative step at a time towards Kelly. She still looked like an unexploded bomb, though.

She couldn't be left with the rope halter on - it was made out of a continuous piece of rope and the spare end was several feet long. So the next task of the afternoon was to replace the rope halter with a head collar. We had learned from past experience that a head collar with buckles on the nosepiece as well as the headpiece makes this process a lot easier, as the whole thing can be opened up, and then put on in stages. Now that Martine was beginning to understand how to release herself from pressure, Kelly's chances of success were significantly improved, but it was still a big challenge for them both. Within the confines of the small round-pen, and now with the rope halter on, Martine seemed to realise that her options for escape were getting more and more limited. Under pressure, as Kelly worked to put the head collar on, she even (for one heart-stopping moment) struck out with a foreleg. The movement was lightning quick, and even knowing that Kelly was positioned in the safest possible place, it was still hard for those of us on the outside of the pen not to jump when Martine reacted violently. Staying calm, and persisting, Kelly was able to work the head collar around Martine's neck. Once this was securely attached, she could then gently work the nose-strap over Martine's nose and quietly do it up. A short piece of rope was attached to this, so that the mare could work out by herself overnight how to release herself from pressure when she stepped on it. Kelly felt the time was right for Martine be left alone, so we put hay and water in the pen. The whole training process had taken just two hours.

When we all arrived the next day she was completely unperturbed about the rope on the head collar, and was a lot less worried when Kelly stepped into the pen than she had been before. It was still not a case of marching straight up to her, however, and Kelly spent a few moments re-establishing the trust that they had built up the day before. She was soon able to attach a long rope, and continue the leading work. Martine was so much improved that the consensus of opinion was to keep the session brief and positive, to let her mull it over, and to tackle the issue of the trailer the next day.

The concrete footbridge over the river was still a cause for concern, as it was quite high above the water and had no railings. We decided to bring more round pen panels so that we could build a chute leading from the pen, over the bridge, to the trailer. One difficulty was that the round pen containing Martine was too far away to join it to the chute. The solution we came up with was to move the round pen, with her inside. With one or two students and the odd cameraman on every panel, we were able to "walk" the pen over to the bridge.

Martine seemed to know she was being helped, and Kelly didn't need to put any pressure on her at all, letting her work out what she needed to do in her own time. It took her a few moments, but she took the plunge and tiptoed nervously out of the pen and over the bridge. Even to the humans, the trailer didn't appear a very attractive prospect, in spite of having had all the partitions removed. At one stage Martine decided very clearly against going anywhere near it, and looked for a moment as if she would go straight back to the round-pen. Astonishingly, it only took her a few short minutes to follow Kelly tentatively into the trailer. Everyone was spared being overcome by emotion, however, by seeing her re-emerge backwards just a few seconds later, somewhat faster than she went in! However, Kelly continued to help Martine calmly work out what this was all about, and after going in and out a few more times, she'd settled enough for the back ramp to be put up and for Kelly to come out. Martine was driven off at a top speed of 10 mph. She went off to her new yard, to be handled and to have her feet seen to. By the time we'd loaded up the pen and followed her over there, she was settled in a stable, eating hay, looking as if she'd been there all her life.

Kelly kept in touch with Martine's new owners, and we heard that with more careful, considerate training she did in fact become a rideable, handleable horse, albeit still a sharp and lively one. Without Kelly's skillful intervention, however, it's clear that the only real alternative would have been a bullet. For such a magnificent horse to have met this fate would have been tragic, but the real tragedy is that she was allowed to get into such a state in the first place. Of course, there are many such cases in Britain today, and working to help and educate owners is one of the core concerns of Intelligent Horsemanship. Kelly even runs specific courses on handling untouched horses, in the hope of ensuring that these animals have a fair start and avoid the otherwise brutal methods sometimes employed in "taming" them. Working with the RSPCA and other rescue organisations is a key part of this strategy. But tradition fights back, and some of the "time-honoured" practices, such as the forcible branding of Exmoor ponies, continue to be done with no thought for the future training of these animals, whose early negative experiences make gaining their trust much more difficult later. The techniques we use are so effective that they can help many a remedial case, but our greatest wish is that we could prevent such suffering or the need to learn these kinds of skills in the first place.

FIVE

The Horse Who Thought He Was A Rock
(Adam)

As I had discovered when I met the Dark Teen, you never know when you'll meet your greatest teachers in life, and it often seems that they come from where you least expect them. I feel greatly honoured to have helped so many deserving and gracious horses and the people who care for them, and I honestly think every one of them taught me something. They probably also tried to teach me a lot more than I noticed or gave them credit for, but sometimes you're just not ready to learn.

As they say, when the student is ready, the teacher will appear. The problem is, unless you have your mind even more open than your eyes, you could easily fail to notice the Master Teacher standing before you. It was down to good fortune and a series of happy coincidences that I came across a fellow called Peter, who has probably had a more profound impact on my horsemanship than almost any other horse, even though I never rode him and only knew him for a few months.

It started with a phone call from his owner, Kate, and I went up to meet them on a yard not very far away. The problem appeared to involve halter training and napping, as he would not walk across the yard or load into a lorry, and he also refused to go out for hacks, although he was easy to ride in the school. I assumed that he was lacking in confidence and that Kate simply had not found ways to communicate with him clearly, or that like many owners, she was not prepared to use force to make him comply with her wishes, and didn't know any other way to be effective.

To be honest, I got it so wrong. If I could go back to that first day, and stand in his shoes, I wonder what it must have felt like - to stay late in the stable and then have this skinny bloke turn up who

41

spent lots of time evaluating me and talking to Kate before putting on a head collar and watching me again as I was let out of the stable into the yard. Hopefully, I would have been grateful for the new way of leading that he was teaching Kate, but the more he concentrated on improving her leading skills, the less I might have felt listened to. Pretty soon I probably wouldn't have expected this guy to help me out either, as I tried again to get someone to listen by politely refusing to cross the twenty metres of concrete leading to the school.

Here was a true gentleman of a horse, for as we only later realised, he was in terrible discomfort, but he only showed it by patiently trying to get someone to pay attention, and finally copying Ghandi and refusing to work, by means of a non-violent protest. And it truly was non-violent. He just stood there as if he were made of stone. I can't remember him even curling a nostril in anger, let alone threatening to kick or rear. Maybe he was too sweet natured, or perhaps he had completely given up and was just waiting, devoid of hope, for whatever was coming. "He's only living up to his name," I joked, adding when Kate looked at me with a quizzical expression, "Peter - Petra is the Greek for rock. He's literally petrified - turned to stone!"

Once in the school, on a soft surface, he was ready to move more freely, but what must he have thought as I sent him away to begin join-up? My problem was partly that, as a result of the more effective method of leading that I showed her, coupled with the pressure halter I was using, he improved rapidly to the point where he reliably followed her across the yard several times without making any protest. The lead rope never once became tight. But I couldn't see the wood for the trees. Having met so many horses who have (I think) simply been so poorly trained to lead - all I could see was what I could do, and teach Kate to do, that would get him to follow her with a minimum of fuss. He didn't appear to be lame at all. The nappy behaviour under saddle, I reasoned, was hardly surprising given that here was a horse whose apparent lack of faith in his owner was such that he wouldn't even follow her across the yard.

Having done join-up, I did some further groundwork and then gave Kate a riding lesson. He seemed to be improving so much, and was probably glad that she was not kicking or pulling any more and was in better balance, but what I completely failed to take into account, however, was the possibility that he was only being so compliant because the excellent surface in the school was so much more comfortable for him.

By the end of that first session a lot looked like it was well on the way to being fixed. He consented to walk across the yard again, without resistance and when she rode him out around the block, we were able to keep him from napping without use of any physical force. She was delighted with the progress we had made and asked me to come back again and work on his loading, which was somewhat of a nightmare for her.

The yard and the whole surrounding area was covered in so much concrete and tarmac that I asked her to book the school and get permission for me to drive the lorry into it, and do the loading training there. Being on a hard surface is not safe when training a bad loader, as it is not unusual for them to slip or even rear during training and it has been known (although it has never happened to us) for a horse to go right over backwards and injure or even kill itself falling onto concrete. Kate didn't have a lorry and used to hire one when she wanted to go anywhere, which she seldom did because it caused them both so much upset getting him on board, so when the day came I somehow managed to get my consistently unreliable lorry started and set off in the 'Big Green Monster' to our appointment.

When I arrived I was relieved to hear that she had been given permission to do the loading inside the school, so I drove right in and began working. Join-up was exemplary, he was still extremely responsive to the halter, and backed up fluently. When I felt we were ready I began to approach the lorry and soon had his front feet on and off the ramp. He was hesitant to go for it and come all the way on, but we were looking pretty close to a result when a young woman, who was evidently the yard manager, appeared and interrupted us, taking Kate to one side and beginning what looked like an awkward conversation. I stood with Peter, remembering how Kate had told me how difficult she found it to tolerate the atmosphere around the yard and wondering whether I should continue to work or wait. I decided I should not go any further without her attention, not least because I thought it likely he was just about to go in.

Their conversation went on quite a long time and was becoming quite heated, the theme appearing to be, "What on earth are you doing in my school?"

Kate was understandably quite upset, having arranged in advance for us to drive the lorry into the school to do this work. It was hard to work out what the yard manager's objection was: the work was unlikely to cause as much disruption to the school surface as a horse going over a jump a few times. Besides, now that the lorry was actually in the school there wasn't much point in us moving it out before we had finished. Loaded or not, we had to move the lorry unless she wanted us to leave it permanently there, which, given how unreliable it was at starting, was a distinct possibility. I decided against mentioning this point. Their discussion was clearly not getting any calmer, and after waiting silently for quite some time thinking how awkward I felt, and how much money it was costing Kate to have me stand there, I thought I would pipe up and try to settle the thing, reasoning that if the yard manager didn't like me that was not a big deal, but that if Kate had a falling out with her, it could be really disruptive for her and Peter.

Well, my father was a diplomat but judging by the result of the next few minutes, I didn't inherit the gene. It turned out that the subtext for her complaint was that the girl didn't like what I was doing to load Peter, despite the fact that it had nothing to do with her. We were told to move the lorry. Kate and I were both very unhappy about it. Peter had gone a long way towards loading and now we were going to disrupt the training yet more, put him back in his stable and spend ten minutes cranking up and moving the Green Monster after finding somewhere to finish the work. "Are you really sure you can get him in?" Kate said, seemingly on the verge of tears. When I assured her that we would be fine, she said decisively, "If you can, then can you take him home with you and look after him until I find somewhere to keep him? I've had enough of being around here." I agreed, quietly crossing my fingers in the hope that the Green Monster would start again, and get us home.

The only remotely suitable place I could find was a sloping field gateway, which was ridiculously difficult to get the lorry into. Having done so, it seemed ages later that Peter was back with us. Thankfully, he went straight in, almost as if he had heard our conversation and knew how lovely Moor Wood is. He never resisted loading from that moment on, but unfortunately the girl from the yard never had the opportunity to see how the work we'd done had made such a difference to him.

So, more by luck and lack of tact than the intent of any of us, and thanks to the uncharacteristic goodwill of the world's most obstreperous lorry, Peter arrived at the yard that evening, much to Nicole's surprise, and he soon continued to give us his lessons. A day or two after he arrived, Kate arranged for him to see a registered farrier who specialised in barefoot care.

When Nicole and I saw the degree to which Peter was lame on the removal of his shoes, we were horrified. He was immediately too sore to move at anything more than a desperate hobble, and did his very best to avoid even that. He couldn't walk on the gravel in the yard at all, and could barely move from one patch of grass to another in the field. He suffered from several abscesses, which it was clear he had developed well before the removal of his shoes. "I don't understand," Nicole said. "If he was fine with his shoes, and is so lame without them, why not just keep them on?" It was only then that it really dawned on me. He wasn't fine with his shoes. He wasn't fine at all. That's what all the napping and leading difficulty was about, and why he was so much better in the soft, forgiving surface of the school. All the time he was on the tarmac and concrete, the concussion was causing him extreme discomfort. He didn't appear lame, but only because he was equally lame on all four feet. The shoes, however, were masking the true extent of the problem, and when his damaged, thrush-infested, abscessing feet were exposed to the concrete for the first time, he just couldn't cope. Removing his shoes wasn't the problem, it was the damage that the shoes had caused, and also covered up, that was the issue.

The farrier pointed out the signs that we now recognise as being common in the shod hoof: under-run and contracted heels, putting pressure on the tendons at the back of the lower leg and the navicular bone; poor hygiene, indicated by the presence of thrush; contracted, small, infected frogs with a very deep slit in the middle (the central sulcus), into which a hoof pick could be inserted, coming out black with thrush; flat, very thin soles; forward migration of the hoof capsule and collapse of the 'internal arch'; a loss of circulation resulting in a noticeably cold leg compared to unshod horses, contributing to slow growth of horn which is therefore more stressed and weaker. For the first time I was forced to accept the fact that shoeing gradually destroys the structures of the hoof.

Now that we knew what to look for, we felt compelled to look at our own horses. It was a sickening moment when we realised the same features were present to some extent in all of the ones who had shoes on, and none of the rest. Like so many horse owners, we were doing what we thought was best for our horses, and had never questioned the necessity - and benefit - of shoes. We had even felt a bit guilty that our ponies Misty and Finn didn't have any, and perhaps had we had unlimited funds, they would have been sporting dinky little shoes, too. I could only conclude that in spite of his best care and efforts, our own farrier, of whom we were very fond and whose manner to us and our horses was always extremely polite and friendly, was gradually laming our beloved animals. When the specialist, barefoot-oriented farrier elaborated on some of the longer-term issues commonly associated with shoeing, such as arthritis, ring bone and side bone, hoof deformity, 'navicular syndrome' (which he told us is so rare in well maintained unshod horses as to be almost unknown), over reaching, and pulled tendons, I found myself wanting to object, but not so much out of a reasoned and well supported argument based on facts. I wanted to disagree simply because I didn't want to acknowledge responsibility for damaging my own horses the same way. Most of them were fully shod, and had been continuously for years. Worse still, we had presided over the first shoeing of more youngsters than I care to think of. How many of them are now getting into the same difficulties that Peter did, I can hardly bear to imagine.

Shoeing is so often referred to by farriers as a "necessary evil", but if it's an evil, why is it that shoeing is so commonplace? I believe that the answer is of fundamental importance in understanding a great deal of commonly accepted equestrian practice, not just shoeing. The sources of equestrian wisdom can largely be traced back to the military. Nobody would argue that the cavalry should go barefoot. It would be supremely impractical. Imagine the story. The horses leave barracks and are loaded into trains and taken to Southampton. They set sail, and spend the next few weeks standing in stalls full of their own excrement, from which ammonia exudes, eating away at the structures of their hooves. When they are unloaded in, say, South Africa, they face a totally different climate than the one they came from. They now have a forced march of several hundred miles across the harshest terrain, on tracks of abrasive sand and sharp gravel, weighed down with a rider and equipment, after which they are required to charge across the veldt to instil loyalty in some of Her Majesty's less co-operative subjects. I expect there would hardly be a horse capable of such a feat without shoes. The military need shoes. They can't be expected to take weeks out of their campaign schedule to acclimatise the horses and strengthen the hoof structures, allowing the odd horse not to continue when the rest are ready to go. So, it made sense for them to shoe every one of their charges. And anyway, if a horse and rider are being subjected to cannon fire, who in their right mind would be concerned about the chance that the horse may get arthritis in a few years' time? If he did, he could count himself lucky! But what's right for the military isn't always what's right for us or our horses.

For centuries, of course, people relied on horses as our only form of speed transport. They acted as tractors, cars, and coaches. They pulled heavy loads, and travelled many miles. They had to be sound and fully useable in the short-term even if the long-term consequences could be fatal. In essence, what was asked of them often exceeded the natural ability of the foot to recover, because owners did not have the luxury of giving them sufficient time to adapt to new conditions, and without shoes these horses would have had over-worn feet and been unusable. Since traditional shoeing practices solved the immediate requirements of their clients, there was very little perceived need for farriers to research into the function of the various structures in the hoof.

There was so much we didn't know, and I know we were not alone in being unaware of these issues. Like so many others, we assumed that barefoot was fine as long as you didn't want to do any significant roadwork, and that a horse in any kind of serious work had to have shoes. We were surprised when 'walking out on roads' was actually prescribed as a necessity for barefoot horses - to stimulate appropriate hoof growth. It's a bit like doing yard work. If you have really soft hands and you suddenly do a lot of sweeping, you will end up with sore, blistered hands, with the skin removed. If you just do a bit of sweeping, and do a bit more every day, you will build up callouses and not get sore. The same is true of the horse's feet, except that they will be building up strong hoof rather than just skin. The shoes can have the same effect as gloves, in terms of keeping the foot soft, but they would be more like really tight, stiff gloves, that impeded circulation and made it hard for your hands to move properly.

What we failed to recognise about the working horse was how much the environment they were in caused the necessity of shoes. As Black Beauty points out, London cab horses virtually never saw a green field; when they weren't trotting around the city streets they were tied up in stalls. Most racehorses and many competition horses don't get any significant turnout. Their feet therefore don't receive the necessary conditioning. Wild horses who spend their entire days roaming over harsh rocky terrain, however, are often cited as an example of just how tough feet can naturally be - it's hard to imagine a mustang or a brumby struggling with a bit of gravel. Of course, breeding is part of it, and the endurance horses who regularly compete in 100 mile races without shoes tend to be Arabs, but we also discovered a racehorse trainer who successfully competes his horses barefoot over hurdles, so even thoroughbreds can do it. As time went on, we heard more and more examples, including horses hunting and competing barefoot. It's not to say that every horse could do what their owner requires of them without shoes, even if the owner is committed to correct conditioning and care, but certainly many more horses than we would have thought have proved capable.

For quite some time, though, I wasn't convinced that the decision to go barefoot was right for Peter. Although I accepted that he had been lame on all four feet when I met him, and that this had been caused by shoes, there was no doubt in my mind that barefoot he was in great pain, much more acutely than before. It took a couple of weeks before he began to look even a bit less footsore and it wasn't till a couple of months later that he was rideable. But gradually he got better, and by the end of the summer when he went to live at another yard, he was sound and his feet had changed a lot. Where he had been walking on his soles, there was now some concavity and the walls had grown stronger and longer so he was protected from the pressure of stones, although he was still being careful not to stomp around on gravel. His frogs were far harder and no longer had fissures and slits in them, nor did they exude the black, stinking thrush infestation they had previously. His abscesses had cleared up, his heels were coming back and his toe was not pushed forward and flared outwards.

In addition all our horses were barefoot, although I would hasten to add that none of them suffered anything like the same degree of difficulty in transition.

Looking back on it, I realise that the farrier who worked with Peter did not know all that much about what he was doing. The transition period was made much worse by the fact that we were not warned to protect the feet against any chance of bruising on stones in the initial days. This caused a few instances of small-scale bruising that led to unnecessary abscesses, which weaken the hoof structure a lot. We were asked to soak the feet in water every day, which was extremely tedious and ultimately of little or no value. The horses were generally footsore for a few days after every trim, which is extremely rare with the Applied Equine Podiatrist we have these days. He also did not give us reliable advice about how much work we should do and of what kind, which meant that sometimes we would do too much and damage the structures. Equally important, he did not give us a programme to follow in order to condition the feet on sand and on the road, so the hooves did not strengthen as much as they could have done. At least he didn't do the sort of catastrophic damage we know to have been done by some extreme trimming methods.

In the end, we were badly let down by this farrier, who at the time of writing is about three and a half years late for an appointment. We've no idea why he never turned up, since he seems unable to return a phone call (which is something not uncommon among farriers - perhaps this is something they learn at farriery school). We'd certainly never exchanged a cross word with him. Although it's really shocking that he should apparently care so little about the horses he trims, we will nevertheless forever be grateful to him and especially to Peter for the learning we got from them. I am absolutely confident that our horses' welfare has been hugely enhanced by going barefoot, not least because we have hardly seen a cut or bruise on them, even when they have kicked one another. I am even grateful to that farrier, albeit through gritted teeth, for not turning up or replying to our calls. Otherwise, we still might not have come across a much better methodology, which, put into practice by our Equine Podiatrist, has made it a rare event for our horses to have abscesses or be footsore, and enabled us to give helpful advice to many clients who have followed the same path.

As for Peter, he is no longer the horse who thought he was a rock. The last we heard, he was sound and successfully competing in one day events, despite the occasional comment that he has lost not one or two but all four of his shoes!

SIX

Tazman And The Green Monster
(Nicole)

Having seen Kelly work with Martine, and achieved a lot with those wild little youngsters at Willow Farm, I am always delighted when the phone rings and a flummoxed owner offers us the challenge of catching a completely raw horse. Whilst most people are too sensible to let slip the opportunity presented by some early handling while a foal is particularly impressionable as well as small, one of the hardest 'untouchable' cases Adam and I have ever been involved with was actually caused by early handling. Someone had managed to get a head collar on a yearling, called Rocky, and then left him in the field thinking that it would make the horse a lot easier to catch. Sadly, as time passed, this owner was unable to get near him and, as he grew, the head collar got tighter and tighter until it had started cutting into his head.

It was the first time we had ever been asked to remove a head collar from an otherwise completely unhandled horse. Rocky's owner, Barbara, had a number of horses, all of whom had been rescued from some dire fate or another. Unable to catch him, she was hoping we could remove this head collar and get him into a stable so she could continue to work on him without the interference of the herd. She had been attempting to bribe Rocky with treats, and had got him comparatively comfortable with her presence over a gate, but whenever she tried to touch him or even the head collar, let alone attach a rope to it, he would leap away. The worst thing was that because it was so tight, there was by now no slack anywhere. Even trying to attach a rope to the ring at the bottom was really difficult, as it was almost part of his chin.

We loaded some round pen panels into our "trusty" lorry, and along with our working pupil at the time, a considerably more

51

trustworthy and, just as importantly, nearly as strong Dane called Brian. Together we set off to a field near Windsor. The six steel mesh panels we took were an absolute minimum but were heavy enough all the same. However we knew from so many situations that they could be invaluable, in spite of how awkward it was to get them on a lorry, and how awkward the Green Monster was, too, for that matter - a temperamental diesel-guzzling money pit capable of eating a thousand pounds without any discernible improvement in its performance or reliability. This time, the green was with us, so to speak, and we arrived without a hitch.

The first step was to separate Rocky out from the others and into the small pen. A job, as we explained to Barbara and Brian, requiring great skill and care, and one which might take a considerable time. Precise positioning was paramount, and knowing when to stand still, when to move a little, when to stand your ground, and when to step aside, would be essential. In short, all the subtleties of body language would need to be observed, as the slightest mistake could mean the difference between success and failure. Stay very alert, we cautioned, and listen very carefully to our instructions. We positioned Brian on "gate" duty - a whole round pen panel, as an actual round pen gate would be too narrow an opening to be inviting, and we started to gently 'haze' the horses, working our way behind the herd with the intention of driving them slowly, quietly, unsuspectingly, towards the pen. Although we didn't feel we moved too sharply, the horses abruptly stopped grazing, and moved off at a brisk trot before wheeling around. Our "target" picked up speed and even began cantering towards the pen. Seemingly unaware of what he was doing, he went straight through the entranceway. The others, who were following, swerved aside at the last moment. "Close the gate!" we called to Brian, not an instruction that he needed all that much, and without further ado, there was our horse, separate from the others, in a nice small pen instead of in a big field, and the whole process had taken no more than 20 seconds. He settled down to graze, seemingly unperturbed, and his buddies kindly hung around on the other side of the round pen, while Barbara looked suitably impressed at our professionalism. It was hard not to feel a little smug.

But the feeling was short-lived. The head collar was so tight there was no way to undo it. Even if there had been a pair of scissors sharp enough for the job, we couldn't have got the blades underneath the head collar to cut it off, and the likelihood of him standing still while we attempted this was remote to say the least, while the chances of him (or one of us) losing an eye in the process were considerably higher. We managed to get close to Rocky, to stroke his neck and his shoulders, to desensitise him to the rope, but every time we touched his head collar, it caused him pain, and he would break away. Time was ticking away, and it was clear we weren't making any progress.

There was a stable which had been hired for him on the other side of a very quiet lane and we repeated the ingenious solution Kelly had used with Martine. As well as both of us and Brian, and the owner, there were two others watching. Cheerfully explaining that one person should be able to carry one panel of the round pen each, with the horse in the middle, we got to work and without too much difficulty, negotiated our awkward load through the gate, over the road and to the entrance to the stables, from where it was extremely easy to herd him into the stable allocated to him.

This hardly felt like an ideal outcome, but the owner had learned a lot about how body language works with horses and things to avoid and use. Rocky had actually learned a lot more than it appeared, for nobody had tried to grab him or become aggressive. The next day Barbara was able to get a vet in to sedate him and cut the head collar off. Once the wounds had healed, she was able to fit him with a bigger head collar, and he was never an issue to catch again.

We had the opposite experience when we were called out to another untouched horse: Taz. Donna, his owner, was quite experienced, around thirty years old, a British Horse Society Assistant Instructor, but she'd not found much in the BHS curriculum about wild horses. Taz was one of a group of seventeen horses and ponies, saved from the meat trade. They were in a large field - about 70 acres - but there was dilapidated barbed wire fencing around the edge and in several places within it, and the horses were not receiving any attention, except from people making use of the public footpaths across the land. One by one, they had nearly all been sold to concerned horse lovers. Thirteen horses had already been paid for and removed, and Taz was one of the remaining four.

Buoyed by our recent experience of getting Rocky into the

pen, we set off with great confidence on a quiet, late summer's morning without a breath of wind. It was a perfect temperature, so there wouldn't be too many flies. We had spent yet more money on the Green Monster, which had the good grace to start first time, so we rolled up in it, met Donna, had a little look around and chose a corner of the field which seemed to have good features. Driving the lorry in, we set up our round pen panels, then set about persuading her horse and all of the other untouched horses, if necessary, into the enclosure. What we hadn't really fully appreciated was why these particular horses were still left in the field, while the others had gone. They had proved to be the most suspicious and wild, and being herded up along with their more gullible, soon-to-be ex-field mates on numerous previous occasions had made them very wise to the experience. The moment they saw the pen, they knew exactly what it was for, and took every care to avoid going anywhere near it.

Our job was hampered too by the size of the field, the problem with the dodgy fencing, and the fact that there were so few of us. It was just Adam, me, Donna, and her partner Dennis, who hadn't had a lot of experience with horses. Some of our first instructions about herding may have been novel for Donna, but to Dennis the idea of using his body to direct a horse was completely crazy. He was fine when they were moving away from him, but as soon as they turned to challenge him, which, sensing his vulnerability, they did at will, he would immediately step aside, and create a gap which they found most convenient to escape through. It was hard not to become exasperated at these moments. We started with helpful comments like "Whoops! Never mind," but were close to sarcasm by the time we were explaining that the whole idea was to block the escape route, to turn the horses back. We were spending a lot of time traipsing to the furthest reaches of the field, and starting yet again the painstaking process of guiding them carefully back to the corner of the field with the round pen in. Rather like, it occurs to me now, the process of setting up a goal in football.

Football?! Perhaps a strange analogy, but let me explain. When Adam took up riding, I agreed to learn to play the guitar. It has to be said that he has kept his side of the bargain rather better than I have. I can, if pushed, strum my way inaccurately through a few basic chords, and now he makes a living teaching riding and working with horses. I've always felt a little guilty about my commitment failure in this regard, particularly if Adam reminds me, so when, to my alarm and consternation, he became interested in football, I decided I had probably better do so too. And not just for the big matches, either. Nor just the highlights on "Match of the Day". I've been known to sit through an entire 90 minutes of a Champion's League match, with stoppage time. Sometimes even extra time. And I think I've really got the hang of it, too. By the end I have almost always known which team we're supporting and what colour their shirts are. I know when to groan at the missed goals, when to say, "Ooh, just a bit too much pace", and "REFerEE!". I've learned that you can say "it's a game of two halves" too often, and that comments such as "that was a bit high/wide/left" are not considered to be entirely appropriate. I can say "offside!", "Dive!", and "that crossed the line!" with conviction, if not accuracy. More worryingly, I know the names of more than just the obvious Man United or England team players, and much to my alarm, I've found myself listening to the post-match interviews and analysis, and finding a name passing through my mind, and finding out it belongs to the manager I see on the screen. I didn't deliberately set out to know who Harry Redknapp is, but somehow, through osmosis, it has infiltrated my brain. What concerns me most is what other information will have leaked out of my brain to make way for this sort of thing? Will there be some obscure bit that I will no longer be able to name? What if I forget the difference between a trace-high or a blanket clip, or can no longer remember the protein content of barley? How did it happen that I know about aggregate scoring?

Anyway, those concerns aside, it has occurred to me through the hours of watching football (perhaps I should be practising my chords at the same time), that getting a goal is very like herding a wild but wise-to-it horse into an enclosure. You have to work together as a team, you have to get the ball/horse to the end of the pitch/field that you want, you have to retain possession, and then even when you've got it all lined up, there's no guarantee you'll score. You have to stay focused and committed, and there's no value in giving up before it's over. At least in the horse scenario, there's no-one defending the "goal mouth" (although on this occasion perhaps we would have been more successful if Dennis had been in goal!). On the other hand, it could go on for a lot more than 90 minutes. Extra time, in fact, could have gone on forever. And just like in football, a miss is as good as a mile.

People often talk about the patience required with horses. On the phone, people will frequently mention that there's no point "losing it" with their particular horse, as if "losing it" would usually help with all the others. Sometimes, clients who have spent well over an hour each time they load their horse will comment on our patience during a loading session, in spite of the fact that the horse is already loading well, in less than the time it usually takes the owner, and we're just having fun with the consolidation. We sometimes point out that actually it indicates a lack of patience, that it's precisely because we wouldn't want to have to repeat the bad loading experience every time we took the horse somewhere that we would want to spend the time really consolidating the work to avoid an otherwise predictable and embarrassing confrontation beforehand. There's also the fact that it's easy to be patient, stay calm, when you have utmost confidence in your techniques. Part of the reason people get so stressed loading - like we used to do with Sensi - is that they just don't know if they will get the horse in or not. And if they don't succeed, then the hours they are currently spending are effectively wasted. Knowing that you have lots of options, effective strategies for dealing with different situations, not just plan B's, but plan C's, D's and E's, is immensely empowering, and reassuring, and goes a long way towards staying calm.

But there's a point at which that confidence can turn into delusional wishful thinking. You always have to keep in mind the question, "Is this going in the right direction? Are we making any headway at all?" In the loading example, it's not uncommon for someone to say, "That horse is really thinking about it, you can see how hard she's trying, she's looking in the box, she's looking at the ramp, I think she's about to go in." But the horse can stay suspended on that moment of "being about to go in" for a surprisingly long time, at least an hour. We've learnt now that if the horse has been on the absolute verge of going in for more than about 5 minutes, there's no harm in fetching the panels from our round pen. If the horse really is about to step in, she'll be loading before we come back with the first one. If she isn't, then the panels will be helpful!

So, realising the enormous advantage these horses had over us, we decided to deploy the horsebox as part of the rounding up team. Adam got in and, with less than the usual difficulty, got it cranked up and began heading off around the field like a big and extremely cumbersome green lion, bumping over the turf, chasing the horses towards the corner where we had the pen set up. This worked slightly better than might seem likely, as it was very effective in bringing them back to the part of the field we wanted them to be in. There were a couple of disadvantages though - having only 3 people for the delicate maneuvering required to usher them into the round pen enclosure was a real "understaffing" issue, and the horses' adrenaline was definitely being raised. One horse in particular, not the one we were after, made a heart-stopping challenge to a particularly dodgy bit of barbed wire fencing, going more through than over, but somehow managing to avoid any discernible injury, at least from the distance we could see her from. There was another problem with using the lorry in this way, too, that didn't become apparent until much later.

Not wishing to risk a repeat of the "fence"-challenging incident, our next strategy was to move the pen. It was at this point that we thought to ask if there was a particular part of the field the horses usually favoured. There was, it turned out, and it wasn't where we had initially chosen to place the pen. We both made a mental note to ask that question rather earlier on in the proceedings in future. A different corner was chosen, next to a gate that the horses were comparatively used to going through. If they were in one field, we could open the field gate, open the pen, and encourage them through. If they were in the other part of the field, we could open up another side of the pen. It seemed to offer most options, but the field they would most logically be approaching through was the biggest, and when they went to the furthest end of it, it was a very long trek indeed.

Time hadn't stood still for our various attempts so far, it certainly wasn't standing still for our new ideas, and in fact it could be more accurately described as "marching on". Dennis had to go back to work. There was the issue of impending darkness, not too imminent, but there was a definite pressure in the backs of our minds. We sensed there might be some real benefit to our new pen arrangement, but if we couldn't capitalise on it on the first attempt, the advantage would slip away. While we had been moving the pen, the ponies had moved away to the furthest reach of the field, hiding in a hollow, munching grass and calming down. We approached one more time, this time without our unsubtle green companion. We moved very slowly. They started drifting towards the corner of the field, the gate and the round pen, at almost grazing speed. We talked on the way with Donna about the need to stay calm, to keep breathing, to move swiftly but quietly when necessary, to avoid ever letting the word 'gotcha' cross your mind, to keep focusing on where we wanted the horses to go, to keep looking at each other, and to work as a team. The horses approached the corner of the field. The mare in front, the one in charge, the one who would challenge any obstacle, saw the round pen panels, and hesitated. We waited, we breathed, we thought mellow 'It's okay' sort of thoughts. She took another step, her friends took another step, we each took another step. We needed to be close enough to get to the gate, to shut it behind them, to stop them coming straight back out when they realised they were trapped. But too much pressure, too much haste, and we would blow it. We had set the panels up in such a way that the gate between the two parts of the field, which was five barred, but hung a long way from the ground, simply needed closing to keep the horses in the pen. Afterwards, we reasoned, we could swing the panels around and close them up to make a complete, definitely unjumpable, enclosure.

There can be a moment when you see what's going to happen before it happens. The ball that passes through the defender's legs, straight on target, blasting through the goalie, defeat for one team, victory for the other, stolen perhaps in the closing seconds of the game. Watching the mare, I knew, beyond the odds, she was going to walk straight into the pen and the others would follow her. I felt a dreamy sense of unreality as I saw her cross the threshold, saw the others follow her calmly in. That dreamy sense gave way instantly to intense focus as we moved swiftly to the gate. They saw the trap the instant before we got there, but they were too late. Knowing how much depended on it, we slammed the gate shut as though there weren't four horses galloping full pelt towards it on the other side. We breathed a collective sigh of relief. Five hours into the job, and we had only just achieved the objective that on our last job had taken less than a minute. And we hadn't even got that far. We had four wild horses in an uncomfortably small space, and we still needed to separate Taz out, to release the other three so we could get near him, put a head collar on, teach him to lead, load him up, and travel him to his new home. Releasing the other three without letting him go was the sort of procedure that the courses at Willow Farm had prepared us for. It was simply a matter of one of us going into the pen, and getting between Taz and the other three. The other person would man the gate, opening and shutting it at precisely the right moments. If all three would go out at once, that would be fine, if they went one at a time, that would also work. The key is getting the horse to believe in the reality of the barrier. You can't be thinking "ooh, I could get hurt here", nor can you be too concerned that you might shut the gate on the horse's nose. You absolutely have to believe that the horse will see that there is no opening, and respond accordingly, taking their nose out of the way in the same way that they would avoid a kick. A moment of doubt, of hesitation, and the whole thing could be lost. And if we were foolish enough to let them out of the pen, there would be no way we would get them back in again, not in that session, anyway.

It's hard to really know who had the shorter straw, but Adam manned the gate, and I took my chances in the pen. Taz was keen to follow the others, but between us we managed to keep him in. His friends more or less left him to his fate. There were a few moments in which we could observe that the mare who had gone through the fence was unscathed, and then they took their leave. Taz might perhaps have been calmer had they stayed, but in some way being abandoned may have helped him to see that humans could be some sort of alternative company. As I recall, I was all up for giving him ten minutes or so to settle, but Adam was keen to crack on, seeing perhaps that there was an advantage to be had in the horse's distraction. And he was right: as long as he moved with the horse, and avoided being squashed in the changes of direction as Taz fence-walked and called for his lost friends, he was actually able to slip a rope around his neck, tie a bowline knot, make a wild-horse halter, and then ask Taz to really pay attention to him. It wasn't long before the pony was following him nicely, responding to pressure, enjoying having his neck scratched, and forgetting that he had been abandoned by his field mates.

We then swapped the rope halter for a dually, which only took a few moments. After the hours we had spent trying to get Rocky to let us handle his head, it was astonishing that within half an hour of his being enclosed in the pen, Taz was easily catchable, touchable and halter-trained. Adam was doing a great job, but Taz was also remarkably easy to achieve progress with. I opened up the lorry, dropping the ramp down into the enclosure, while using the round pen panels as wings. Taz took very little persuasion to go up the ramp, and once he had worked out how to negotiate the slope, was very happily going in and out, or staying on board if requested. We worked for a fair while on this, wanting to make sure that he had really got the hang of it, and then he would remember his first loading experience as being positive. When he really could be no better and was in fact loading better than most horses at the local show, looking like an old pro stomping up and down the ramp, we closed up the partitions, and went to do up the ramp. "We'll be off in a minute," Adam said to Donna, as he reached for the button which operated the hydraulic lift.

We were greeted only by an ineffectual electrical hum. The ramp stayed firmly on the ground. This wasn't simply a minor inconvenience. It wasn't just a bit heavy, it was very solid wood, without springs to assist lifting it manually, and with a hydraulic system now devoting itself to holding it down. It was now that we discovered what a bad idea it had been to use the lorry like a ranch horse. Bouncing over the field had damaged the hydraulic pump, almost completely detaching its cylinder, which was now hanging off at an angle that was obviously not how it had been designed. The lowering of the ramp had drained all of the fluid. There was no way the three of us could possibly lift it without risking serious injury, and not just through strained muscles. If we dropped the thing it would kill us. There was a huge sense of anticlimax. We let Taz out of the lorry to graze in the pen, and Donna called Dennis. He went out on a mission to get more fluid, to get some advice, to find someone who might be able to help, but in the end it proved fruitless. I rang Kelly to see if her lorry was anywhere nearby, but it was impractically far away. There wasn't anyone on the yard who could come out and collect him. The sense of elation and purpose we'd felt when he was going up and down the ramp gave way to despondency, and a growing awareness that we hadn't had lunch and were both very hungry, tired, and although the darkness was beginning to close in we were still a long way from being finished and going home.

Eventually, Dennis returned with about eight strong men, who, being bribed with the prize of a crate of beer that we happened to have in the back of the lorry, and with much grunting and sweating (but great good humour all round), succeeded in lifting and closing the ramp, while Taz stood there as if he'd seen this a thousand times before. They then followed us to Donna's yard, where they then managed to lower the ramp without crushing anyone or breaking the ramp axle. They even managed not to drop it with too much of a bang. Taz was then led out of the lorry and straight into his stable. It was large, and banked up deeply with fresh, clean straw, but it had a low overhang, and to get to it he had to step over some strange piping, and some very uneven surfaces. He picked his way through gingerly, snorting, but followed Donna into the stable, saw a huge pile of hay in the corner, had a wee, and started munching as if this, too, was nothing out of the ordinary. We would have loved to stay and watch him, but instead it was back to the field to pick up the panels, with the eight strong men, who had been rounded up, it turned out, from the local pub, and were "very keen" to return.

We stopped off at a pub on the way home, in a village we had ridden through with Sensi on one of our long autumn trips in the years before we had moved to Moor Wood. It seemed a lifetime since we had been a one-horse family, with one riding and the other cycling through the Buckinghamshire and Oxfordshire countryside. Going by car or lorry through or around places we had ridden had always seemed strange to me, a bit like the way floating around Cambridge in a punt and seeing the city from a completely different angle made it feel like a different place altogether. Driving along a motorway that we had passed under or over didn't seem like a different perspective to me - it actually felt like another world. Almost as if travelling by horse gave access to a different Earth that didn't exist unless you were with the horse. But back in the 1990s when we did quite a few long distance trips, riding the 70 miles or so along the bridleways to a friend's farm felt like we'd been to a place further than abroad.

We got to the pub just before they stopped serving, and had one of those meals that was common to us at the time - so infused with tiredness that ordering, consuming, and paying for it felt like an ordeal rather than the privilege it was. We were aching after the hours we'd driven, the miles we had walked, the panels we had shifted, the strain of staying calm and optimistic. We knew we had made some major mistakes in our strategy, and needn't have taken quite so long, but we also knew that what we had achieved was no mean feat. Nobody had been hurt, and Donna now had a catchable, touchable, leadable, loadable horse in her stable, who was even beginning to get the idea about picking up his feet for us, and whose first trip in a lorry had been positive (for him, at least). Their situation had been transformed in a day and they now had a potentially great future ahead of them.

We tried not to count the cost. For some reason, I had negotiated a very modest flat rate for the job. By the time we paid the £300 for the ramp to be fixed, as well as fuel for the lorry, and overtime for the workers at home whilst we were both away for twelve hours or so, we didn't just not earn any money, we were well out of pocket. To cap it all we had no crate of beer to commiserate with. Even taking out the lorry repair costs, caused by our own carelessness, our hourly rates might not have matched the abject rates which we earned on our very first jobs. We didn't really mind. As usual, we'd learned a lot. But it was clear we were going to have to adopt a different pricing strategy if we were to continue paying the rent!

SEVEN

The Pig Who Learned To Fly
(Adam)

The first thing I remember thinking was how inappropriate a name for such a magnificent animal. A dark bay gelding with a small white star in the middle of his forehead, standing over 17 hands high, he was as impressive a horse as I had ever seen. A German Hanoverian, only seven years old, gleaming with a glossy sheen, he was obviously a horse of great breeding with the potential to be successful in competition. You'd have to admit his eyes were a bit small but I was still kind of taken aback to hear his name - Piglet. But his owner, Jo Clark, who had only had him a few months, and was clearly as sweet as could be, broke into a hearty smile and fondly said that it seemed to describe him or at least his appetite. Apparently he seemed content with it, and I had to admit I preferred it to his "proper" name, Delta.

The difficulty was, although he was only seven, he had almost every problem in the book, and nearly all of them could be attributed to him being such a valuable horse, which is exactly why his troubles had begun right back when he was a little baby, just four months old. One day he was in the field with his mum and the next thing he knew he was in a lorry, alone, being transported across the Channel, which must have been nothing short of terrifying for him.

I remember at the time being bowled over by this piece of information, which goes against most professional advice (not to wean before six months). I was immediately ready to accept that almost everything about this little piglet must have been shaped by what he had to undergo in that lorry. But the magnitude of it was just too horrendous to contemplate, and I couldn't begin to take on what he must have been through. Now, some years later, knowing all that's gone into putting that horse back together from the state I met him in, I still can't really bear to think how he must have felt, stripped from his mother, removed from his home, and left to lurch around in a tiny space for many, many hours.

A horse could hardly get off to a worse start and almost every one of the problems he had seemed to stem from it. Basic things like catching him in a stable were an enormous issue and, equally understandably, he was an appalling loader and generally highly strung. He could be ridden, and you could say he had been schooled, that is if you could get him to stand still by a mounting block long enough to mount, or find another way to get on. Taking him out with another horse was a major drama, and his napping was so bad that he could not even be led out alone from the yard. Catching him in the field was also very difficult. Being turned out by himself in a small enclosure proved futile - he was too scared of the electric tape to approach his neighbour and used to stand there looking miserable, then attack whoever came to catch him. However, if his head collar was left on, this could be achieved relatively painlessly by means of food. He was not happy about having rugs put on and would often threaten or try to bite, but that behaviour paled in comparison to his reaction to the sound of plastic. The slightest noise of a plastic bag or crisp packet and he would bolt uncontrollably.

This was the horse Jo had bought - her first ever horse - and for a sizeable price, especially given that he came with such a catalogue of issues, although of course none of them had been obvious when she went to try him out. Fortunately, being a former Olympic rower, she was athletic and, although very gentle and kind, she was also very determined. She knew how to ride reasonably well, was unbelievably keen to improve and had managed to find a place at a supportive yard. However, when she took delivery of her dream horse, she found that her dream rapidly turned into a nightmare. His behaviour was really frightening and even though she did have some help, the yard was more focused on the riding side of things, which was about the only part of his behaviour that wasn't absolutely pathological, apart from picking up and shoeing Piglet's feet, which he seemed reasonably happy about. Ironically, those feet would turn out to be by far his biggest problem. Fortunately the yard, half an hour's drive from her home, was managed by a good rider - a gently spoken man who acted confidently around Piglet. He was also assisted by a number of dedicated working pupils, all of whom were conscientious and keen to learn. Jo was, therefore, able to get from day to day with their support. However, by the time she began to discover how scary her horse could be, she found that the hours she worked created a further difficulty. Most evenings, by the time she got to the yard, the head trainer and yard manager, as well as all the working pupils and even all the other clients, had left for the night and she would often find herself alone up at the yard, dealing with some really hair-raising behaviour from this huge horse.

Hearing such a litany of troubled behaviour about one horse was unusual even for me, but I was cheered by the knowledge that although this was her first experience of horse ownership, Jo had been riding for years and was very keen on Monty's work, and that this yard was a place where I knew it would be welcome. I met Piglet one afternoon and talked about body language and emphasised how important it was, especially with a horse like him, not to get your intentions misinterpreted by unintentionally appearing to act aggressively. Looking him in the eye should be avoided unless her intent was to get him to back off. Advancing on him and moving too quickly had to be guarded against so as to put him at ease, but if he turned his quarters to her she could make him feel uneasy about doing that by raising or waving a rope. The instant he turned to face her, she should instantly make a very noticeable change to a non-confrontational stance. He was extremely responsive to this and I hoped she would be able to improve things from there. I spent a lot of time showing Jo how to lead him more safely and effectively. She had never had any groundwork training in her life, so it was not surprising that she didn't have answers for any of his groundwork issues.

This was a yard with a well-earned reputation both for caring and competence. Jo was unhappy with the saddle Piglet had arrived with, even though it was not cheap and had, as is usual with ill-fitting saddles we have come across, been made to measure and fitted by a qualified saddler. With the help of the trainer at the yard, she arranged for a suitable replacement. There was an immediate improvement in Piglet's behaviour under saddle, but things were only getting worse in the stable. It might be that, having finally got someone to listen to one of his complaints, he was determined to speak up about his other ones.

I was going through a particularly busy period and it was ridiculously difficult to find time to go back again. The next time I could visit, I asked Jo to go off and get Piglet but she soon came back, looking distraught and shocked. "I can't catch him. You'd better come and help."

He was in a state of terror, moving round his stable as fast as he could, completely unable to settle. I stood well outside his door, and made no effort to go any closer, so I could stay beyond where he could hurt me. Occasionally he came and stuck his head over the door but was so agitated by me and the few others standing there very quietly that he even tried to bite. I didn't do much about it. There wasn't anything useful to be done. I was only just starting to get my head around what a massive problem he had about everything.

Again I went about explaining and demonstrating the way body language could be used to disarm his frightened behaviour, for that was what it was, although it was hard not to see it as aggressive. But the previous attempt Jo had made to put on his head collar had got him so worked up that it was not as simple as it had been the first time, when we had been able to open the door and work with him in the doorway. For some time I just worked over the door, as both he and I could both feel relatively safe thanks to the boundary it created. Fortunately the stable had bars along the front so we could still see and interact with him when he was not looking out, but even with very careful, non-confrontational body language, it took a long time until I could touch him. When I could stroke him around his face I decided to open the door although, with hindsight, perhaps the best way that I should have approached putting on his head collar was over the closed door.

This completely set him off again and he began circling his stable once more, clearly anxious about the impending episode of catching. As I stood just outside the open door, he tried to come through it a few times, but found that I would hold my ground and raise my opened hands if he did so. This got a major reaction, even though I made no effort to move my hands towards him and was never in danger of touching, let alone hitting him. It frightened him, but it was better than me getting run over by about 600 kilos of horse. Whilst trying to remain impassive and unemotional in the face of all this stress, part of me was filled with sadness and more than a tinge of anger at how appalling and unnecessary it was to see a horse in this state. He continued to circle and think about running through me as he got round to the door and suddenly he made a major lunge to get through. When my hands flew upwards in a blocking action, this time I looked in his eye and made a loud kissing noise and he pulled himself back from the doorway and reared to his full height, exposing his huge underside as his front feet pawed the air.

I do not remember feeling any fear, but the sight of his belly and flailing legs above me is clearly etched on my memory. He seemed to stay in the air for ages, before coming to the ground and heading off round the stable again. I think at this point, many trainers would react and "chase after" the horse in some way, to make the horse realise the behaviour is unacceptable. Not doing so can reap enormous rewards, however. If you protect yourself but then let the horse have space to think about what happened, instead of forcing him to think about your reaction, that might provide a window through which the horse could learn that you won't hurt him, even if his behaviour is extreme, and so the need for extreme behaviour may diminish. Explosive though his reaction had been, I could also see that what I was doing was beginning to work. When he came to face me, I was still blocking the space and if he tried to blast through me I was ready with my response. If he paused even for the briefest moment, I went into a more passive stance, chest turned to the side, eyes down, keeping my hands still and closed, inviting him to come up and making no effort to approach or encroach on his space. This was a form of reward, which gave him a chance to slow up and find an alternative to flying round the stable again. Eventually what had been a momentary hesitation was becoming more pronounced, and he finally began to become comfortable simply to stand with his head towards me, in front of the open door. Within a short space of time I was able to touch him gently on the forehead, after which I moved away quietly to my space outside so that he could see there would be no attempt to pounce on him. His trust began to build steadily as I repeated this process until I was able to move towards him relatively quickly without a fearful reaction.

Shortly after, I put the head collar on, using an alternative technique to the one I most commonly see being used. The normal approach is to slip the head collar over the horse's nose, and then, using the right hand, to flip the headpiece over behind the ears.

There's an awkward moment when you are positioned under the horse's head, and also for a second or two you have to let go of the head collar with your right hand as you bring it around to join your left hand, so that you can do the headpiece up. In most circumstances with most horses, this really isn't a problem, but with a difficult or untouched horse this approach is much less likely to succeed, and puts the handler in a more vulnerable position. Instead, I stood in a more passive position by his shoulder, held the head collar in my left hand and put my right hand over his neck to hug him softly. I then passed the poll strap of the head collar under his neck to my right hand. Slipping the rest over his nose was easy enough and once I could do it, I removed it and stroked him and moved back out of the door again. We practised it several times, and he rapidly got better and better.

It was a long time before we got into the school that day but we had done what I believe was the most important schooling session of his life. While it was obvious his problem in the stable had been a long time in the making, I knew that the actions of the yard manager were - completely unintentionally - part of the source of his worries. I had seen on my first visit how he would deal with putting on Piglet's head collar. Without hesitation, he simply walked into the stable and, although the horse panicked and did his best to run, in such a confined space he couldn't get out of the trainer's reach. Staying in the middle, the trainer was able to put on the head collar whilst moving alongside Piglet. You couldn't fault him for his bravery, nor the skill he showed in doing up a head collar on a horse who was trying to canter. He was not trying to be aggressive, quite the opposite, and in many situations this approach might have worked fine. We've put many a saddle on a remedial starter in this way, and as often as not, the horse soon realises that they didn't need to be afraid. It can be better than going more tentatively and prolonging the horse's anxiety. In this case, however, Piglet wasn't improving with this approach, and he obviously felt he was being assaulted. Having his stable and his personal space invaded like this was only making it worse both for him and Jo. She clearly wasn't happy to do it like that and risk being bitten, trodden on or kicked whilst trying to copy it. For all its efficiency, getting the job done in this fashion was causing her horse at best to remain trapped in his phobia and, at worst, to become even more worried about it.

Meantime, whenever I was talking about Piglet, I just found I could never remember his name. I am notorious for forgetting names, but this wasn't because of my usual forgetfulness. I was aware of his name but I couldn't find it in my mind, even when I had just used it, which I avoided doing. It just wasn't the name I thought he belonged to, and I said so.

So we got over the worst of P's catching and some of his leading troubles that day. We reviewed the leading work we had done on the first visit, emphasising the careful use of a much longer lead rope, keeping him further away from her and rehearsing how to use safer options available to her if he did act out in some way. We agreed that the next step should be for us to sort out his loading, as Jo wanted very much to learn to long line him, and the obvious thing was for her to do so in our round pen at home, rather than the huge arena at the yard. So we would have to get him there by lorry unless she was going to hack the most nappy horse in Gloucestershire halfway across the county, when he wouldn't even go down the drive by himself. She decided the best thing to do would be to take a week off work, and dedicate herself to sorting out some of the handling and behavioural issues which were making her time with him such a nightmare.

Loading him was quite an episode. I went up again to begin sorting it out. The yard owner kindly let us use her box to practise, as Jo didn't have one. It took some time to get him on, and then he panicked. He was simply too big for me to hold and he launched himself at the gap between me and the side of the lorry. What happened next was terrifying for us all. He got a hoof stuck between the ramp and the lorry, and ripped his shoe off, which flew through the air, passing only inches from Jo's face. The next thing we knew, he landed with a crash on his side at the bottom of the ramp. Somehow he was not badly injured beyond leaving bits of fur on the ramp, and having torn some of his hoof wall away, but we were all pretty shaken up. It was about the worst thing that has ever happened to a horse when I've been working and we decided to leave the loading for another day. Instead, we took him for a little walk down the drive, to the village green, and let him have a graze on the lush grass there, just spending some peaceful time together. Before we'd done the leading work, even this simple activity would have been highly stressful. When we got back to the stables, I encouraged Jo to take off the lead rope, while I followed behind to stop him in the unlikely event that he decided to make a run for it. Without hesitation, he followed her placidly into the yard, while Jo quietly shed a tear, not for the first or last time.

By now, Jo was beginning to rethink his name. She didn't share the superstition some people have that changing horses' names brings bad luck. If that were the case, then among several others, we have apparently jinxed Cobweb, a horse we have had for about fifteen years, who is now well into his thirties and about as healthy as you could hope to be at that age. Nobody has ever fallen off him and he has hardly had a day's lameness in that entire time. I think it is much worse luck for someone to persist in calling a horse by a name which doesn't belong to him. Piglet just didn't do him justice. He was altogether more magnificent, more significant a presence, especially in Jo's life - and she was only at the beginning of the journey he was taking her on. Eventually, a name came to her that seemed to fit him much better. Reflecting her passion for wildlife, and especially birds, she decided to call him Perry, short for Peregrine Falcon, a bird of unsurpassed elegance in flight and whose peregrinations in life bring it to many different places. And so, he became the pig who learned to fly. The first place he had taken her was this yard, at which she had learned a lot. The next stop was a trip to Moor Wood.

The next time I visited, we were planning to get him loaded and take him back to mine. In spite of the incident where he had fallen down the ramp, I was confident we would get the job done, but this time we used a different lorry, with stronger suspension, which would rock less when he got on. Working systematically and patiently, I got him aboard, and immediately led him off, as I had been planning to do the first time, if he had not beaten me to it. The better lorry probably helped some, and in common with most horses, once he had been given the chance to do the task in smaller increments, he began to load much more confidently. When he was completely calm, we closed the ramp and took him off for his week's holiday.

He never went back.

EIGHT

Life's Greatest Pleasure?
(Nicole)

Moor Wood is such a special haven that it would seem wrong if it didn't have contented horses gracing its slopes. We have a dog here for much the same reason, and many people have commented on what a wonderful place it would be to bring up a child.

The problem is, I always knew that I didn't want children. As a child, I had no interest in those baby dolls that pee and cry, and was far more interested in the litter of kittens that our cat unexpectedly produced. I wasn't quite as adamant as my childhood friend, Ciara, however. One ill-fated Christmas she was presented with a Sasha doll that her mother considered "exquisite", and she cried inconsolably, for hours if not days. Cruelly, the box had been the exact size and shape that would hold a "Happytime" horse, and the disappointment was unbearable.

As I grew older, and perhaps better informed, I became even more adamant. The feminist in me was offended by the assumption that this is what all women would automatically do, and that somehow life as a childless person had little validity or purpose. The thing was, I didn't really like children. And more particularly, babies. They always looked a little strange to me, not quite entirely human, and always somewhat moist. The whole not-being-able-to-eat-with-their-mouths-shut thing always disturbed me too, and those parents who insisted on involving toddlers in family meal times always struck me as particularly insensitive. I didn't ever feel that there was anything inherently wrong with having children. In fact, I acknowledged the obvious fact that somebody has to. I just never felt it should be me.

When I looked at my life, I couldn't see a space that a child would fit into. Not that, as horse-owners and trainers, we led the sort of jet-set life that children interfere with. But working long hours, and having activity-crammed days, just didn't leave space for a child, and the pace would be completely incompatible. I remember going for a walk with my brother and his first-born son, Colin, one time. I was pushing the stroller. Every time Colin made a move to get out of the seat, I would tip the stroller up a little, and accelerate. "You aren't perhaps as good at reading children as you are at horses," my brother suggested gently. "Can't you see he wants to get out and walk?"

"Of course I can," I replied. "That's why I'm going faster - to stop him. If he keeps getting out, it'll take forever to get where we're going." My brother, who had always walked so fast my lungs burned to keep up with him, had adjusted to a different pace of life that, at the time, just didn't appeal to me.

But it wasn't just the twenty-four hour duty, the sleep deprivation, the crying, the nappies, the vomit, the drool, the monosyllabic conversations, the constant clinging and interruptions, and the resultant relationship strain that put me off having children. It was that I didn't want to accept the reduction in status that I perceived would go with it. I'd heard it said that parenting is the most important and difficult job you can do. I'd heard one or two people speak of mothers as revered members of society. I understood on an intellectual level the value of bringing children up in an intelligent, kind and considered way, and how society depends on an ongoing supply of well-adjusted, happy, achieving, balanced people to flourish. It's obvious that the conditions for this are best set out in childhood, rather than extensive therapy later on. But I saw no evidence of this belief being played out in daily life in our society. Mothers still did their extremely difficult mothering jobs that were largely unacknowledged by anyone, including, quite often, their husbands. No-one celebrated the stay-at-home mum, or advocated the stay-at-home dad, and there seemed to be nothing set up to allow mums to keep sane and still be primary care-givers for their children. It seemed as though everyone said that being a mother was a most valuable role, but no-one actually believed it. Not even the mothers themselves, quite often. Otherwise, why would anyone say: "Oh, I'm just a mum," when asked what they do for a living? And the response always seems to be, "Oh, no, don't do yourself down, that's an incredibly valuable job," but I always got the impression that the person was secretly thinking, "Huh, must be nice to stay at home everyday, watching TV," and that there was more than a hint of condescension in it. Much in the way a lawyer might tell a refuse collector that they respected and appreciated them for keeping the streets clean, while privately thanking God they didn't have to do it themselves.

If we really appreciated how important child-rearing was, it would be reflected in the way our society is set up. For example, surely the best way to arrange the whole child-rearing thing would be for both parents to job share, preferably in the same job, or at least both work part-time. Then they would each have time alone with the child, each have time out of the house using their brain in a different way and interacting with other adults, and in the evenings (or whenever) they could both have time together with the child. With a trusted caregiver, such as a grandparent, stepping in occasionally, they could also both have time together and pay attention to their relationship. In fact, this didn't strike me as the ideal situation, it struck me as about the only way it would be truly tenable.

When a friend of mine announced she was pregnant, I immediately asked, "What will your husband do?" He worked extremely long hours, including some weekends, and had a long commute. It didn't occur to me that continuing like this was even an option. She looked at me blankly, and asked what I meant.

"But he can't keep working those sorts of hours!" I exclaimed. "He'll hardly ever see his child. He'll come home exhausted. You'll have been alone with the baby all day, going quietly mad. He'll wonder what you do all day, and why you haven't got around to some task or other, and you'll resent him for being able to get out of the house and leave it all behind. Surely it can't work? He must reduce his hours!"

Thinking back to this exchange now, I realise that I wasn't being very supportive as a friend, and that perhaps all this had already occurred to her. I'm not even particularly good normally at really saying what I think, so this was quite an outburst from me, but I felt I had to say something. She just calmly explained that she didn't want to get a job, she couldn't earn anything like her husband, he really couldn't reduce his hours, and it would simply have to work out. She was right, of course: there would have been no sympathy for this idea at her husband's firm, and his commitment would have been seriously questioned. But even though I knew at the time that I didn't want a child, I also knew that if I did change my mind, I wouldn't want to do it like that. It felt as though feminism had never happened.

Then, social considerations aside, there was the whole pregnancy and birth thing. If ever, as the years went on, I found myself mellowing on the whole idea of children, I only had to think about the prospect of giving birth to abandon the idea immediately. The whole procedure just terrified me and was an ordeal I didn't ever want to go through.

The other negative factor - assuming you survived the birth - was the seemingly inevitable change in the relationship with the child's father. It seemed obvious to me that once the baby was born - maybe even before then - it would become the most important person in your life. Adam had occupied that spot pretty much from the moment we'd got together (well, sharing it with Sensi - and how would I find time for her if I had a baby clinging on to me?). I just didn't want that to change. Taking all these considerations together, I found myself very clear that I didn't want children. Neither did Adam.

So much so that when we did accidentally conceive, about five years into our relationship, the decision as to what to do about it didn't really seem like a decision at all. I was aware that twenty four was a comparatively reasonable age to have a child, that I was very confident in my relationship with Adam, and that if I were ever going to have a child, it would be with him, but I just felt no maternal feelings at all. The little being growing inside me felt like an invader. And I believed without question in the woman's right to choose.

So I went ahead with the operation, and felt traumatised and remorseful, but somehow it still seemed right. Afterwards, I often felt the presence of a little spirit with me, and I always thought "she" understood. I could imagine a little being looking down at my life and saying "Yes, I can see there wouldn't have been space for me. Just don't forget that I existed once, and remember me."

So the years went by, and as the inevitable question "So, do you think you'll ever have kids?" was repeated with increasing frequency, the answer remained the same adamant "No". I had two lovely nephews, who, although they lived in Canada, felt as if they provided an adequate child "fix" (by this time, I had conceded that children could actually be lovely. I just didn't want any of my own).

And even when our great friend and colleague, Julia, who lived here at Moor Wood for some time, gave birth to the very wonderful Emma, I wasn't really tempted to follow suit. Mind you, her experience of pregnancy was so awful that it hardly seemed appealing, a bit like how easy it is to resist the temptation to swim in the English Channel or trek across Antarctica. I also felt that Sensi giving birth to Karma was a pretty good proxy, and was always a bit disappointed that my mum didn't seem to count her among her grandchildren. But the years were passing, and although I still couldn't hear any actual ticking, I became aware that the time was fast approaching when the "We'll never have children" statement could easily become a reality.

When I mentioned it to Adam, I really wasn't at a place where I felt I had changed my mind at all. I just wondered whether we needed to have a quick look at our feelings and see whether we were operating an automatic response. When we looked carefully at the situation we realised we still really didn't want children, but there was a "yet" beginning to come into it, and yes, we hadn't really thought about it seriously for a while. We sort of promised each other to keep an open mind. One thing we did agree on, though, and it felt a bit like crossing the Rubicon, was if we had another unplanned pregnancy, we wouldn't terminate it.

I'd always thought there were two distinct ways of looking at your life and the potential role of children in it. You either saw a gap that only a child could fill, where all other activities were really just empty substitutes. Or you examined your life and thought, "Where's the space for another person? The car's full enough with just the two of us, the dinner table is lovely and intimate with just us two, and the bed is certainly just the right size." I had always seen it like this, but gradually there seemed to be a gap appearing. I don't know if it had to do with the death of both our fathers, but all of a sudden all the family gatherings that didn't involve my brother's children seemed much too small, much too quiet, and much too peaceful. Everyone got on too well. The challenges involved in the minefield of bringing children into the world began to seem exciting. And I began to think that maybe, just maybe, by remaining childless I was copping out in some way, and avoiding one of the biggest and potentially most rewarding challenges that life has to offer.

I had read once that people never think about having children, instead they imagine having babies, and don't project much further than that. This certainly wasn't my experience: I found myself imagining what it would be like to be going through life with a five year old by my side. What questions would they ask, and how would I answer? What family traditions would we start? How would I explain the world? In fact, what is the world about? I was beginning to see the appeal of babies - they were even starting to look less like damp aliens to me - but what really interested me was the new personality we could bring into being, someone with their own thoughts and way of looking at the world, who would, for a few years at least, want to share that world with us. (I had no illusions about the teenage years - no doubt we'd be exasperating and embarrassing and very annoying to a teenager, who no doubt would appear ungrateful, unruly, lazy and rude to us.) I began to really wonder what it would be like, in a way that suggested my development as a human being would be less complete if I didn't find out.

So somehow, nearly a year after deciding to think about it, we found ourselves agreeing that we would in fact try to have a child - or at least, start trying before another year had passed. We were thirty five.

The excitement we felt at even just having made this decision is hard to explain. It was nearly as thrilling as when we got Sensi. We told lots of our friends and family, even knowing, as we did, that there were no guarantees, and that we might open ourselves up to unnecessary pressures. I think we felt that even if it didn't work out, we had at least taken the life affirming and - to us - highly radical step of having a go, and we wanted to share that with people. The joy spread by even the possibility of bringing a new being into existence was amazing. We felt as if we had taken a leap off a very tall waterfall and were exhilarated and terrified all at the same time.

Of course, life doesn't stop even when you make such a momentous decision. The horses still need mucking out, and money still has to be earned - even more so. Teaching on the clinics and improving my horsemanship was still a major priority for me. Exploring new trainers and their methods was as stimulating as ever. The only area in which I felt I really needed to make changes was in my commitment to touring with Monty.

From the time I finished my course, I had been on every single

Monty tour, and to every one of Kelly's demonstrations too, only missing a couple of dates when they clashed with Karma's birth. I'd missed Adam's sister's wedding and countless other family events, as we charged around the country on a schedule that often involved ten venues in as many days, all over the UK and occasionally abroad. Although I found being Head of Merchandise quite stressful, I was happy to do it because it meant having the privilege of watching Kelly and Monty work their magic night after night. I also felt very honoured to be part of the core team. Deciding to step down was a sad moment for me, but I knew that the unpredictability of trying to conceive would make committing to a particular tour very difficult, and I didn't want to let anyone down at the last minute. I was pretty certain that morning sickness and touring would be incompatible, and not knowing if I might experience it, or how badly, was just one of many uncertainties around the whole having children thing. It was easier to give Kelly plenty of time to find a suitable replacement, and I would just have to go along to as many demonstrations as I could, when I could, and try not to feel left out!

The first demo I went to and watched someone else do my job *was* strange, but it was lovely too. I didn't have the worry of whether or not the figures would tally at the end of the night, nor the responsibility of going around with several thousand pounds of someone else's money in my bag. Nor had I spent hours setting up and then dismantling the stall, with the enormous task of counting all the stock out at the beginning and end of the demo. I helped out with the selling during the break, which had always been a part I'd enjoyed, and then could walk away. Best of all, I could really concentrate on the horses, and enjoy the demo for the stunning spectacle of horsemanship skill that it was.

NINE

Coaching With The Enemy
(Adam)

When Perry arrived at Moor Wood for his week of intensive training, he had such a catalogue of problems that it was hard to know where to start. In fact, since it was precisely his early intensive training that had created so many of his ridden issues, a week grazing out in the field might have been most appropriate. But Jo had taken the week off work and we were keen to make enough of an improvement in his behaviour that she would be able to cope with him when she took him back, so we cracked on.

We decided to avoid the school, however, since he had such negative associations with it, and instead to take him out for a hack. Ideally, he would have been much better schooled before we took him out and about, but it was a bit of a catch-22. He wasn't very responsive to the aids, so he shouldn't be taken out until he was much safer. On the other hand, he hated being schooled so much that working on his responsiveness and obedience was counter-productive. Very often, the best way in with a horse with schooling issues is to find something they like doing and make progress with that first. When there's enough of an improvement in their attitude, you can look at the areas where they are more negative. With Perry, other than eating grass, there really didn't seem to be anything he liked doing. He even hated being groomed. But by changing the circumstances in which we took him out, we hoped to change his opinion about hacking.

Whenever Jo had attempted to take him out before, it had been a complete nightmare. He did just about everything in the book, planting himself, running backwards, spinning, and spooking. When he did finally get the nerve to move he was usually uncontrollably forward going, bolting and bucking. He was so tense that even a

79

short walk around the block would bring him home dripping with sweat and quivering. Jo and Perry certainly didn't fit the description of "happy hackers."

That first ride out from Moor Wood started with a join-up in the round pen, which went quite well, for he seemed willing to listen and communicate. We then spent some time reminding him about the groundwork he had done, concentrating particularly on backing up. The emphasis was on calmness and precision, getting him to concentrate on moving his feet exactly where we asked him to, and praising him generously for complying. Since this work was new to both Perry and Jo, it gave us a way in to Perry's issues - it was different enough that he didn't switch off to it, whereas twenty metre circles in the school would probably have had him thinking, "Here we go again." We tacked him up, putting his bridle on over his halter, and repeated the exercises, helping him to work out that the same ground rules might apply under saddle. We led him down from the pen to the grass by the yard, and I held him while Jo mounted. She immediately did something we do a surprising amount of in our work - nothing. She didn't pick up the reins, she didn't even adjust her stirrups or girth, she just sat there, until he relaxed enough to stretch his long neck down to the grass and start eating. In fact, he could only do this because we had taken off the flash strap of his noseband and attached it to his reins to use as an extension. This doing nothing, these pauses, are a crucial part of training, for they allow both the horse and the human to slow down, relax, and think about things...to be "present in the moment" as the popular phrase has it. The circular route I was planning to take Jo on takes between twenty minutes, with some trotting and cantering, to an hour, at a leisurely stroll. We were allowing the entire afternoon to tackle it.

When I was sure Perry was settled munching the lawn, I fetched my trusty steed, Finn. Being an Exmoor, he's very easy to hop on and off, and he's not at all intimidated by big horses. He's also very comfortable to ride bareback, and reasonably brave out and about, so he was the perfect choice. He's only about 12 hands high though, and Perry is a good 17 hands, so we must have looked pretty comical going out together.

Reminding ourselves that we had all day, if necessary, we set off, with Finn in front. If Perry stopped, we gave him a moment. Very often, this is all a horse needs to work out that going forwards is safe after all, but it can be hard to do. A couple of seconds seems like a long time in this situation, and it is very tempting to jump in and chase after the horse straight away. Of course, it can be best to help the horse out by giving him some appropriate direction, too. If he did seem to be stuck, I instructed Jo to use the reins, steering him to the side, at a sharp angle if necessary, or in circles. Moving a horse in this way often seems to unstick them enough that they'll then move forward. At the slightest approximation of 'correct' behaviour, she would reward him with a release and a rub on the wither. Rather than pressuring him to comply to the aids, we wanted to give him the chance to work out that he was safe, and to stay calm. I didn't want her to have to deal with rearing, spinning, and running backwards. Behaviour like that would indicate that we had pushed him too far. I didn't mind if it took all day, just so long as we could do it calmly. If we reached a real impasse, Jo would be encouraged to dismount and lead him, hence the dually halter under the bridle. It astonishes me that anyone would think it was 'losing the battle' to get off and walk, unless they are talking about an internal battle with their own nerves. The horse certainly isn't thinking like that, although he knows when he's being fought against. To me, if you're having a battle, you've already lost it.

Of course, it's easier to have this attitude when you have set aside time for a proper training session. Much as it's true that "All the time you're with your horse, you're training him, whether you mean to be or not," when you're out for a quick hack before work in the morning, it's hard to see the training opportunity in your horse deciding not to go past a dustbin. It's certainly difficult to go about solving the issue as if you had all day when the clock really is ticking against you. In this case, the expedient of turning the horse around and backing past the scary place can work well. Making appropriate decisions in these situations is what successful training is all about. Seeing it from the horse's perspective can really help.

In the napping example, it's worth remembering that if the horse is comfortable, enjoying his work, and is confident in the rider, he wouldn't nap. If he's in pain, or frightened, it's no wonder he doesn't want to go out. Using force may work initially, but it's likely to give the horse negative associations with being out and about. Resisting, particularly to the point of rearing, takes a lot of energy, so a horse wouldn't do it without good reason. A lot of it comes down to trust.

Imagine that you're at a party, enjoying the company of friends, snacking and drinking, and another friend comes up to you, attaches something to your head, and drags you away from the party. If you're hesitant, she pokes you in the ribs. If you still don't want to go with her, she pokes you harder, perhaps even with a pointy piece of metal, and then hits you with a stick. She then pushes you ahead of her out into the street, and insists that you keep moving quickly, even though you're worried about the neighbourhood she's making you go through. As you get more and more nervous, you just want to stand still so you can assess the dangers, but she insists you keep moving. She won't let you look around, either. You would feel more confident if she would go ahead, or even stay next to you, but she insists on being behind and making you go first. Every time you try to turn around to go back to the security of the party, she hauls your head around to face forwards again. She's still poking you in the ribs and hitting you with the stick. Eventually, your journey takes you back to the party, where she makes sure you're clean and comfortable, have plenty to eat and drink, and are happy with your friends. But the next day she wants to put you through the same ordeal again. How would you feel? I think this is quite close to some horses' experience of hacking out, and it's not surprising they struggle.

Perry's first hack out was comparatively uneventful. Given time and space to work it out, he was able to go forwards, albeit tentatively. In spite of (or perhaps because of) us allowing all afternoon to get the job done, it didn't take long, and he got back to the yard without a bead of sweat.

One of the things which had bothered me right from the start was the state of Perry's feet. If we hadn't met Peter and learned so much from him, I don't think I would have known what I was looking at. Perhaps the fact that he would frequently trip over his own toes, even on the flat surface of a manège, would have seemed wrong, and I might have blamed it on the upright profile of his hooves. But Jo wasn't yet ready to listen. I was told that Perry's feet had been much worse when he'd arrived there, and that the farrier they used was one of the best in the country. There wasn't a lot I could say to that, so I just quietly suggested we agree to disagree, and mentioned that all my horses were barefoot. Fortunately, we were soon to be given a very good opportunity to investigate the state of Perry's feet more thoroughly.

Jo was particularly keen to learn long-lining during her week with us. It's one of those traditional skills that has gone somewhat out of fashion, but is now enjoying a renaissance. Not just useful for starting youngsters, or breaking to harness, it can also help all sorts of remedial issues, such as napping, and is an art in itself. It involves driving a horse from the ground with two lines, either with or without a saddle or roller. One line is usually placed behind the horse, falling on to the hocks. Some people walk behind the horse as if they were in a carriage, although this has the disadvantage that you have to travel at the same pace as the horse - not a problem if you are only working in the walk (and it's probably the best position to take to rein back or train the airs above the ground), but going at the same speed as the horse can be a big issue if you want the horse to trot or canter and you aren't in training for the marathon!

The difficulty with long-lining, which is one of the main reasons why we had decided to bring Perry down to Moor Wood from his yard, is that some horses panic when a line is placed behind them - especially if they have ever been whipped on the hocks when being lunged. This panicking about the lines can be very dangerous if you are not in a suitable enclosure, because if the horse gets loose, he will find himself pursued by lines trailing on the ground behind him, like a pair of super-fast, extra long snakes. Many horses will kick out and can get their feet tangled in the lines, causing burns and other injuries, and they can even run through fences, after which who knows when they will stop. Since our round pen is about twenty-five feet in radius, it is possible to stand in the middle holding thirty foot long-lines without moving much, allowing the horse to get used to the feeling without being stimulated into running faster by the movement of the trainer. This isn't to say things can't go wrong, but it generally makes the introduction of long-lines a lot less stressful for all concerned. It's also comforting to know your horse is in an enclosure made with eight-foot high wire mesh panels, rather than a small, wooden fence.

As we had anticipated, Perry did have a momentary panic when he felt the lines go down the back of his legs, but like most horses, instead of kicking out at them, he tucked his bum underneath him, clamped his tail down, and moved forward in an extremely collected fashion. The next thing that happened was that he over reached - stepping with a hind foot on the shoe of one of his front feet. Since the shoe was protruding behind the end of his heel, he pulled it off. I immediately stopped working and we had a look at his hoof.

What we saw made it obvious to us both that his feet were seriously in trouble. The nails had torn away large chunks of weak hoof wall as the shoe came off. There was evidence of severe thrush infection, and the hoof was so compromised by poor balance that the two sides of his heels were destabilised. His narrow, infected frog was clearly not functioning properly, and was allowing a degree of independent movement through his heels. The wall on either side of his heel was so weak and compromised with white line disease that I was able to take chunks out of it with my fingernail. He also wasn't weighting his heels properly, probably because of the pain of his infected frogs. He was immediately lame. As is frequently the case, the shoe had been holding the hoof together sufficiently for him to appear sound, while further weakening its ability to function as it should.

Aghast as I was to see the situation, I was pleased that there was no further resistance from Jo to the idea that we have his hooves looked at by someone else. Fortunately, this happened before the damage was irreversible, but our barefoot farrier at the time was of the opinion that it had been a near-run thing. It turned out that pulling off that shoe probably saved Perry's life. What I didn't have any idea at the time was how much he would affect mine.

Perry had immediately settled at Moor Wood. It was obvious that the better turnout, and stables that looked out over the yard and wood were much more suitable for him than the stables at the barn he'd come from, which only looked into each other. In spite of the fact that it would mean a drive of over an hour each way to see him, and in spite of how difficult it might make relations between various humans, Jo decided that she could not ask Perry to return to where he had been. We were uncomfortable with how this might look to the people who ran the other yard, but we felt we couldn't turn down her request. His happiness was more important.

A week or two later, I was having a well-earned rest. This had become a rare luxury. The yard, emails and the telephone were all so busy that it had become almost impossible to have a day off without working in one way or another. In fact, most "days off" were more like days working without getting paid, and the thrill of that was beginning to wear thin. We had reached a point where it seemed the only solution was to go away, but it was more to escape being caught at home than from a desire to go somewhere special.

One of Moor Wood's many glorious features is that the gardens on the estate host the National Collection of rambler roses. There are about 120 different varieties here, which involves a lot of pruning, and I try to help our landlord out with the ramblers around the stables. So I was having a hack at one of these, and short of wearing a T-shirt with "Day Off - DO NOT DISTURB!" on it, could not have made it plainer that I was not in a sociable mood. You might say I was doing my best to avoid meeting another of my Master Teachers.

For the first time, Jo had come up with her husband Derek. He was totally 'non-horsey', in fact he had an all-consuming obsession of his own. As well as running a software business with Jo, he was a consultant coach for the Oxford University Boat Club.

Now, rowing and I had what is known as 'previous'. My older sister, who was at Cambridge at the same time as us, was a cox (the person at the back who steers and shouts commands - something my sister was always particularly good at - in fact, you could say she was born to shout!). In her final year when I was also at Cambridge, she was cox for Gonville and Caius College men's first eight. Caius (pronounced "keys") is one of the oldest and most prestigious colleges in Cambridge, nestling between King's and Trinity College in the very centre of town. Their boat club had recently won the big inter-collegiate competition, making them 'Head of the River'. I had endured a bellyful of rowing banter every time I visited her room. There always seemed to be several enormous, super-fit healthy men there, members of the club, and all they ever talked about was rowing. I'd knock on the door and she'd say, "Come in!" and the conversation would go something like this:

"Oh, hi Adam, I thought it'd be Steve. He's keen to move to bow but I think Brian is going to get that place, even though he really let the crew down last year and it's not as if I can influence the Captain that much...you know I'm only Secretary. Anyhow, Brian had to be in London for an interview last Friday so Steve took the bow seat, and..."

Half an hour later, and after Steve, Brian and several others had come by for a quick chat, which seemed to go on forever, I still hadn't got a word in edgeways, and wanted nothing more than to take the plug out of the damn river. I'd sometimes just butt in to try to make the point that this was not a real conversation, by saying something like, "Yeah, it's just like my band, we're learning this song by Eric Clapton, and I want to play the solo but Dom wants to play it on his sax, I mean..."

At which she would look at me with a surprised, puzzled expression, and then continue banging on about rowing.

So in the end I decided that the best way to rile her would be to play her at her own game. Nicole was a member of possibly the University's least prestigious crew. We were at Robinson College, the newest college in the University, a 1980s construction looking more like a motel than the ancient portals of Caius, and situated a demeaningly long way out of the centre of town. As if that weren't bad enough, she wasn't even in an eight, but part of a four-man crew, except that they weren't men, they were women, and you don't need me to tell you where they stand in the rankings. They were so low, they didn't even have anyone to cox them. As soon as I realised that they didn't train often, and never in the pre-dawn hours like my sister and her overkeen buddies, I volunteered for the job on the condition that we never had to talk about it afterwards.

In the end, on the dozen or so occasions that we went out, I could not say that it was any kind of an imposition. I didn't have to exert myself and didn't even need to be especially sober, which was convenient given my commitment at the time to avoiding being in that state whenever possible. The river meandered through a beautiful stretch of countryside, with only the occasional road bridge or industrial building to disrupt a scene which otherwise seemed to have been there since the first rowing boat floated down in the Middle Ages. I only had to sit there and try not to let the sight of four young ladies in skimpy singlets heaving backwards and forwards distract me so much that I hit the bank or steered us into an overhanging willow. Best of all, I could keep an eye out for my sister, or rather an ear. Her sharp orders, needlessly projected through a small PA system, preceded the boat by several leagues.

As you might imagine, rowing at Cambridge has a venerable history, so much so that a whole language has developed around it, and an etiquette to match the most sophisticated court of Renaissance Europe. It all seemed like no end of pretension to me, so I made sure I just spoke English - the cruder, the better. If we were in someone's way, I'd just wave and say, "Sorry, didn't mean to bugger up your ride, guys! Have a nice day!" while their irritated cox admonished me in incomprehensible boat-speak. So, aside from the lovely views I had, the thing I most looked forward to was standing up in the boat waving as my sister went by and shouting, "Hey Venetia, look, we're out too, fancy a race? Hang on, give us a chance!" as her boat shot out of view while she screamed at them, "Ten stokes full pressure! MOVE IT! That's my brother!"

So I was not especially keen to meet Derek. I can distinctly remember thinking, "Bloody hell, here we go again!" when he strolled up, introduced himself, and started talking about rowing. I wondered whether I could get rid of him by making sure a nice long thorny rose stem flew into his face but thought better of it, because being an ex-Oxford crew member, he is about six foot twenty

Much to my surprise, in contrast to every conversation I'd had with my sister over several years, rowing turned out to be only one aspect of the conversation. He was just as interested in what we do, in how we were getting Perry to reassess his ideas about life and people, and in particular, Monty's ideas about motivating people and horses. He had been tolerant of, but not remotely interested in his wife's healthy interest in horses for years, until the season before, when Monty had, in a roundabout way, helped Oxford win the boat race.

In my opinion, the Oxford vs. Cambridge Boat Race is the world's most difficult amateur sporting event, with the possible exception of the Marathon Des Sables, which takes place in the Sahara, and in which competitors run six marathons in five days. The latter, however, clearly only allows certifiably insane entrants (who have to pay a large amount of money and carry their own gear as they run) to compete, whereas the contestants in the boat race, being Oxbridge students, are supposedly sound of mind (not that many of my contemporaries at Cambridge seemed to fit this description), and they certainly have to be sound of body. Compare it, for example, to the Olympic races, which is the milieu in which Jo and Derek met, for he was her coach when she was in the GB women's national team. They race on a purpose-built lake, flat as a pancake without a current or the rough waters of the Thames, which can swamp a boat. The Boat Race course is three and a half times longer than the maximum 2,000m raced in the Olympics. But perhaps most difficult of all, the Universities only begin their training in October, for a race in March - while the Olympic teams have four years to select and train their crews. Certainly, no-one can question the level of fitness and effort required to win the race. It's nearly twenty minutes of total exertion, which also requires a very careful use of technique - something easy to lose when you are close to blacking out towards the end of the race.

Technique is something which Derek was particularly interested in improving, and the previous year he had found himself up against a brick wall. A member of the club, who was one of the strongest and potentially best rowers, was not willing to listen to the coaches and remained impervious to attempts to get him to change his ragged technique, which was reducing the potential speed of the boat. Every effort he made to push this rower into changing seemed to make him listen less. In frustration he mentioned the situation to Jo, who simply handed him a copy of Monty's book, *Join-Up: Horse Sense For Humans*. In it, Derek found ideas that were really effective in helping this individual to work more as a team player. It also helped him notice that some of what the coaching staff preached they didn't really practise. For example, their reliance on mechanical 'ergo' machines on which rowers often train, which were known to give measurements that did not necessarily always reflect the real effectiveness of the rower out in the boat and thus could give a skewed impression of the actual value of that athlete in contributing to the boat's speed on the water. Derek noticed that in spite of everyone knowing that the single-minded pursuit of high scores on these machines often had the unintended side effect of making permanent the flaws in the athletes' rowing techniques, the data recorded on the ergo was still given a heavy weighting when deciding who would be selected to take seats in the boats. By altering the emphasis on aspects of the coaching like this, he was sure he had increased the chances of Oxford winning, and he was prepared to put their recent victory partly down to the changes he had been able to make as a result of coming across Monty's work. He was interested in having us host a day of team building and mind opening for the next year's squad.

Nicole and I had never done anything like this, but with our impeccable rowing credentials, we knew that we were perfect for the job. Just as we were proficient at helping horses like Perry change their behaviour, to the extent that their personalities seemed to alter, we knew that one of the most important aspects of our work is to help riders to improve their performance, even if many of them are simply 'happy hackers' with no desire to compete. Although we knew it was going to be a challenge and a major departure from the norm, we agreed, and after many hours of planning and a visit to see the club training on the river near Oxford, we designed a day-long course. It might have been seen as treachery by my sister and anyone else who had been to Cambridge, but given the many times she'd bored me to tears by banging on about rowing, it felt like completely justifiable revenge.

Of course, the people we help with their horses know that they need help, and actively seek out our advice. These rowers, on the other hand, were not necessarily convinced that a couple of "horse-whisperers" could help them win the Boat Race. Worse, they had to come on a Sunday, their only day off from lectures. At least, we thought, they won't mind if it rains, but apparently we were wrong about that - they may well train in all weathers, but, we were told, were prone to complaining about standing around in the cold and wet. We had to get them on board, and fast. To do that, we also needed to avoid using phrases like "You need to get on board, and fast". In particular, we couldn't say "We're all in the same boat", since at this stage it hadn't been decided who would go in the first boat, and who would be relegated to the much less prestigious reserve boat. The fact that this selection was yet to occur surely worked in our favour: the candidates must have been aware that the decision might partly be based on how enthusiastic and committed they were during this training day.

The experience of having around thirty rowers, coxes and coaches coming to our yard couldn't have been more out of the ordinary. The first thing that struck me was how tall most of them were, much taller even than Derek. They could hardly fit in the house, and had to stoop to avoid bashing their heads on the beams. We had been warned that they would eat everything in the place, and had laid on extra supplies, but still we were staggered by the number of loaves of bread they devoured, and that was just for their mid-morning snack. Perhaps the biggest difference, compared to our usual clientele, was that all but one of them, a tiny coxswain who only came up to waist height on most of the rowers, were men. I guess I had become used to being the only man in a room full of women, and now the shoe was on the other foot. Nicole seemed in her element, much the way she had been back at college where the ratio of men to women was four to one. I resolved not to be jealous or to make too much of it the next time we had a riding clinic.

What we most wanted to impress upon the rowers and their coaches was the importance of communication, and how easy it is to think you have understood someone when in fact they meant something completely different. This is bad enough when the only consequence is that your partner didn't get the milk on the way home from work because he misheard you, and thought you were getting it. It's far worse if it leads to losing a race. Or even, as Nicole pointed out in her introductory talk, to a horse or rider losing their life.

We had taken the group out to the school, where Nicole was going to do join-up with Karma, Sensi's daughter, to illustrate non-verbal, inter-species communication. As Nicole led the horse around, the boys seemed polite enough, but there was a sense of it all being a bit of a lark, and I was worried about how seriously they would take us. I could hear a little bit of chatter going on, and I hoped they would settle down quickly.

"Sometimes horses are sent to us as a last resort," Nicole explained, coming to a halt with Karma in front of the group. "We might be their last chance. If we get it wrong with them, it could be the difference between life and death for the horse. If we seriously misread them, it could also be the difference between life and death for us. They can't speak to us and tell us how they're feeling, so we need to be able to communicate in other ways."

At this point Karma, who wasn't used to being in the school, and certainly not to sharing it with so many young men, started to prance about on the end of her lead rope. The space around Nicole grew by several feet as the entire group stepped back.

"It's obvious with horses that we can't communicate in English," Nicole continued. "We may be able to teach them a few simple commands, but that's it. With humans, the difficulty arises when we share a common language, and because we know what we said we assume that the other person understood what we meant. As a result, we don't notice all the opportunities for misunderstanding."

Karma, meanwhile, seemed to grow by about a hand and was looking decidedly frisky, so we asked everyone to leave the school so that Nicole could set her loose. The group vacated the area readily, one might even say hastily, and as soon as the gate was secured, with everyone safely on the other side, Nicole unclipped

Karma's lead rope, stepped back, and sent her away.

Karma exploded. She really is quite a mellow horse, but on this occasion decided to play the part of a wild youngster. She reared, kicked, bucked, spun, and galloped around the school. Nicole, meanwhile, calmly explained about how horses use body language, and that there were signs to look out for. Karma duly displayed them all, almost on cue, and when the fireworks had subsided, Nicole invited her in. Karma followed Nicole in exemplary fashion as she walked around the school, considerably happier but still looking like a lot of horse. Nicole looked over at the rowers for the first time since she had started working, and seemed surprised to find them so quiet, even subdued.

"Walk with confidence, give the horse something to follow, be calm, and they will follow you," she said. "Now, who would like a go?"

There was quite a long pause before anyone volunteered.

In the end, though, everyone had a turn. We brought another couple of horses up to the school for the leading practice. Some people found it very easy, and the horses followed them eagerly, others struggled. Being hesitant or self-doubting usually meant it wouldn't happen. The horse would stand still, while the person continued getting more and more self-conscious. It was one of those situations where technique and attitude mattered more than physical strength, and the parallels with the race situation were obvious.

Physical fitness and strength would be in place for Oxford by the time the race took place. The problem was, it would be for their opposition too, and this year Cambridge would also have a huge advantage in height, weight and experience. What would make the most difference on the day, and also in the run-up to the race selection, was attitude. Not only did the rowers need great mental fortitude to stay focused and calm during the race, even if it seemed to be going against them; they needed the right approach throughout their training. This essentially meant being willing to do something differently, in order to do it better, even if this change felt weird and strange to them. They really had to trust what the coaches were telling them, and this was a big ask. If they changed their technique, they might feel it made them row slower, whatever the truth might be. They would certainly have to concentrate even harder during training and the race itself. With the horses, however, they had nothing invested except a little pride, so they had nothing to lose by making changes. With just a little coaching from us, everyone managed to get the horses following them. It might well be harder to implement such changes in the boat, particularly with their current techniques well and truly embedded, but at least it showed what a huge difference a few small alterations could make.

We did some other exercises on body awareness too, but what probably had the biggest impact was getting them to do some coaching themselves. We chose the rising trot mechanism as the subject, not least because it has a slight similarity with a rowing action, but also because you can do it in various ways, just as you can apparently row in various ways. We didn't set them loose on real horses, of course - we rigged up some barrel horses and put saddles on straw bales, and then showed one person in each group the technique we wanted them to teach the others. Most found it really challenging, and some got quickly frustrated when they couldn't explain what they meant in a way that the other person could understand and implement. It seemed to give them some insight into the difficulty of coaching well, and how much it is a two-way process, with the necessity that the person being coached be willing to be directed and pipe up when they don't understand what's being asked.

We hoped that these exercises had made more difference to their chances of winning than yet more sessions on an ergo, as Cambridge were probably doing that day. Several of the feedback forms we gave them to complete at the end of the day reflected this. One member of the eventual first crew wrote, 'From now on, I will actually listen to the coaches and try to do what they are saying.' In spite of what Derek had told us previously, we were both breathless with amazement when we read this statement. Then we reflected that in the end, these rowers were little more than big, strong kids with superhuman appetites, for whom a rowing coach was just another teacher. We could easily remember how through most of our academic careers, all teaching staff had appeared as a form of enemy whose influence should be thwarted at every opportunity. Nevertheless, we found it incredible to imagine that what we had done with the boat club that day could have an effect on the outcome of the race. A few months later, we were to discover the results.

The race took place on a cold, blustery day in March. I went down to London to watch it with Jo, while Nicole attended her grandmother's ninetieth birthday celebration. It was a difficult decision to make - which of these unique events to attend - so in the end we decided to split ourselves so we could at least tell the other what they had missed. Unlike everyone else involved with the teams, I was in the enviable position of being able to feel happy whichever crew won. If it were Cambridge, well, that was the team I 'belonged' to, and had always supported, if you could call my total apathy about the result in every previous year 'support'. If Oxford won, I would be able to claim a small part in their success, and revel in teasing my sister about it.

However, I was by now aware of how much this meant to my new friends Jo and Derek, and to everyone involved. As they had explained to me, this is the cruellest of races. There is no silver medal. You either win or you lose. Coming second is to be a loser, a nobody, even a disgrace. The whole University loses face. There is nothing but misery to reward all those months of gruelling training, getting up at four o'clock to row on a half-frozen river, burning every muscle on ergo machines, lifting weights, and possibly sacrificing your chances of academic success, or at the very least, your entire social life. And for most of the competitors, there isn't a second chance as there is in other sports. They'd have graduated and left before the next race. The after-race party would be like a funeral procession.

To add to the tension, Oxford's chances looked very slim. In a race where the heavier crew wins more than 70% of the time, Their crew was over a stone per man lighter, significantly smaller, two inches per man shorter and several years younger than Cambridge's, which was composed almost entirely of recognised international rowing stars. If they were to win, they would have to overturn a record weight deficit in the 150 year history of the race. On paper they looked as though they hadn't got a chance. The bookies had Cambridge as hot favourites. In addition to all this, Cambridge had won the toss and so were allowed to select which side of the river they would row on. This makes a big difference, because the boat on the southern - Surrey - side, has a great advantage in the middle of the race, where the river takes a huge left bend, nearly turning back on itself. At this point, the boat on the Surrey station rapidly gains a three-quarter length advantage just from the turn of the river, making it the ideal springboard for a race-winning 'push' from a strong and powerful crew.

In spite of these factors all working against him, Derek gave off an air of complete confidence about the race. Every disadvantage was twisted to serve his optimism in some way. Since Oxford were the underdogs, how much more painful it would be for Cambridge when they lost. Smaller and lighter, they would instill doubt and fear in the minds of their opponents when, in spite of rowing as hard as they could, Cambridge still weren't able to break Oxford around the critical 'Surrey Bend'. Being on the Middlesex station, the glory of beating the 'scum', as Jo venomously described their opponents, would be that much the greater. (Jo herself had rowed and won for Oxford in the lowly women's boat race three times, so her intense feelings about the opposition were understandable, if somewhat surprising, given what a lovely person she otherwise is). In the way he approached the psychology of winning, it was clear that Derek had a lot in common with Monty, who has deleted the word "failure" in all the dictionaries in his house, and replaced it with "opportunity to learn".

After watching the crews get into their boats and head off down the river to do a little warm up, Jo and I got into the Oxford team supporters' boat. For the first time, the boat club had arranged to let the families of the crew and coaches follow in a large riverboat, behind the flotilla of small motorboats in which the coaches and a select band of 'Old Blues' and supporters who help keep the club running follow hard on the heels of the crews. Our boat was supposed to follow close behind, but in the event, it was far too slow. Alongside at the start, we were completely unable to see a thing almost as soon as they got going, and the crews rapidly became no more than specks in the distance. We could not tell who was in front at all, and could barely hear ourselves speak above the din of the straining engines. But it was fun all the same, because Cambridge's support boat was even slower, so we took great glee in gesturing to them how inferior they were, and whipping up support from the thousands of people lining the banks to help us in our little sub-race. Occasionally, through the dirty, spray-strewn windows, we could catch a glimpse of the racing boats, beyond the line of motorboats following them. It was clear that the race was very competitive. As far as we could tell, it was neck and neck. Then the boats would go out of sight again, around another bend, while we chugged frustratingly behind.

It seemed to go on and on, and I found myself suddenly really involved in the outcome. It was agonising to be following a few hundred yards behind, but to have no idea what was going on up ahead. Finally, the boats reached the finish line, although by now we were so far behind that we could barely make out that the race was over. There was a moment of supreme tension while someone with a radio told us that, as the boats were so close, there was a photo finish to determine the result. Then he erupted in a cheer. Oxford had won by a mere one foot - the smallest winning margin in history.

Of course, the local media were all over us when they heard that this historic victory had been won by a whisper. We had more publicity as a result of this one event than all the really meaningful achievements we had managed over the years - the horses we'd saved from the bullet, the owners like Jo whom we had helped to enjoy being with their horses again. It seemed especially inappropriate given how few of our clients are intense competitors. Not that we really minded.

While Oxford went wild with celebrations, and Cambridge were plunged into miserable recriminations about what went wrong, Perry continued quietly munching grass in the field at Moor Wood, his bare feet recovering, as the layers of trauma that had shaped his early years gradually washed away.

TEN

A Right Poppet
(Nicole)

Poppet was a black Arab, utterly adorable, with a blaze and one eye showing white all the time, which many people feel makes a horse look a bit wild. In fact, much of the time his other eye was showing a lot of white as well, because he was a turbo-charged bundle of nerves. He had belonged to Gypsies, who by all accounts had not been too gentle with his early handling and "breaking in". In fact, it seems he had never been ridden successfully, and attempts to break him to harness had spectacularly failed. He had a phobia of just about every piece of training equipment - long-lines, ropes, saddles, and rollers.

He had been sent to someone else who had tried to overcome his problems, but without any success, and as "a last resort" he was coming to us.

His owner, Bridget, was understandably anxious, and wanted assurances about how likely we were to succeed with him. She had seen him at his worst, and couldn't really imagine him ever becoming a calm, ridden horse. We were confident. We'd been at Moor Wood for a few years by now, and had already dealt with quite a number of such remedial horses. Jo (not Perry's Jo, our groom Jo) was still working for us, and was shaping up well. We more or less promised that we would 'fix' Bridget's horse, or else we would refund her money. In recent years, we have spent more time cultivating realistic expectations, especially of what work will be required of the owner to step up and consolidate what we have started.

One of the difficulties is that owners understandably don't want to pay to get a horse to the stage where we can ride it successfully - they want us to get it to the stage where they can. Of

97

course, this can be a tall order, especially on a limited budget. Bridget worked several not particularly well-paid jobs to keep her horses, many of them rescued, in very comfortable conditions, and only wanted to do the best for Poppet, but she didn't have unlimited funds, and couldn't really commit to spending money on her own learning too. This didn't bode well. To make matters worse, she lived more than an hour's drive away and had so much going on in her life that finding time to come and watch or work with us was a real issue for her. We would have to concentrate on turning Poppet, a highly strung, adrenaline filled, six year old Arab gelding with a whole heap of negative baggage, into a plod. Agreeing that he would stay with us for six to eight weeks, which was all she could realistically afford, she brought him up to Moor Wood.

The first session Adam did with him made us wonder if eight weeks would be anything like enough. Join-up seemed to trip a wire in Poppet's head, and instead of trotting calmly around the pen, he took off like the very devil himself was after him. Although he stopped careering around and ventured into the middle when asked, he was paying attention to everything except Adam. The idea of putting on a saddle and then some long-lines, and seeing where we could get to that day, suddenly seemed absurd. We took him and the tack back down to the yard, trying not to look downcast, and explaining to Bridget as we went that we would have to go at a speed that he found acceptable, and that once we gained his trust, we could expect real progress and accelerate on from there.

She had been doing some work with the saddle, and said he was fine with it. Well, he was fine in the sense that he didn't immediately explode, but he did curl up like a cannon ball when the girth was done up, and if let loose would hurtle erratically around the pen at a terrifying speed. By this time in our careers, we had learned that some horses are better not let loose with the tack, and that with some horses - Arabs often fall into this category - it wasn't a question of letting their adrenaline peak and then watching it come quickly down. Rather, the best strategy was not letting the adrenaline get high in the first place. Shutting down their explosive movement can be the key.

Keeping his adrenaline low and doing any sort of training, however, were more or less mutually exclusive. In preparation for riding, we really wanted to long-line him. It's such a useful thing to do with starters and remedial starters, and has plenty of benefits for calm, sane, normal ridden horses too. But sometimes it creates so much anxiety in itself that one has to question its worth. Usually, once you can show a horse that something doesn't hurt, they'll accept it pretty quickly, but if a horse has been whipped across the hocks, or worse still, had its legs tied up with ropes to restrain it whilst it panics, then the mere presence of ropes on the hocks can appear to be an act of aggression. It can take quite a bit of work to develop sufficient trust to allow one to 'go there'.

Poppet hated the long-lines, and would kick at them, charge around the pen, tuck his quarters under him to the point of almost sitting down, and generally resist them in every way possible. In spite of his extreme reaction, I felt there was a reasonable chance that with a few successful sessions under our belts, he would be alright with the lines. He never really relaxed into the process, however, and it became clear that if we wanted him to be perfect - or at least reasonably calm - before we got on him, we would have no time left to work on the ridden stuff. It was time to move on.

Poppet responded pretty typically to our initial work with bellying over: he tensed up and held his breath as, with Adam's help, I drew myself slowly up his body, and relaxed when I let myself down again. Occasionally he shot off like a cork out of a champagne bottle, but would stand still again afterwards. He never showed a tendency to buck or rear, and didn't even waste time leaping up and forwards when he went. No, his trajectory was as fast as possible away from us, in as straight a line as the short hold Adam had on the dually would allow. He did improve quite quickly with the repetition, however, and I was feeling quite optimistic that perhaps the riding would turn out not to be so difficult after all. Sometimes, the horse seems to know that the preparation work is building up to something, and the anticipation can be worse than the event. Lying on my belly over his back, with my right hand on the saddle near the knee rolls on the off side, my other hand firmly ensconced in the neck strap and grab handle, keeping my hanging legs well away from his sides, I was just contemplating this pearl of wisdom when all hell broke loose.

Suddenly I found myself lying on a horse cantering sideways into where I knew Adam had been standing, and then hurtling around in a very tight circle. Gravity took over, and I found myself on my feet, while a ballistic Poppet charged around Adam (who had somehow managed to stay upright) and me, who, under the circumstances wasn't sure that being on the ground was any better an option than being on his back had been. When he finally managed to bring himself to a panting, sweating stop, Adam and I looked at each other with astonishment.

"What on Earth just happened?" we asked each other. His reaction was so sudden and so severe we wondered if he'd just been stung by a bee. It's the sort of thing that can happen, and which could ruin an otherwise great session, but we weren't sure how likely it was. We couldn't see any signs of swelling either.

Working together over the years Adam and I had become pretty good at backing horses. We knew when to keep going, and when to back off, and we never did anything that we knew could lead to a reaction without letting the other know. "I'm just going to touch him on the shoulder now" from the rider, would give the person on the ground the warning they might need to make sure they were in the best position to direct the horse's response, if there was one. "Unclip?" from the person on the ground let the rider stay in charge of the process, and decline or accept the suggestion as they saw fit. In this way, we had managed to keep each other as safe as possible. Had I done something that had caused such a strong reaction? I remembered I had just slightly re-adjusted my grip on the saddle panel. I definitely hadn't touched Poppet, but maybe he had seen this minute movement? I mentioned it to Adam, and we decided to check it out. Slowly and carefully, we repeated the bellying over process a few more times. Apart from a few snorts of anxiety and a little fidgeting, Poppet dealt with it well. When he was feeling calmer again, I warned Adam, and just moved one finger half an inch off his saddle. As I hit the ground beside Adam again, we looked at each other - "That must have been it!"

Hmm, so as long as there wasn't even the faintest whisper of a movement, Poppet could bear having someone belly over him. Any movement at all and his reaction was explosive. I dreaded to think how he might have responded to me had I got on and then sneezed. We would clearly have to do a lot of de-sensitising before we got to that stage. I was confident in my ability to sit still, but at some point I was going to have to move, and it would be better for all concerned if he could handle it a little better.

Interestingly, once I was moving my hand, he could cope with it. I soon found it was better to touch him on the shoulder, quite firmly, and to keep moving it even if he reacted. Once he realised that what I was doing was not so terrible, he could relax. Of course, it wasn't particularly difficult to see where such behaviour had come from. Horses that have been beaten are often most frightened of that moment just after movement starts and before contact is made, for this could be the strike they're fearing. Once you have made contact, and it isn't aggressive, they know they can relax. I guess no lioness on the African plain has ever stroked a zebra before going in for the kill. Poppet quickly became quite comfortable with having his off side stroked and rubbed while I lay for many uncomfortable minutes on my belly over his back.

We had done a lot of this work in the school, because he had begun to associate the round pen with the unpleasantness of the long-lines, and we knew that for a few days at least, bellying over was the only thing on the agenda. Once we felt we were ready, however, we decided to go back to the pen and commit ourselves to the next step, actually getting that leg over.

I have the session on video, and it went incredibly well. We kept it all very calm, I kept very still, Adam did an excellent job being very quiet and reassuring, and the only moment there was any reaction at all from Poppet was when it came to dismounting. As soon as he felt me begin to lean forward he tensed up and threw his neck up so there was almost no space for my body. However, I was fully committed at this point, and was able to dismount just before he shot forward about 10 feet. With all he had been through, there was no malice in Poppet, and he didn't look at all like he would kick out at me. It was still a bit worrying though, because if he had done so I would have been in a very vulnerable position.

In a way, it's hard to describe what made Poppet such a difficult horse. In all the time we worked with him, he never bucked or reared. It was just that he felt so much like an unexploded bomb and his flight reaction was so very strong. We had seen him bolt off at impressive speeds, and the thought of careering endlessly around the pen or worse, the school, with him in a state of absolute panic was not entirely appealing. Then there was the issue of dismounting. His ability to raise his neck vertically like a giraffe meant he often missed my nose by mere millimetres as I was getting off. However, over the course of a fortnight or so, Poppet did improve, to the extent that I felt confident that Jo, our groom, could ride him. She did a great job, and I was delighted, as I really needed a break. We were having to work him every day, because if he had any time off it was as though we had never done anything with him at all, and it was disheartening to seemingly go back to square one. We had done a few sessions in the pen, and decided it was time to go to the school. The first session went well and was uneventful, but the second school session was considerably less successful.

Bridget had come up to watch, as we had urged her to, and we were hoping she would be pleased with his progress. We were a bit more than half-way through the allotted time, and we were doing well. Perhaps our desire to show her just how well he was doing meant we read the signs less well than usual. I did have my doubts about how he was going to be, and suggested a return to the pen, but Adam seemed confident, and as I'm often a little over-cautious, and he was doing the session, I decided to butt out. Poppet seemed on edge, but as Jo got on and he didn't react, I thought perhaps I had been worrying over nothing. Adam began gently patting him all over, to desensitise him to the eventual movement of the rider, as he had done several times already, and Poppet seemed to be coping well right up to the moment he freaked.

He took off with his trademark astonishing acceleration, and as Adam pulled him sharply around on the circle to prevent him from charging off in what would have been a disastrous straight line in the school, the centrifugal forces took their toll on Jo and the saddle. She stayed on for a circuit or so, and then as the saddle began to slide around his barrel-like belly, she went with it and hit the ground, none the worse for wear, but needing to get out of the way of a thoroughly frightened horse who had already completed one circle and didn't look as if he planned to stop just because his rider had dismounted. Adam thankfully managed to bring him to a halt before the saddle slipped any further. Bridget had turned white, her worst fears realised, and as much as I tried to downplay the situation, I was gutted. The weeks of painstaking work we had already put in had gone as well as we might have hoped, and yet here we had a totally terrified horse, a dearly loved groom who could have been seriously hurt, and an even more traumatised owner. This was another session I had on video, and I wished I could just rewind reality and start again. But sometimes these things work out better than you think. The terrified horse who realises that no-one is going to hit him can begin to calm down and trust these people who never get cross. The rider realises that the worst reaction the horse exhibits is really not so bad after all. The owner perhaps recognises that these things are to be expected on the path of training a remedial horse. The situation you've been so careful to avoid can actually be a turning point when it happens.

Not so with Poppet. Jo and Adam worked quietly and carefully around him, going back to bellying over, and when they judged him to be calm, Jo slowly swung her leg over his back. This time he reacted almost as soon as her bum came to land gently in the saddle, and without her off side stirrup this ride was even shorter than the last. I wasn't sure how much more of this Bridget could take, so we abandoned the session as soon as a little progress had been made. We all tried to keep positive about a session that was barely the right side of disastrous. Feeling like total muppets, in an attempt to placate Bridget, we admitted that we had made a mistake, and that when we came to the end of the agreed training time, if he still wasn't ready, we would carry on working with him for free until he was.

After that, I decided to do all the riding myself. It wasn't that Jo had done a bad job, or that I necessarily believed I could have stayed on better, but I disliked feeling that she could do something that would set us back; at least if I made a mistake, I had only myself to blame. I devised a clever system with the reins, so that if Muppet panicked, Adam could simply let us go, without any of us having to worry about a long line getting tangled up anywhere. We used two pairs of long, synthetic, endurance reins. I had one pair, with a knot tied at the end to reduce some of the length, and passed through the grab handle and neck strap at the front of the saddle, so that there was no way that if I accidentally let go of them, they could get in Poppet's way. Adam had the other set, secured in the same way, but without the knot, so he had more slack to play with. This way, it was also very easy for Adam to transition from leading us to walking beside us, to backing away, to coming back to us again, without too abrupt a movement.

We went back to basics and clocked up lots more small successes. Riding Poppet every day put me continually in my stretch zone. I really worried about whether we would be able to achieve our goals with him, and the prospect of sitting on a jet rocket every day was daunting. I lost about a stone in weight, just through the worry. I felt I was up to it and knew I was the best option out of our team of three for riding him, but the relentlessness of doing it day in and day out was wearing. A day off was a lovely prospect, but we still had to pay dearly for one, as he would go backwards by about a fortnight if we did. I spoke to a colleague at Witney about it, and she had some good advice: "You've just got to work him through it. Never give him a day off - if anything, see if you can work him twice a day. And push him a bit. Don't hang around at any one stage for too long."

I thought about it: I could handle anything he had thrown at me. His tendency was to bolt off, but in the confines of a round pen, there wasn't really anywhere he could go. The footing was good. I loved going fast in other circumstances. What was I so worried about? I didn't want him to feel unduly anxious, but anxiety was inevitably a part of his everyday working experience, as we were asking him to overcome deeply ingrained fears. It was extremely important that we had been very still and quiet in the early days, but perhaps it was time to just cut loose a little, shift around a bit, let him go.

Adam was a little surprised, I think, by my new cavalier approach, as I explained that I was just going to go for it, and asked him not to worry or try to intervene if we ended up going quite quickly around the edge of the pen. I hadn't ever been holding tightly on to Poppet's head (we weren't using a bit), but I was using my body to contain him and slow him down as best I could. He immediately noticed as I slackened off my riding "framework", and felt a bit wobbly as I made less effort to stabilise myself fully. He shot forward, and I went with him, pushing him on as we leapt erratically around the pen for a couple of circuits. I soon felt his adrenaline come down and he slowed to a much more sedate canter, and then a trot. I repeated the process a few more times on each rein, each time with less adrenaline, and although he was a bit hot and breathless at the end (well, we both were), he really seemed to have turned a corner.

The difficulty with working on such a remedial horse is that Adam and I both needed to be there. There was very little I could do on my own. Usually, with say just a normal starter, we could be mounting and riding without assistance after a couple of weeks' training. With Poppet, I needed a second person, and I needed it to be Adam, but with callouts and clinics and the usual demands of life on his time, it could be tricky. I had been working on getting Poppet to stand near a mounting block and tolerate me stepping up and leaning over for a couple of weeks, in conjunction with the other work, but it was time to take the next step.

The problem was, he was still very volatile in the pen. He associated it strongly as the place where he had to deal with his fears, and he was very concerned about the work I was doing. Reasoning that I wasn't planning to actually mount him, just do the preparation work, I decided to see if he was any better in the yard. It was enclosed, and he could be near all the other horses in their stables, and not have any negative associations.

It worked beautifully. He was completely calm there, and I was able to get him to stand like a rock while I hopped up and down the mounting steps, leant over him, patted his saddle and sides, and generally did a lot of desensitising. I was really confident that he would be fine if I got on, but the problem was that if he wasn't, the consequences could be really serious. The yard is surfaced with gravel, and there's a concrete apron around the boxes, so if he rushed over to get reassurance from another horse, there was every chance he could slip over, although mercifully he was barefoot, so losing his footing was considerably less likely than had he been shod. I could make sure there were no wheelbarrows or anything to get in his way, but there was a post to hold open the yard gate which he could trip over. If he really panicked and tried to jump out, there was a massive drop down to the muck heap, the drop Sensi had managed to tear her stifle on, attempting to escape. So a Health and Safety Risk Assessment didn't designate the area as a good one to work in, but I knew in my heart he would be fine.

Adam helped the first couple of times and after that I was able to mount, from either side, ride him around the yard, dismount, mount again, all with almost zero signs of anxiety from Poppet. I could pat him all over while I was on him, do up his girth, and generally treat him like a normal horse. At this point, we had been working on him for free - not even charging livery - for about an extra six weeks. I felt it was time to have some fun, and to take him out for a bit of a blast.

Jo accompanied me on her pony Molly, and we set off for "the wheat field" - a huge expanse of eroded soil on the neighbouring farm, that had been created by ripping the hedgerows and stone walls out of five fields, before the practice became illegal. Nevertheless, for about a week in early autumn, it was an asset we appreciated, for the gap after the harvest and before ploughing proved a great time to canter around it. The hill was so steep that any horse not currently in training for Aintree or Badminton would run out of steam before they ran out of space. Poppet was calm on the way there, and as soon as we got to the field we stepped off the bridleway and let them go.

The weeks of work in the pen had made Poppet quite fit, and we had a lovely gallop up the first steep segment. A second wind carried him more slowly, but still very willingly, up to where it levelled off, and we continued sedately until there was no more field to go. He didn't put a hoof wrong, didn't spook at the ubiquitous pheasants, didn't nap or pull, even though he was still being ridden without a bit. He was an absolute dream. We walked the rest of the way home, chatting like normal people on normal horses. I couldn't wait to get out on him again.

Now that we had made such a breakthrough, Poppet could have a day off, and come back to work where we had left off. I took him out for plenty of long rides with Jo and with Adam. The only time I had a moment's concern was when we were going down a steep hill in the neighbouring village, and someone suddenly started sweeping their alleyway. They were concealed from the road, and the noise was very startling. Both Poppet and Molly took off for a few strides of canter, but came quickly back to us. Again, I was thankful that neither of them was shod, otherwise the gradient would almost certainly have caused a slip and possibly, a fall.

Bridget came to watch me ride him out, and rode him out herself. She was delighted, but still found it difficult to believe he wouldn't revert back to the horse he had been. Poppet did his absolute best to convince her, however, and never did anything wrong. Once he had overcome his fear of being ridden, he seemed not to fear anything else. He had turned into a fantastic little horse, and I was sure he would be very suitable for what she intended to do with him - endurance riding.

So, having been with us for eighteen weeks in total, ten of them for free, he was going home. The nights were drawing in now, and Bridget's opportunities for riding him would be limited. She also had not much in the way of facilities, but I implored her to sit on him every day. Just to get on him by the light of her barn, sit there for a while, and get off again. She had people who could help her on the weekends, and she could do more with him then. What she did instead, which was sort of fine, was to get someone else to ride him in the daylight every day for a couple of months. Only sort of fine, because she was by all accounts blasting him around the roads at a spanking trot, with no walking, but he was coping alright. Then Bridget decided she had better get on and ride him and, in two short sessions, undid the work of months.

The first time she got on him she lost her balance as she began to swing her leg over. He moved forward slightly, and she landed heavily behind the saddle, on his loins. Understandably, he leapt forward, and she fell straight off. The next time she tried getting on was on a windy day. The huge wax jacket she was wearing flapped out around her, and already unnerved by her previous attempt, he shot off again, with the same result. As she told me the details on the phone, my heart sank. Reluctantly, I agreed to visit her and see what I could do.

I was secretly hoping that when he saw it was me, he would remember the literally thousands of times I had mounted him, and quickly calm down. As it was, he was difficult for either of us to catch, and when I stood him by the mounting block to gauge his reaction to the prospect of being mounted, it was as if we had never done any training at all. Bridget's finances were exhausted, and I simply couldn't face the prospect of doing it all again if he were going to go straight back to her. I knew of one person who would have been really suitable, and I would have been happy to put in a few weeks work if he could go to her, but she wasn't interested. Bridget would have given him to me, but we already had eight horses, of whom only three were rideable, and finances just didn't allow another. Not just the ongoing upkeep, but the work we would have to put in again would seriously cut down our earning potential. I couldn't think about it without feeling sick. Each tiny step of progress had been so painstakingly earned, and been ruined so quickly.

I still think about Poppet often, but I know he's okay. He's still with Bridget, and just spends his days hanging out in the field with his mates. I'm not sure it was the best outcome for him - I'm certain he would have loved doing endurance rides - but at least he didn't change hands and go from pillar to post. His future seems safe, unlike so many similar horses. But I remember those fun rides we had together, his eager little body powering beneath me, and I wish it could have turned out differently.

ELEVEN

Paradise Found
(Adam)

I can still remember how scared I was. My heart was beating fit to burst my chest. I'd have been less freaked out on the back of a horse bucking to save his life. And all I was doing was walking up to a building, ready to spend a few days attending a seminar that Annabelle had recommended to us.

By now Annabelle had given up her high-powered job (she'd worked very successfully for the huge accountancy firm Price Waterhouse, and had rescued several companies from bankruptcy), and she was living at Moor Wood, learning about training horses and learning rather more than she ever wanted to know about shovelling muck. It would be a massive step down in most people's eyes, going from a high salary in a prestigious company, to living in a tiny room and continually mucking out stables. But she had volunteered for it, had consciously chosen this lifestyle, and didn't seem to regret it in the slightest. Although her previous work had been well remunerated, it had also been very emotionally taxing and stressful and, perhaps as a result, she had become ill. There must be a lot of jobs in the city which are a lot less interesting and more impersonal - after all, even my most anti-materialist streak has to recognise that there is personal value in helping rescue a company from liquidation, given that this means saving people from losing their jobs, their dreams. But she had not been satisfied with that life, and had taken radical steps to follow her dreams and become a horse trainer, thanks in large measure to the work she had done on herself through the Insight seminars she had attended.

Actually, Annabelle, gentle and charming as she is, wasn't the only one we knew who had 'done Insight'. Back in 1998 when I had done my ten-week course with Kelly, learning the art of 'horse-

109

whispering', I had become close friends with a man called David, an interesting character whose story I went into in *Whispering Back*. A colourful childhood in Argentina was followed by six years' service in Israel's messy war in Lebanon, and after a long time in the both a literal and figurative wilderness, David had made the effort to move on in life, and had met his remarkable wife, Ruth, at an Insight seminar. I had a lot of respect for the journey he had been on.

It was neither at his insistence, nor even his suggestion, nor Annabelle's, that I decided to go on the seminar, however. All the personal development books that Nicole spent so much time reading failed to impress either. I couldn't galvanise myself to read more than a few pages of most of them. In the end, my decision came as a result of David's fortieth birthday party. We had made the effort to do the journey to London to celebrate it with him. But I wasn't up for a self-help "journey".

And yet, that party was enlivened by some of the most exceptional people I have ever met. We'd never met a single one of them, except David. The atmosphere was very welcoming, but nobody was indulging in the false camaraderie of drinking heavily or taking drugs as a means to break the ice. There were people of all ages, many cultures and colours. Nobody tried to dominate the conversation - even David, who is one of the most talkative, lively people I know - or impress everyone with their intelligence, or the brilliance of their repartee, or anecdotes of adventures they had experienced in far-flung places. There weren't the usual 'So, tell me, what do you do for a living?' type of conversations, let alone the 'What car do you drive?' posturing. In spite of not knowing anyone there, it was so easy to talk and to listen. They really tried, but without forcing it in any way, to engage on a deep level with both of us. I don't think I've ever felt more welcome at any gathering before. And the one thing almost everyone had in common was that they had all completed, or led, Insight seminars. Even so, you couldn't tell who were the big shots. I figured this had to be worth a few days of my time.

Even so, when it came to the crunch, I put it off for many months - I always thought I had something more important to do than to pursue the most important thing most important in life - happiness. I found so many reasons not to go to the next seminar I heard about - it was too expensive, it would mean I couldn't go to this or that horsemanship demonstration, I had too much work to do, and I had to save this or that horse, or person, instead. It was all a way of putting off the day of reckoning, of facing my own inadequacies.

For years I had been irritating Nicole by grumbling about how much everything costs. I'd see how much other horse trainers charged, whose work I thought was no better and often much worse than my own, and be resentful. I'd begrudge the cost of almost everything except the rent, because I knew any amount of money couldn't really be compared to the value of living in such a special place. So I figured that one of the main things I should work on while on the Insight seminar would be my relationship with money, which I was discovering really means investigating one's self-worth. In the end, by the time I actually was stepping down the stairs into the conference centre where the seminar was held, I had already got my head around it. I had put my prices up, and restructured my working life, enabling me to enjoy myself more and also do more for charity. I had discovered what many participants have found - that the seminar really starts when you make the commitment to do it, when you see that you are worth it, and that there isn't anything more important than the quality of life you live, and the love you give. And the seminar certainly doesn't end on the last day. You're still on it, for the rest of your life.

From the moment I walked through the door into the seminar rooms, I found myself engaged in a series of 'processes' which opened me up to the most intense and enlightening introspection and personal journey I had ever undertaken. Success in this context was such a different experience to anything I had done before, and a world away from the sort of emotionally stifling 'education' I had undergone at the leading public schools I attended. To me, it was also a vastly more valuable form of education than what I had been exposed to at University. Everyone should have the chance to do one.

The processes were widely varied and involved many diverse group sizes. Some work was done in pairs, some in small groups, and some by individuals speaking to the whole group of fifty-five. Some parts involved simply listening to the facilitators, and some took place behind one's eyelids in guided meditation. Every process seemed perfectly to complement the one before and after, leading us individually and as a group towards a profound internal shift. To me, it was sometimes surprising where the sources of learning and inspiration could appear from. A great example was the process involving the matchsticks.

I had always been conscious that it can be valuable to 'listen also to the dull and ignorant; they too have their story.' In spite of the underlying, perhaps unintended elitist message which permeated the public school ethos, I had always tried to pay equal respect to everyone I met, but I could not honestly say the judgmental attitude hadn't rubbed off on me. I wasn't consciously trying to be patronising or superior, but I didn't really see how I could learn much from someone less intelligent than myself. The matchstick process showed me a lot about what I was missing, and how my education had failed me, and had helped make me into a person I did not entirely like.

The facilitator began to outline an exercise which involved making a new shape from some matchsticks set out in an original shape, by moving only a certain number of the matches. The answer came to me instantly, with no effort at all, before he had even finished explaining what the task was, I don't know how. It just popped straight into my head.

We were each given the requisite matches and shown the pattern in which they should be placed to start with, and were told we could have as long as we wanted to solve the puzzle, and also that we could ask anyone for the solution to the problem at any time. If you had finished the puzzle, you were invited to watch others trying to solve it, but you should not tell them what the answer was unless they asked. We were invited to notice how we felt as we did this.

Since I had already worked it out, I was immediately, and somewhat smugly, watching others writhe as they tried to do so. I soon noticed how hard I was finding it to let them take their time and not tell them the solution. Part of my reason for this was, I think, because I simply wanted to help them as they struggled. I didn't want to be in their position - that was for sure. But my desire to intervene was not without a tinge of condescension, as I noted shamefacedly. Clearly, someone somewhere had convinced me that to take longer over a problem like this was a sign of inferiority.

A few of the other participants had also got the answer quickly, and after about five minutes almost everyone had. We began to congregate noticeably around the rest of the group, those who had not got it yet. Once again I noticed how glad I was that I was one of those standing, not those still kneeling on the floor in front of a handful of matches. I realised that if I had not been so fortunate as to see the solution immediately, without any effort, I might well have been struggling desperately by now, because I'd have felt a great deal of pressure and judgement simply from the presence and scrutiny of those who had worked it out. Having people stand over me, who were apparently more intelligent and therefore in my warped mind, more valuable, successful, and worthy, would have made me so stressed that I'd have been unable to think. I would never have let myself be one of the last to get it. Well before that, I would have copped out and asked for someone to tell me the answer.

Eventually, there were only two people who had not solved it, and after a few moments one of them asked for the answer. But the last person, Trevor, stuck resolutely to the task. With over fifty people crowding around him, he stayed kneeling, eyes glued to the floor. He would deliberate for what seemed like ages, then pick up a match and put it here or there, or sometimes, straight back to its original place. But whatever he seemed to try, he would only be able to solve the puzzle and make the new shape by moving too many matches. In many different ways he came to the same incorrect solution, at which point he would simply replace the matches and go back to staring at them. Several times he began moving the same matches, even though they had not got him a result before.

They say a good definition of insanity is to try the same thing again and again and expect a different result; in this instance I was thinking it was a better definition of stupidity - at least, that might be what I'd have been thinking in normal times. But instead I was awestruck, overcome with respect. I could hardly bear to watch him. I couldn't believe how he had the bottle to stick to this task in the face of so many onlookers, managing to stay unconcerned at the judgements that people like me were potentially making. My sense of superiority in having been so quick at solving the puzzle was completely overcome by an intense admiration for how well he was coping with the weight of people's judgement.

The seconds seemed to hang endlessly, as if time were standing still, and yet Trevor just stuck to the task.

Finally, after what seemed an eternity, he found a way to

make the required shape. To my surprise, he had come up with a second solution for the problem, and it was not one that I had seen yet. This forced me to reconsider just how clever I really was. But the facilitator told him it wasn't the right solution.

I was astonished by how calmly Trevor responded to this decision. Very calmly, he initially queried it, pointing out that it fulfilled the requirements which had been laid out. But when told it wasn't what they were after, he simply said, "Oh, OK," and replaced the matches in their original shape and spent about another ten minutes - it felt like hours to me - working out the other solution. Even though I hadn't been the one under examination, I was riled by the injustice, felt that there was no greater merit in one solution than the other and would have been up in arms about it, making a protest and missing my opportunity to work out the other solution, as well as my opportunity to learn, grow and expand emotionally. It turned out as I got to know him later, that Trevor actually had a huge amount to teach me, and that he was competent and wise in many ways in which I was not. Although he later acknowledged how hard it had been to ignore the crowd watching him, he stuck by a decision he'd made at the beginning, to take as long as he needed to work it out, and not to ask anyone for the answer. It was enlightening to realise that the judgements of those watching him, if there were any, were generally supportive and positive, not negative and derisive as I would have assumed, if I had been on my knees struggling to work it out in front of everyone as my brain turned to static and my skin turned hot and cold with shame and embarrassment. Looking back at my 'top class' education, it was not hard to guess where those emotions had been formed.

There is a lot that gets left out in a classical education, I would say, if that's what they gave me. I didn't tend to know what was happening inside me, or outside the school grounds, as well as I might. In many ways I was pathetically weak. But I was about to move on a lot, at least with regard to a childhood event that I had tried to forget, but which still affected me every time I tried to dance.

Dancing - there's no more natural human behaviour in the world, it's one of our most basic instincts. You don't need to teach it to a baby. Just let them hear a beat, and watch. It is a source of wonderful joy, to move, and not just for people, for horses as well.

In fact, I'd say what I most aspire to do with horses is to dance with them, from the ground or on board - and for the horse to enjoy moving with me as much as I enjoy moving with it. I'll never forget the first time I showed a client that I had 'taught' her horse to do piaffe - trotting on the spot. She said, "Wow - it's like she's dancing!"

In my early teens, I discovered dancing and parties, and I loved them. Living in Lagos, Nigeria in the mid-80s, there wasn't much else to do, since it was dangerous to be out in the daytime, let alone at night. There was no TV, no cinema, nowhere the expatriate and diplomat kids could go except to each others' houses. So there would be a party every single night of the holidays, at each of which I would get ridiculously over-lubricated, flirt, and dance with complete abandon. I won't pretend I was cool, although I did at the time. But no matter what you do on the dance floor, not everyone will think you're cool anyhow. These days I think the really uncool ones are the people who are too cool to look like they are having fun, and don't let go. But at one party something happened that put a major spoke in my wheel.

I was about fifteen or sixteen years old, ridiculously oversexed and I was at an all-boy public school, so I had naturally acquired an idealised notion of females - in fact you could say I just about worshipped the ground they walked on, as well as desperately fancying nearly every one I saw. Which partly explains why, when one night a girl made a very sharp, vicious comment, along the lines that I was an awful dancer, I was so upset. It hit me with a physical force. To this day I can remember the feeling I had, deep in my gut, as if she had plunged a knife in there.

I can still remember pouring whisky into my litre of Star beer, and downing the lot, although the rest of the night is a bit of a blur, up until throwing up in the bathroom. But no amount of alcohol could erase my memory of what she had said, and every time the words went round in my head, I was tormented. I didn't dance again, not for many years. I'd just get blind drunk at every party I was at, and pretend I had something better to do than enjoy myself dancing. When I performed in my various bands, I'd 'do a Pink Floyd'- stand there, look at the floor and hope the light show would take the stage. Not that our lights were ever good enough.

Maybe lots of people have had a similar experience with dancing, or at least feared some negative comment if they did put themselves out there. Certainly, listening to people on our riding clinics, plenty of people have had a similar experience on board a horse - and worse, they've usually paid an instructor for this criticism. Riding in front of others can be such a big deal that it literally seizes people up, and takes all the pleasure out of it for them.

I'd sort of got over it by the time I was attending the Insight seminar, nearly twenty years later. That's to say, I'd used aggression to mask my inability to deal with it and move on. I told myself that the girl was a complete bitch and I hated her and what the hell - if it was New Year's Eve and everyone else was drunk enough - I was going to dance, or at least shuffle as inconspicuously as possible.

So, imagine how I felt when I discovered, towards the end of the seminar, that we were all required to dance, at two o'clock on a Sunday afternoon, in a brightly lit neon environment, without so much as a sip of beer. And the music - well, it was disco stuff like Abba and Madonna. I normally wouldn't have been seen dead on the dance floor if that was playing.

But I was completely elated, utterly liberated. I hadn't danced with real joy like that for years - not since that cutting comment on a sultry African evening. I simply didn't care about what anyone else saw or thought of me, because I had really worked something out, thanks to the seminar. Instead of hating the girl who had so venomously criticised my dancing almost twenty years before, I had turned it around completely. Certain processes we'd been led through had helped me to see something I had been blind to for so many years. Whatever my sensitivities, she hadn't intended to deprive me of the pleasure of boogying around on the dance floor. In fact, the only thing that was really wrong about the whole incident was that I had listened to her. She wasn't really saying anything about me at all. I suddenly realised that she was actually describing herself. I can't remember her in any other way, not her name nor her appearance, which is interesting given how long the words she said affected me. But I do remember one thing about her. I never, ever saw her dance, not once. Now I found myself able to look through her eyes, and I think she was terrified about being seen to be dancing, in case people thought she was uncool. How sad that she should feel the need to protect her own inadequacy by stabbing the knife into me. I wonder whether someone had said something similar to her some time earlier. For the first time, I felt a shift in my feelings towards her. Instead of hating her, I began to feel a kind of warmth towards her.

That wasn't the most important personal shift that I took away from my Insight seminars, but it serves, I hope, to show what an extraordinary and liberating experience it was to participate in one. It might seem a small thing, but to me it was huge, and it's lasted. Recently I went to the inaugural gig of a band and found there were not many people there, and most of them were hanging around the bar at the far end of the room. The band was great and I spent the entire show dancing away by myself, miming and singing and playing air guitar right in front of the stage. I was delighted when a cute girl came up to me afterwards and said she was so jealous of what I had done, that she had really wanted to dance but couldn't bring herself to do so in front of everyone like that. I badgered the band till they played another number, and danced with her and her boyfriend. It felt like a liberation - finally I didn't give a fig whatever anyone thought about it.

The seminar had deep and lasting, very meaningful effects on me, and helped me to experience so much more abundance in my life. But it also helped me to see that most of the time, everyone is just doing the best they can. It's worth trying to see things through other eyes, and to take what you can from each person's interpretation of the truth - a very helpful attitude to have where horsemanship is concerned. Not only that, but I came to the realisation that I had often tried to protect my ego even when I didn't know what I was talking about, even at the cost of truth. Thus I made a huge step in opening myself up to learning about other approaches to horsemanship. I also realised that actually, it was OK for me to go and do something I hadn't felt I deserved.

My working days were usually deeply fulfilling, rewarding and interesting, but there was something missing. The perfect world we shared had lost a bit of its lustre due to the sheer hours it all took. We almost never got a break, apart from visiting family. At the end of the seminar, we were asked to stand up in no particular order, and each say something that we were going to get more of in our lives from now on. The facilitator had barely finished speaking, when I was on my feet, dancing, saying, "I'm going to have more holidays!"

This was the start of a love affair between us and the paradise called Hawai'i. In just over a year, we were to visit three times, spending more than two months there, and we've since been back a fourth time. By the end, we knew the islands better than many residents.

It was an easy twist of fate that brought us there, to the most remote place on earth. It all began with a pretty random phone call out of the blue. "You coming to my leaving party?" It was Chris, whom we had met and lived with at University. Not knowing that he was leaving, I enquired where he was going, but had no idea of the significance those words would bring. "I'm off to live in Maui. Going to learn to surf. Leaving in three weeks."

Chris had been travelling before, quite a bit in fact, including a six month stint in India on a motor bike, but since then, a bike crash in London had left him in hospital for months with serious injuries, and he had been somewhat brought down to earth. He had been working in the City for a hedge fund, gambling on the markets with other people's money. We had always kept in touch since leaving college ten years earlier - this was in summer 2001, just before the events of 9/11 wiped 20% of the value off the stock market. Chris had clearly had enough of that life, and the person it was turning him into, and with the proceeds of an absurdly large bonus and other assets, he was heading out to what I would discover is the actually the closest thing there is to a wild west.[1] But instead of

---

[1] Hawai'i has more cowboys than any other state, as well as the largest cattle ranch in the US. You might wish to consider for a moment the land that has been used for this burger-building bonanza. This was not some open, grass-covered plain like those of the Serengeti or American Midwest, already grazed for aeons by wildebeest, bison or buffalo before man brought fences and cattle. In the time of Christ before the island was discovered, it was a unique ecosystem, stranded on the lava of a huge volcano in the middle of the emptiest stretch of ocean in the world, never set foot on by any land mammal, and mostly covered by impenetrable jungle. Untouched, Hawai'i had lain for millions of years without contact with the outside world. A few Polynesians, only a few centuries ago, found and colonised the islands, introducing a small number of edible plants and both domestic and farm animals. But the natives who lived there had not often ventured far inland, instead colonising the shoreline and leaving the forest largely intact. The islands contained an amazing collection of sea life, birds and land fauna, many of which were endemic - unique to Hawai'i. Much of the land which was pristine, unique and irreplaceable rain forest, is now plagued by feral goats and pigs, or has been turned into cattle ranches - acres and acres of virtually sterile, featureless grasslands which the tropical rains are quickly eroding away,

serving as a cowboy on one of the numerous Hawaiian cattle ranches, he was going to ride another kind of beast. He was going in search of that wonderful Hawaiian export, her greatest invention - surfing. He was going to learn to surf, but not just any old waves. He was hoping to accomplish what many would say is the ultimate ride - perhaps more terrifying than the wildest bucking bronco, or even a bull. He wanted to ride the biggest wave that has ever been surfed, on the north shore of Maui, the one they call Jaws. He had seen films about it on the TV, and was heading off to live his dream.

Now, at the time he left the UK, I obviously was thrilled about the fact that Chris had given up what I considered to be a soulless existence in the city for a life of adventure. But I did have my reservations, even before I heard about Jaws. After all, there had already been the horrendous bike crash in which he'd broken his pelvis and smashed up a wrist and shoulder, and a five week long motorbike ride across America to California, the whole length of Route 66, en route to Maui was obviously going to be an adventure with its fair share of perils. But that wasn't the only thing which made me hold back a bit from total encouragement (not that he was seeking my approval). Somewhere inside me an alien voice, definitely not from my heart, was making a comment along the lines that it wasn't right for him to be going off to have so much fun. Although I did not reject his generous invitation to stay for as long as we liked ("But obviously you'll have to make it at least a month"), I replied with words to the effect that a month in Hawai'i sounded like a splendid idea - and of course, who in their right mind would argue with that? But I knew as I said it that I had no real intention of following it up, so I was very vague about when this might happen. We were on too much of a mission to help horses and there was the other more obvious hurdle...we didn't have any money. It would cost us extra to be away from home, as well as a lot to go. We didn't want to leave anyone with the responsibility of looking after the horses for such a length of time, and there wasn't any point in going so far away for anything less. All in all, it was too much of a dream. But to tell the truth, the reason we hadn't gone anywhere like that was because we didn't think we deserved it.

---

and whose runoff now chokes the once-pristine coral reefs. Of all the extinctions that have occurred in the US, 75% of them have been in Hawai'i.

Insight seminars blew that resistance away and our first mission to Maui in Feb 2004 was an incredible experience, which coincided, not coincidentally, with our first active attempts to create a new human being.

That month in Hawai'i was more than a holiday, it was one of the biggest adventures of our lives together. We grabbed every opportunity that came our way, including late-night skinny dipping in the flooded lava tubes of Waianapanapa, hikes through tropical rain forests, up waterfalls and across lava fields, and horse riding across the spectacular volcanic crater of Haleakala. We went whale watching, saw dolphins and snorkelled with giant sea turtles. We even indulged in a helicopter flight around the island, reasoning that it would probably be our very last chance to have such experiences before our lives were changed forever by the addition of a little person.

TWELVE

Pregnant!
(Nicole)

Pregnancy is an altered state of almost everything. I should have known I was pregnant the moment I was shopping for test kits and thought, hmm, this brand hasn't worked so well. I've used it before, and the result's always been negative. Perhaps I should try this one instead. But I'd been certain I was pregnant before, and been wrong, and I've even allegedly had the occasional illogical thought in my time, so I went ahead and took the test. It was first thing one morning, before I was really awake. I snuck back into bed, and forced myself not to look at the test. I even gave it an extra 30 seconds, just to be sure. I squashed down the mounting feelings of excitement, as they'd been misplaced before, and resignedly peeped at the stick.

"Flipping heck!" There was a cross where I was expecting a line. A plus sign, a positive. I was pregnant! This could account for my polite exclamation, rather than my more usual sailor-like expletives. I didn't want to swear in front of the baby. I really did say flipping heck, and loud enough to wake Adam up.

"What?" he asked, peering over. He thought I might have been looking out into the field and seen something odd with the horses, but I wasn't in quite the right position to see out of the window. "What is it?"

"I'm pregnant," I told him, not quite able to take it in myself. "Oh my God."

He grinned, snuggled up, and said, "That's wonderful. I knew you were." A short pause. "Now, let's go back to sleep." Before I could protest, he explained: "Soon we'll need all the rest we can get."

Sleep?! Absolutely no chance. Along with a feeling of

irrepressible joy, I felt shocked. What on earth had we done? Shouldn't there be some official present, perhaps an angel of some sort, asking, "Are you really sure? If so, tick this box, and the pregnancy will continue. If not, we'll take it away and bring it back when you've had a bit of time to think about it." I'd been thinking about nothing else for months, and the fear, the irreversibility of it, was all part of the adventure. I felt calmer, but sleep was still out of the question. I lay there being hugged for another hour or so, and then crept out to let Sensi know.

She seemed mildly pleased, sniffed my belly for a moment, and then went back to munching the grass. But I spent the day walking around with a huge grin on my face. I felt excited in a way that I hadn't felt since I was a child. Or at least, not since getting Sensi. Everything seemed so vibrant and alive, and the future stretched out ahead, challenging, difficult, demanding, and real. I knew it wouldn't be easy, but I knew already that there would be immense joy. From the moment I realised I was pregnant, I felt overwhelming love for this little person growing inside. "I will look after you," I promised, "in every way I can."

I wanted to tell everyone, and I didn't want to tell anyone. It was a wonderful secret I wanted to keep to myself, and a joy I wanted to share with the world.

The usual advice given in books and magazines about sharing the news with the world is, "Don't." Wait until week twelve, as the chances of a miscarriage are so high in these early weeks. The logic is that the fewer people you have told in the first place, the fewer people you would have to tell the bad news to. They do sometimes concede that hiding the facts might be a little difficult. You've suddenly stopped drinking - coffee, let alone alcohol - and started looking green around the gills alarmingly frequently, while no longer having the energy to pick up the phone, let alone go to the gym, or long-line that horse, as well as suddenly becoming less inclined to ride those youngsters.

So, we followed advice and decided to wait until twelve weeks before we told anyone but closest family and friends, and those whom we felt needed an explanation for my otherwise odd behaviour. This resulted in some participants on riding clinics knowing before family and good friends whom we didn't see very often, which felt very strange. And telling people wasn't always the joyful experience I expected it to be. Friends and family mostly managed to get the balance right of being sure that everything would be fine, but keenly counting the weeks with us in the first trimester. Otherwise, people occasionally seemed to assume blithely that all would be fine, and couldn't understand the worry, or else felt obliged to point out the number of pregnancies that don't make it through, which always resulted in making me want to wail: "I know!" A quarter of all diagnosed pregnancies, and a half of all total pregnancies (this includes those that miscarry before the woman even knows she is pregnant) end in miscarriage. Suddenly, all our friends who had children dragged their own stories out of the woodwork, counselling us not to be too complacent. And no-one, absolutely no-one, except Adam, expressed any confidence that I might be able to undergo childbirth without drugs.

One of the things I found hardest to deal with in pregnancy was people dispensing their advice. There seems to be a sadistic joy that some women take in trying to destroy your happiness about the expected baby. Adam told one client, who, although she dutifully said, "Congratulations!" had to follow it up with a gleeful, "She won't know what's hit her!" Given that this woman hardly knew me at all, I found myself offended by this little piece of wisdom. Quite calmly, given the circumstances, and admitting outright that there was a distinct possibility that I might be feeling a little hormonal, I said to him, "What she meant was that she didn't know what hit her." I was very well aware of the fact that it isn't possible ever to be completely prepared for the experience - or indeed, any experience - but I really felt that I had done about as much preparation as it was possible to do. I'd thought about all aspects of it very carefully, and had always done so from the perspective of why having children was like dropping a bombshell on your life. I had read exhaustively on the subject, from American sugar-coated books that made "mommiehood" sound like the most fulfilling and wonderful state of being possible, to hard-hitting feminist polemic that raised and addressed all the issues I had ever thought of, as well as a few more. More importantly, I had seen the impact that children have on people's lives, and had seriously considered at length if I could possibly cope with that. I had finally concluded that I was ready for this challenging journey, and I didn't feel I needed anyone saying, "Ha! She doesn't know what she's let herself in for!"

But in truth, it's very hard for people to respond in just the right way. And although truly insensitive comments were rare, very few people really could understand the experience unless they've already been through it, and even then there seems to be a kind of collective amnesia, which is probably a natural defence that ensures the species continues to reproduce.

What surprised me a little was the universal sense that this was extremely good news indeed, and very exciting. I mean, it was very exciting to us, but I was surprised at how genuinely delighted so many people appeared to be. I could understand how many women felt that it was all very well to say "how wonderful" when they weren't facing endless sleepless nights and soiled nappies. But I felt I had reconciled myself to the prospect, and could just enjoy the process. It did, however, make me feel justified in taking every possible opportunity to grab a lie-in, or an afternoon nap, or read an endless list of books, not all pregnancy or baby based, reasoning that I wouldn't be able to do it after the baby arrived.

All the books I read on the subject seemed to be very understanding about the changes that I would be experiencing, and all advised that feelings of ambivalence, or even depression, were quite normal. Having had so long to get my head around it, I didn't experience ambivalence at all. I think the strain of worrying about the foetus surviving the first twelve weeks maybe did make me feel a little depressed at times, but it was more like a constant anxiety companion. Pretty much every hour of every day I would feel twinges bordering on cramping. I read that these were most likely to just be ligaments softening and expanding, and moving around the growing uterus. All the same, every single time I went to the loo, I couldn't stop myself checking for blood. I didn't want to be wishing my life away, but I really was counting the days until the twelve week Rubicon. There was also the promise that the nausea and vomiting might stop then, which would be very welcome. It seemed astonishing that any book could write: "but don't worry, in most women these symptoms cease after a couple of months, although for the unlucky few they continue right throughout pregnancy," as though a couple of months was an insignificant amount of time. I refused to acknowledge the worst-case scenario of "morning" sickness only going after the baby was born. It just didn't bear thinking about. In reality, although I continued to choke up stomach acid and bile every morning until the 14th week, once I stopped feeling peculiar and nauseous absolutely all the time, I really didn't mind too much. In fact, I had made a deal with myself that although it was alright to feel a bit sorry for myself, I wouldn't go on and on about it, and that although it seems crazy that just when you should be eating optimally, and exercising well, you can't keep anything down and have the energy of a sloth on downers, that is nevertheless how it is, and there's no point complaining.

I decided to ride throughout the pregnancy. I knew that not everyone would endorse this approach, but I thought it through carefully, weighed it up, and decided that not riding would compromise my sanity much more than riding would compromise our safety. I was pleased and reassured that neither my doctor nor the midwife thought this was unreasonable. I decided I wouldn't sit on any starters, however calm they looked, nor any horse that made me feel anxious in any way, and that I wouldn't be jumping. I looked back over the last fourteen years of my life with Sensi and realised that she and I had hit the ground twice in all this time (once when she had fallen off a small footbridge, and once when she slipped on ice while I was tightening her girth), but that I'd never actually fallen off her. I concluded that driving my car was significantly more dangerous, and no-one was questioning whether I should continue to do that. It was probably a mistake to ask her to look after me, though. "You need to be very careful," I told her. "It's very important that we come to no harm." I swear she understood me, but misunderstood what I meant her to do in response. She became even spookier than normal, taking extra care to ensure that nothing could get close enough to harm me. I had to explain that I was happy to take my chances with the lions and tigers and bears she was spotting behind every blade of grass, but that her sudden sideways leaps were more difficult to deal with. I think she got it, but I did more work in the school anyway, on the basis that if I came over a bit funny I was never far from home that way.

There was something else about continuing to ride that went far beyond the simple pleasure of doing it. She didn't need to be ridden to maintain fitness (the large mixed herd and steep Cotswold hills where she lives did that perfectly well), nor did I need to be in the saddle to experience the pleasure of her company. Long-lining, walking out with her, or just watching her eat were enough. But part of my fear about having children had always been about the abandonment of self that so many women seem to experience. Time and again on Five Day courses and Riding Clinics, women would say how they had ridden up until the time they'd had children, then had a long gap, having sold their beloved horse, and only got back into it when their daughter started riding ponies. Usually they bought the child a pony, and only several years later realised that perhaps a horse for themselves might be a good idea, and something they might even deserve, after years of unstinting devotion and care-giving. Of course, lots of women on the courses also mentioned how they'd given up horses for boys, in their teens, then gone to University, got sucked into a career, and only later found that they still had a childhood dream to fulfill, whether they had children to delay them further or not. One story in particular haunted me. A woman who had ponies as a child, gave up horses when she became pregnant, and had a fifteen year gap. She was truly making up for it when I met her on a riding clinic, but - fifteen years? Could it really be right that in all that time she hadn't been able to take even a couple of hours a week for herself? Could she not have shared a horse, or had the odd lesson? It seemed impossible that she couldn't have fitted something in. Maybe she was an all-or-nothing kind of person, and I don't want to judge. But it frightened me, the idea that it could happen like that. I knew I was prepared for huge changes to happen in my life. I understood that there would be sacrifices, and compromises, and I was willing to take on the challenges ahead, but I kept thinking: surely I still need to be a person in my own right, able to do a little bit of my own thing, keeping sane and being something of a role model? I wanted to be properly hands-on. I didn't want nannies and day care, but I didn't want to lose myself and my identity either. And I knew of lots of women who had managed it. Riding during the pregnancy felt like a statement of intent, that this was important enough to me to keep on doing it. And even when I felt most nauseous, riding always made me feel better.

At the same time that I was quietly determined to keep riding, I found myself remarkably accepting of the other limitations I suddenly experienced. I went from feeling highly energetic and being very active, to suddenly sleeping for up to sixteen hours a day. Having long-lined a succession of horses around the local villages, up and down the steep hills, I discovered that a walk to the end of the field and back just about did me in for the day. I read a lot of books and watched more garbage TV than is good for anyone, and I felt fine about it. I taught on the Riding Clinics and Five Day courses in the early days, when I just felt a bit odd and woozy, but as soon as I felt properly nauseous and weak and dizzy, I stopped, and did so almost without a qualm. I taught lessons at home, where I sat on the ledge by our school instead of walking around in the middle, and learnt to project my voice. I did the admin. And I felt alright about it because I knew that looking after myself, my body, and my growing baby was the most important thing I could be doing, and whether or not society recognised it, I did, Adam did, and we didn't have to answer to anyone. This is part of the joy of being self-employed, although of course there's no sick pay or maternity pay, and I recognised how incredibly lucky I was to be able to take the time I needed.

The anxiously awaited twelve-week watershed arrived, and I began to relax a little. We told the news to the rest of our family, friends and colleagues. They were all overjoyed, and although it still seemed a bit unreal, we were finding ourselves more and more unable to ignore the impending changes. We began to talk about the bump that was showing as if it were really a human. My day still couldn't get started unless I'd had a quick chat with the porcelain in the bathroom, but I began to feel a little more energetic. I was able to stay awake for a whole eight hours at a time, and could walk to the end of the field to collect a horse without collapsing in a heap. I even took Sensi to her first dressage competition.

In fact, earlier in the pregnancy, I had done my first dressage competition, in Surrey. The anonymity that came from being in another county was very reassuring. I borrowed a horse who had been with us on livery, called Sammie. He's the horse on the front cover, looking considerably more relaxed lounging in our fields than he did that day in Surrey! Astonishingly, we scooped up third prize, but that might have had something to do with there only being three of us in the class. Nevertheless, it had been good fun, and with the opportunity to practise at home, I thought it would be something to aim for with Sensi. I decided to take her a few weeks later.

The nerves I felt were astonishing. It could've been the pregnancy nausea, but I think it was butterflies. I even had to ask Adam to load her, as I knew I would be too jittery to do so calmly. Adam couldn't come, but a very good friend and livery client, Judi, kindly volunteered to help us out. In the past, whenever we'd been to shows, we'd had to hack there, which at least meant we were warmed up and calm when we arrived. I wasn't at all sure how Sensi would handle being boxed there, but she travelled well, and stood impeccably on the box while I got my number. She was perfect to be tacked up in the big, open field. Ever since she had been pregnant herself, some years previously, she'd developed a tendency to be very aggressive to other horses that got too close. Not that she'd ever kicked them, but she would regularly practise the spectacular faces that caused her once to be described as a barracuda witch-pony. Yet at the show, enormous great horses passed within centimetres of her, and she never even put an ear back. She warmed up beautifully, hitting the transitions within a millisecond of being asked, and always striking the correct lead in canter. I was beginning to enjoy myself.

The moment we got near the ring, however, everything changed. She spooked at the judges' Land Rover, then she spooked at the boards, and then she spooked at the bushes. She jumped at least a foot in the air when she heard the horn blow. It was as if she had read some sort of charade card that said, "Do the entire test in the manner of a drunken camel." I had already decided that I was going to ride as if there was no-one watching, rather than sit there stiffly and pretend everything was fine, as I didn't want her to feel that all the rules suddenly changed at competitions, but in any case I couldn't have pretended that all was going to plan. I had to see the funny side as we did a long side that involved us nearly leaving the arena, and then a correction that took us nearly to the three-quarter line, and when I looked over I could see the judges were seeing the funny side, too. I'd have thought they weren't actually allowed to laugh I finished the test nearly shaking with laughter, and poor Judi didn't know where to look. Needless to say, we weren't placed.

The second test was in the outdoor school, which was also quite spooky and new, but I think she had got her head around it all a little better, as we actually did quite well. Not a perfect test, but about a thousand times better than the first. We scooped up sixth place, and I'm sure the fact that there were only six of us in the class had very little to do with our success!

It was a fun day, though, and I felt we did pretty well given my "delicate" condition. I had long vowed to do the odd competition, as it seems like a good way to test the work you're doing at home. In fact, it was quite a humbling experience. It's all very well being able to do half-pass and canter-halt transitions when there's no pressure, but the fact is that in public, especially in a new location, a simple test involving walk, trot, and canter is ridiculously challenging. I found myself with renewed respect for all the people out there having a go at all levels (provided they put horse welfare and ethics above winning, of course).

I realised that having managed to get through a comparatively gruelling day of competition in the August heat, I could hardly justify my prolonged relationship with the sofa anymore, and had arranged to start teaching on the Five Day courses again. I was really looking forward to it, and it meant that Adam was freed up to continue doing his appointments.

'The vet suggested that I could quite legitimately claim loss of use for her.'
Sensi at a clinic following her recovery.

Kelly, Adam and Nicole at the launch party for Whispering Back.

It's amazing how much progress can be made in a single lesson.

Photo ©Peter Spurrier

'The local media were all over us when they heard that this historic victory had been won by a whisper.'

Left: Taz, looking a lot easier to catch than he was when we met him in a large field with three other untouched ponies.

Jo and Perry.

Chris in Hawai'i, after he gave up life as a city trader.

Nicole in a waterfall-fed pool, Hana, Maui.

Adam impersonating Tarzan in the same pool.

Haleakala Crater, Maui, Hawai'i.
Looking down from 10,000 feet into the heart of the island.

And looking back up 3,000 feet to where we started.

Philosopher's Point.

'...We spotted a tiny island of lava which hung off the shelf and was connected to it by three lava bridges...'

Finn and Misty with Monty at Moor Wood, July 20, 2005.

Adam, Monty, the ABC Nightline film crew, Misty and budding horseman.

Misty meets her adoring fans at Kingshurst Junior School.

'Misty and Finn greeted the children like the hosts of a wedding party.'

Photo courtesy of Monty Roberts.

Willing partners: Monty riding his late horse Dually to a sliding stop.

Note the lack of contact on the rein, the raised, open poll, deep engagement of the hindquarters, and forward position of the rider's leg.

Seat training with Asterix, summer 2009.
Photos © Simon Palmer www.into-the-lens.com

'His big, bright eyes and smiley, engaging disposition made it doubly hard to accept that he was due to be put down.'

Adam's first ride on Karma.
Fortunately there isn't a photo of his second ride...

Laden with rosettes, Nicole and Sensi return from their highly successful
competitive outing, Aug 2004.

Nicole and Marley riding Sensi, July 2007.

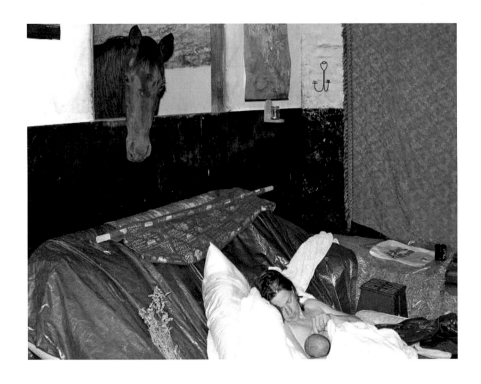

'...If she wanted to check on me, Sensi could simply poke her head through the open window between her part of the barn and mine...'

Marley, just hours after birth.

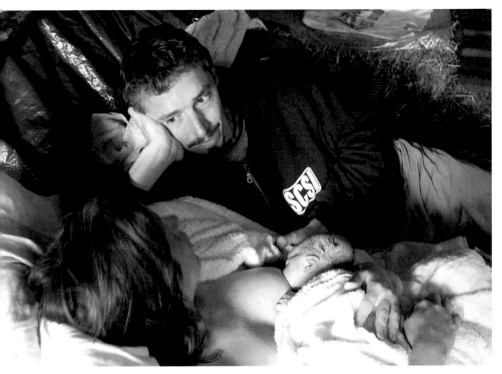

'It'll change your life forever.'

Finn meets Marley, one day old.

'A man has got to have some loud rock, especially if he's going to spend the whole of the rest of his time trying to calm everybody down.'

SCSI, November 2009. Martin Van Dyke, Marley and Adam, Murdoc, Tim Hills and Simon "Siom" Messenger.

Murdoc. 'The pain and pleasure of living such a full life leaches out into his voice.'

Photo Donald Miralle/Getty Images

'This is the wave that had enticed Chris to Hawai'i, luring him with the dream of one day riding that immense power.'

THIRTEEN

A Day In The Life
(Adam)

Up until my mid-twenties I was highly sceptical that there was any such thing as an honest day's work. I couldn't see a way of making a living that didn't create some sort of immoral or wasteful side effect. If it didn't put another person in the shafts to earn your money for you, it seemed to involve being shafted by someone else. Studying social and political sciences at University certainly opened my eyes to some chilling facts, which had been below my radar even when I went off to Africa to stay with my parents in the holidays, and you can't hide African poverty completely, no matter how high you make the walls. It has been estimated that the average consumption of natural resources per capita in the UK is fifty times greater than that consumed by the average African. But then again, turning the clock back to an age where we close down all the shops and factories, dismantle international trade and use horses to replace petrol seems a little impractical. Perhaps the credit crunch might do all that for us, which might not be such a bad thing, since the alternative looks at least as bleak.

I eventually found myself a niche in this crazy world, and am trying to leave it a better place than I found it, by making a haven for people and horses to live in, and helping others to understand and connect with their horses. I'm just hoping to do an honest job for an honest animal, and the people who care for them, who are almost always honest too. One of the best things about it is that there really is no such thing as a typical day in this life.

Take the day I met Dancer. I had scrawled some notes when I had spoken to his owner, Judy: 'DANCER', 10 y.o. mare 17.2 Danish warmblood. Bad loader, bought as a 2 y.o. already had an incident in the lorry, panicked and went literally through the roof

131

when left alone. Also still has problem with stable doors. Rears, bashes head, lashes out and hit boyfriend. Normal width door being enlarged. Want to compete this year, then produce foal. Horse not travelled for years. Bought new horsebox with more headroom. Has pressure halter. Teeth done.

It sounded like a severe case, but it's always hard to know. Problems that sound bad on paper can be comparatively straightforward, and sometimes the issues that don't sound too difficult can prove surprisingly intractable. But it's rare (thankfully) for a horse actually to go through the roof of a lorry, so I wasn't expecting a quick solution. We arranged to meet on what happened to be two days after the sixtieth anniversary of D-Day, 8th June 2004.

Dancer couldn't really have asked to be looked after by anyone more willing to do whatever was necessary to help her. Judy had bought a lorry instead of a trailer, had widened the stable door, and had got a saddler to make the most elaborate form of head protector I have ever seen - virtually like medieval leather head armour.

But she seemed in such a hurry, presumably to get out and start working on the horse and I wondered whether she took the same attitude to loading. I wanted to see what she would do to get me in and out of the lorry first. It was not a bad vehicle, but Judy's loading technique left a lot to be desired. She got in the way, using a very short lead rope, which she pulled on all the time, and frequently looked in my eye. We went to meet her horse.

Dancer was dark bay, huge and powerful, but with a graceful demeanour. I started as usual with some leading work and a join-up, which she took in her stride and soon she was following me around the field without objection. It was clear, however, that she (and Judy) didn't understand how to work with a rope. If I asked her to put her head down by gently tugging downwards on the rope, I got a response which showed me a lot about her ridden and ground work. She immediately braced against the pressure and held her breath, her whole body tensing against my request.

It took a while for me to get her to understand, by very small increments, that I was asking her to lower her head. When I asked Judy to lead her around a bit, it was clear that the habit was as much due to the human as to her own instinct of being 'into pressure' - to resist and push or pull against pressure. Judy held the rope right under her chin, which is common enough, but without noticing it she dropped the whole weight of her arm on the rope, and thus Dancer's head. This habit proved pretty hard to eradicate for Judy, as well as for Dancer. When she was paying close attention, Judy would hold the rope a good deal further down, allowing her horse not to be constantly pulled; but whenever she lost focus her hand tended to have a mind of its own, and it migrated up the rope until it was back under her horse's chin. This issue turned out to be very important for them both to resolve.

As well as improving her head lowering, I also (partly as a way to get her to want to lower it) got her to raise her head up several times. At first she threw it up in the air in a panic, but after a short while she would put it up or down when cued. After the leading work we'd done, she would also follow me when I moved my feet away, and stop when I stopped, staying out of my personal space. Along with backing up, something she had never done under the influence of a human before, this all made her much easier and safer to handle.

Before going to the lorry it seemed sensible to have a look at the issues they were experiencing with going in and out of the stable. I had been aware from the notes I'd taken on the phone that Dancer had a problem with stable doors, but I had no idea how serious this issue would prove to be. The roof was easily high enough for a horse, and it overhung the doorway, so that the frame of the door, which had now been widened, was about 2 feet back from where the edge of the roof came down. It was a modern wooden building, with a pitched roof and no ceiling, so the headroom within the stable was a lot higher than it was under the overhang.

I should have known what to expect when Judy put on Dancer's poll guard. It ran right down her nose almost to the tip, and right up behind her ears, covering the entire poll area. She had previously smashed her head on the overhang numerous times, and her face had several scars on it as a result.

Not surprisingly, on approaching the door, Dancer's adrenaline shot up. Unfortunately, and not coincidentally, at the same time her head went right up too. This put it well above the height of the roof, which she only managed not to bash into by virtue of the fact that she pulled back very hard and retreated at the same time and so was too far away to knock it. She stood with her head right up snorting at the building. It almost looked as if she was trying to graze out of the gutter. Naturally, she now thought she couldn't fit into the stable. It was clear that we had a lot more work to do before we could even consider loading onto the lorry. It was all very well to teach her to lower her head when she was out in the paddock, with low adrenaline, having just done join-up. But here, in front of her nemesis, her adrenaline was making it impossible for her to remember the lesson she had apparently just learned.

I could sense Judy's frustration, even though she was not impatient or irritated. She simply didn't know why this was happening or what to do to make this everyday activity less traumatic. On the other hand, it was also very clear that her horse was feeling just as frustrated. She would plainly have preferred to stay outside in all weathers rather than going in that stable.

The first thing I tried to do was to explain to Judy what I thought was going on here. It's not as if Dancer had woken up one morning and said to herself, "What can I do today that will really annoy her? I know! I'll start messing about, refusing to go in the stable and barge into her as we go through the doorway!" She was absolutely terrified. Evolution had dug a hole for her, which she was getting deeper and deeper into.

Any horse in the wild, alarmed by hearing a noise or smelling a predator, has a better chance of survival if he raises his head as high as possible, to see over any surrounding vegetation. These two instincts - sensing danger and raising the head - had combined to make it a really difficult task to get past this devilish doorway. As Dancer saw it, something was lurking at the doorframe and attacking her just as she was going in, so she had to charge through at top speed to save herself. But sometimes the predator got her, bashing her face or the top of her head. Then Dancer, in a blind panic, had smashed her hip against the doorpost. This only served to fuel her adrenaline the next time she was faced with this danger, so she had got into the habit of hesitating, getting very uptight, then charging through, while Judy, from her position next to her shoulder with her hand holding just under her chin, was in danger of being crushed against the doorway, stepped on, head butted, thrown in the air or dragged under those big, shod feet. It was about the most ghastly combination of dangers she could have faced. When I enquired further, I was not surprised to hear that she had trouble with this every single evening, and then again in the morning. Her boyfriend, who was due to arrive soon, had tried to help but in doing so, had probably made matters worse. An ex-paratrooper, he thought he was strong enough to hold Dancer's head down, but he had suffered a broken hand a little while ago as a result of trying this macho approach. I could imagine how unlikely it was that his attempts to intervene and protect his woman had not been somewhat aggressive. After all, it's as natural for a human male to get aggressive when trying to protect his mate as it is for a horse to try to flee from danger as fast as she can, with her head up in the air. And there's no question this horse was a threat to his partner.

Pete arrived, a surprisingly small, surprisingly soft-around-the-edges and friendly person, but you could also certainly see how he'd got through the Paras. He listened to me and Judy explain what the problem really was and how we intended to solve it. I was trying to like him, but I have to say I found it a bit of a struggle, and felt a bit threatened. It's not because I dislike soldiers. In fact, as a child I always imagined that when I grew up, I was going to be a General. I'd been deeply affected when, living in Turkey in the 1970s, my parents took me to the WWI battlefields in Gallipoli. Now, exactly sixty years after France had begun to be liberated from Nazism, here I was, facing a man who had lived my old dream, and followed in the footsteps of the paratroopers who had thrown themselves out of planes over occupied France all those years ago. I had plenty of respect for that. But there was still something about Pete that made me feel uneasy.

Dancer wanted nothing more than to do what she was being asked, but she had to understand what that was, because at the moment she thought we were asking her to charge past demons. Before expecting her respect, we had to respect how she thought and communicated herself. Using appropriate body language was a natural and effective way to help her to comprehend; force was something which she was programmed to resist. As well as, hopefully, learning by having his hand broken when Dancer had refused to be held down, and understanding how to train the horse in a logical, progressive and gentle fashion, I wanted Pete to become more aware about how he could use his body to communicate. So I asked him, standing about fifteen yards off, to try to run me over as if he were the meanest horse in the county.

It's a little game I had often played, to illustrate to people how your body language is predominantly to do with where you move your feet. When they charge at me I make some aggressive gestures and don't move out of their way, and they always stop, unless they are very recently divorced and I remind them of their ex. Then I get them to repeat the exercise and I make all the same gestures but I retreat. They almost always keep charging, until I tell them I surrender.

So, I was a bit surprised when, as he charged at me, in spite of my holding my ground, facing him and drilling him with eye contact, waving a rope sharply in front of me and making a loud hissing noise, he came charging on like a train. I kept the pressure up but he just kept running, meeting my gaze almost gleefully and ignoring the obvious warning that I was about to hit him if he didn't back off. I kept whirring the rope, and when he got close enough, he hit it hard with his face. He let out a yelp and, to my relief, veered away at the very last second.

I thought this would have been a pretty obvious thing to avoid, and he seemed surprised that I had let him come to terms so directly with the fact that the rope was not a figment of his imagination. I was also a little taken aback, as this had never happened to me before. I mean, even in America, they don't put notices on the side of helicopters saying, "CAUTION! DO NOT PUT BODY PARTS IN WHIRRING BLADES!" and yet he had done something nearly as foolish. I was concerned that this would not get us off onto the right foot, but I was even more surprised at what happened next.

As I say, he was a former paratrooper, who had served in Northern Ireland. The Paras, who were the unit responsible for killing thirteen civilians on 'Bloody Sunday' in 1972, are probably not the most popular regiment in the British army among the Republican community. But his features broke into a sudden expression of enlightenment when I explained that my gestures in response to his attempt to run me over had been intentionally aggressive, designed to keep him from attacking me, and that normally, when I look into someone's eye as they run at me like that, they drop their gaze. At that moment I know I am about to survive the encounter, and they tend not to run into my flailing rope. In his case, he had welcomed my eye contact, appearing to take it as an invitation to join him in an enjoyable fight.

"Oh my God," he said, and began to explain.

During his service in Northern Ireland, he had been involved in confronting several groups of Republican demonstrators, and had been a member of a 'snatch squad'. For this, the police would create a line with riot shields and at a prearranged signal, a gap would be created in the line, allowing the squad to run out and try to nab one of the leaders of the demonstrators. But it didn't always work according to plan. Sometimes the IRA supporters would organise a snatch squad of their own. He held the record for having been snatched more than any other paratrooper in the regiment. Our encounter had made him realise that it was their eyes that gave the game away. If they were genuine rioters, scared of being grabbed, the moment the snatch squad charged out from behind the riot shields, they would break eye contact as they tried to get away. But if there was a gang of big toughs waiting to try to bag one of the snatch squad, they didn't break eye contact. They remained confident to look at the prey they were hunting. That he had never realised this caused him much fear and distress. I felt my earlier hostility melting as I considered what he must have been through.

I left them a while later, with a horse who had not even approached the horsebox, but who had come a long way towards sorting out her phobia. She followed either of them in and out of the stable with her head down and no pressure whatsoever on the lead rope, without rushing or hesitating, although she didn't manage to do it calmly every time. Sometimes she seemed to have flashbacks, but overall she was much improved. Her nose, under the pressure halter (which was not the same design as the one Monty sells, and which I had never used before or since), was looking sore. My arms certainly were, and probably Pete's nose was too. Still, there had been a big improvement in Dancer's behaviour. Judy and Pete now understood some vital principles, and were better equipped to continue with the work. It wasn't the miracle cure I am accustomed to seeing when I go out and help with bad loaders. It was clear that she required many more hours training, and the best thing I could do was to give Judy and Pete a roadmap, a plan of action to follow. I suggested they construct an adjustable imitation ceiling, so they could start with it really high and gradually lower it incrementally, and get Dancer *really* good at walking and standing under it before even considering the lorry. I had no wish for her to repeat her previous experience of actually putting her head through the roof, and we needed to be sure that when she felt her ears brush against anything solid she knew to calmly lower her head away from it. They could only go on to fix this problem completely with common sense, patience and commitment. Of course, I would provide any ongoing support or expertise they required.

I was very struck by how much Pete seemed to have changed his attitude, even more than Dancer or Judy. I was aware how easily frustrated anyone would have been, had they faced such a seemingly insurmountable problem with no method to follow. It's easier to stay calm, focused and patient when you have a plausible, or better still, really watertight plan to follow. I hadn't achieved as much as I'd have liked, as we didn't fix the loading, but we had not had any big setbacks either. Perhaps, I ruminated as I drove home, for the first time in his life Pete had met and gained some respect for a man who was not interested in how strong he was but how sensitive he could be. That, if nothing else, made it a worthwhile visit. All in all, we each came quite a long way that day.

After a couple of hours in the car, I got back to Moor Wood. I hadn't seen my beautiful home or any of my horses all day, but the light in the yard was perfect as the sun dipped behind the redwood trees and I leaned over the gate, savouring a cold beer with our friend Chris, who was over on a flying visit from Hawai'i. As I told him about my day, he reflected that he certainly had never felt he was doing an honest day's work, back when he was a city trader. Teaching people to kayak, and appreciate the marine life as he taught them to snorkel off one of the beautiful beaches he'd showed us during our recent visit to Hawai'i felt closer to the mark to him.

We were particularly pleased to see Chris as we had some momentous news to share with him. We watched his face light up with delight at the prospect that Nicole was now in the process of turning a tiny cluster of cells into a person, a living breathing soul, with all the joy, creation and waste that implies. But all too soon he was off. We didn't know when we would see each other again.

Later, I got in trouble with Nicole for staying up and writing notes about Dancer's story, something I really should do more often. I know it was wrong. I should have been cuddling and loving her, honouring her body, soon to be filled - perhaps even overwhelmed - by that baby she was bringing to life, that new little being half made from me.

FOURTEEN

Philosopher Joe
(Nicole)

The first Monday teaching back on the courses went well, and it was lovely to see everyone again, but I felt quite wiped out on the Tuesday. I thought perhaps with the dressage show and everything else, I had just overdone it a bit, and decided to rest up as much as possible on the Tuesday and Wednesday, so I'd be fit for the Thursday and Friday, which are big days for me on the courses. But having taken it easy on Tuesday, I realised by the end of the day that I wasn't actually very well, and arranged to see my GP on the Wednesday.

The morning started with a shock: that awful moment when, having thought it was all safe, you see a spot of blood on your underwear. There was a moment of panic, and then I calmed down. Spotting without cramping is almost never a cause for concern. When I mentioned it to the GP, he was very reassuring. By now, I had backache to add to the list of symptoms, but that also was quite normal. As a precautionary measure, he phoned through to the hospital to arrange another scan. He more or less had to beg them to do it, as the risk at fifteen weeks is considered so low. It scuppered my plans to teach the next day, but it was good to know I'd be checked out. I had to turn up at the hospital at 8 am, with a bladder full of water, and wait my turn in a sort of "lucky dip". I wasn't looking forward to it.

My back began to hurt more and more, and I decided to sleep in the annexe so that Adam, who would now have to do my teaching on the course, wouldn't be disturbed and could get a good night's sleep. But it soon became clear I wasn't going to get any rest. I tried to ignore it, but there was soon no denying the fact that I was actually in a lot of trouble. I'd started to get very painful

139

abdominal cramps, and was shocked at one point to discover I was actually writhing and moaning. I was trying to distract myself by watching appalling television, but even the abusive alcoholic on a chat show couldn't do it. I realised I had to call the hospital. But I wanted, by sheer willpower, for it to be alright. All I could think was, "Hang on tight, little one, please just hang on tight."

In between cramps, I woke Adam up to tell him we had to go to the hospital. I had imagined this scene before, the "Darling, it's time" cliché having been played out on so many TV shows and movies, but the horror of doing it now, so early, was frightening. It wasn't time. It wasn't time at all. Our baby was weeks away from being "viable". Adam was concerned but calm when I woke him. He did ask, "Are you sure?" but needed no answering when the next wave of pain hit.

We sped along the abandoned Cotswold roads in silence, just offering the occasional word of reassurance to each other as we went. I found a kind of stillness in my mind, in spite of the certain knowledge that something was going very, very wrong, and the overwhelming desire that it not be so. That strange calm when you look into the abyss and see that your very worst fears could come true, and somehow you have to cope.

We had barely sat down in the waiting room before we were shown into a cubicle, and then that strange transformation from "normal person in trouble" to "patient" took place. Reassuring though it can be to be in hospital and in the hands of professionals, being in a gown, with a pulse rate monitor attached to your finger, oxygen over your nose, and an intravenous drip in your arm, you suddenly feel very much less well than when you were clothed and looking half-way normal. I had a nasty fall off our little Welsh Mountain pony Misty once, when she bucked and I shot straight over her head. I thought perhaps I should go to casualty and check there was no serious damage. I was able to cycle there and I felt fine right up to the moment when they strapped my head to the stretcher, muttering about potential spinal fractures. They quickly ascertained that there was no injury, however, and sent me on my way. I was hoping for a similar outcome this time, but it wasn't looking likely.

They were concerned about my blood pressure, which they felt was alarmingly low, and I in turn was alarmed when they saw me experience cramping and immediately offered me morphine. They assured me it was perfectly harmless to the baby, and I took it.

And the second lot. It didn't make the pain go away, but it dulled it, and made it seem more distant. I found it a very unpleasant sensation, though, and it's hard to imagine that people take it by choice, for fun.

With the pain receding a bit, I felt more optimistic. An examination by a specialist was very reassuring, too. Nothing was wrong with the cervix, and the most likely explanation was a harmless cyst, bursting, which would cause a lot of pain. Just to see what was going on, I would have a scan as planned the following morning, although a bit later than suggested, as I wouldn't have to take my chances with the "pot-luck". The cramps happened less and less frequently, and then finally stopped. I was moved onto a ward to await the next day's events and scans. Adam propped himself up in a chair, and we even managed to sleep.

Ultra-sound scans have to be done with a very full bladder, which is not much fun when you're being wheeled over bumps to a far distant part of the hospital. But you forget everything when you hear that "whump-whump-whump" of the foetal heartbeat. Adam had missed the twelve week scan, taking my place teaching on an Intelligent Horsemanship course, and was blown away when he saw our baby, waving a clenched fist. For me there was a rush of recognition, and the overwhelming relief: you're still there! An indescribable feeling. The sonographer pointed out a shadow on the screen, but didn't say much about it, and she could find no cysts, which seemed like good news.

Which is why it was such a shock when the doctor on duty informed us a couple of hours later that there was a 90% chance that we would lose the baby within the next two days.

He explained that I probably had a pelvic infection, and that my cervix had started opening. They'd started me on antibiotics, but there was almost no chance that they could reverse the damage. There was the very slightest hope that it might work out, but we shouldn't expect this. Perhaps they might put a stitch in the cervix, to try and stop it opening any further, but the prospects were not good, and he would have to ask the consultant.

Free of pain and feeling comparatively well, it was hard to believe what he was saying. There was nothing to do but wait, and Adam went home to deal with an appointment and get some supplies to make us both more comfortable for the stay. We were completely shocked by the doctor's news, but it's never over until the end, and we still kept hoping. Then, late that afternoon, the pain started again. It was excruciating, made even more so by the realization of what it meant.

There's a point where denial dies out, and you know what the truth is. It was no good. We were at the end, and this little person and I were about to part company. Adam still wasn't back. The nurses were very concerned, and lovely, and kept ringing him to try to get a message through, but they were very busy, and couldn't sit with me, and could only give gas and air for the pain as they couldn't leave me alone on morphine. I don't know how long it was before Adam made it back. The doctor came in, and patted my hand, and said there was good news. The consultant had agreed we could go ahead with the stitch tomorrow. I tried to tell him it was no good, tomorrow would be too late, but I just couldn't speak. I kept sucking on the gas and air and wondering if I could make myself pass out, craving oblivion.

Then finally Adam was there, and I could stop struggling and let go. Minutes later, our baby left my body. A life ended before it had even begun. It felt like the end of the world.

FIFTEEN

The Ride At The End Of The World
(Adam)

There is a road that snakes along the north shore of Maui, known as the Hana Highway, where the rain forest rushes down thousand-foot cliffs, laced with countless streams and waterfalls, in an area of astonishing natural beauty. Being atop a sudden rise out of one of the deepest parts of the ocean, together with the fact that swells come in from storms in the far northern Pacific with nothing to stand in their way for 3,000 miles, makes for lots of big waves much of the time. All along the coast in winter, although the water is nice and warm (perfect for those hundreds of humpback whales to frolic in the water just offshore), there are big waves and occasionally, monster waves. But at one particular cove, where the shape of the shoreline and the underwater topography combine to funnel the power of the ocean into a concentrated spot, once in a while there are freak conditions. Most of the time there is nothing to see, the waves don't break at all, they just bash into the cliff. But when ocean conditions are right - when there's been a big storm off Japan a few days earlier and the waves from it have come across the open depths, the result is a relatively narrow wave of unparalleled power, literally the size of a large barn, which breaks about a quarter of a mile out. They call it Jaws.

This is the wave that had enticed Chris to Hawai'i, luring him with the dream of one day riding that immense power. Although there is no beach, and the area is surrounded by lava and cliffs, if you come down the coast, you can approach from the ocean side. At the left side, looking out to sea, there is a convenient channel where a person is pretty safe, when only a few yards away a wall of water thirty feet or more in height (the face, from tip to trough, can therefore measure as much as seventy feet) comes crashing down.

The tumbling, the pounding of water upon water, would be astonishing enough to witness even if it weren't for the fact that crazy people actually surf this wave. The wave was so powerful that when surfers first thought of trying it, they knew they couldn't hope to paddle fast enough to actually catch it, despite the fact that these fanatical athletes were unbelievably fit, and could be seen toying with Mother Nature on other waves, like the 18 and 20 footers found at other spots. Top level windsurfers were using their sail power to achieve similar results but, of course, the sail was also an encumbrance when actually riding a wave like this one - and often, when Jaws breaks, the wind might not be strong enough or from the right direction. Added to this, if you got it wrong and fell under the wave, your mast would almost certainly break, leaving you with a slight predicament when the next wave came in. It was theoretically possible to get on the wave and come out into the channel to the side. But to risk experiencing that ultimate thrill - going in on a long surfboard - the only thing heavy enough to prevent you from actually taking off as you come down the face of the wave - meant having no chance of catching the wave, and more than a small chance of being caught helpless by a force beyond your power of comprehension, slammed into the cliffs or the coral, knocked unconscious and drowned by the wall of broken water that surges in thunderous boils around the bay. Then one of the surfers, Laird Hamilton, came up with the idea of attaching foot straps to the board and drilling channels in it, filling them with lead balls to weigh it down, and using a friend on a jet ski to tow him in - into the path of the wave and let him go at speed, right into the jaws of something literally the size of a tsunami.

You have to see it to believe it - there is a link on our web site www.whisperingback.co.uk to some great footage - and in fact you might well have done, for I saw film of it in previews when I was at the cinema recently. As the jet ski drops away behind the surfboard, a wave begins to rear up, slowly, like a monster from the deep, the water rising gradually, inexorably, becoming several times the height of the man, and it also begins to drop below the board, an electric blue mirror with a sharp white channel carved in it by the board's fin, an incredibly short board, and now the man is completely alone with the wave. It's moving so fast, the board pointing almost straight down, as a blue wall twice as tall as a London bus roars behind him, hurling them down, the wind blowing hard in the man's eyes as the air is pulled up the face of the most powerful ocean wave ever harnessed by man, a face of water several stories high, holding itself frozen for what seems an eternity before it heaves itself over the brink, beyond the vertical, and slams down behind him with unhurried power like a slab of mountainside, an avalanche, to be blown up again only a few feet behind him in great boulders of foam, heedless and indifferent to the incredible act of human endeavour and defiance that has been performed on its thundering water.

By chance, Chris had phoned us from Hawai'i almost as soon as we got back from the hospital, having left behind our little baby, and all our hopes and dreams for his life with us. According to Chris, the next step forward sounded so simple. "Come over. Get a ticket, pack your bags, get on a plane," he advised. It was extremely tempting, and although we couldn't quite just abandon everything and go, we did feel it would be a wonderful thing to do, to take his tiny pot of ashes and let him go in Maui.

SIXTEEN

Aftermath
(Nicole)

It didn't feel like it would be right ever to feel happy again, let alone go on holiday.

The sorrow felt as if it drained out of every cell in my body, pooled in my heart and then flooded out, saturating everything around me. It really felt like that. I cried and cried and cried. I washed clothes and sheets when they seemed drenched with sadness. I couldn't sleep for long, or too much grief welled up and threatened to explode. The waking up was the worst. There was a moment, a split-second, a fleeting fragment of time when I forgot, when there was hope and a future and a baby growing inside of me, and then reality slammed in hard and I just wailed. For the enormous loss of that little life, for the potential that would never be met, for the people who would never meet my son, the people my son would never meet, for the trauma of it all, the needles, the blood, the pain. Adam's face when he saw and held little Joe, the love and the recognition - that's him, that's our boy, so perfect, so small, so wise, with an incredible expression somewhere between struggle, acceptance, and simple knowing upon his part-formed features. He was not yet ready to be born and yet had already finished his journey.

Too big to deal with all at once, I divided the sadness into pockets, and dealt with them one at a time. The hardest one, the biggest one, maybe even worse than the enormous loss, was the feeling of helplessness and guilt. I will protect you, I had promised. And begged of him, hang on tight. But there was nothing for him to hold on tight to. I should never have asked him to try. His little world fell apart, and there was nothing he could do about it. We'd seen him, alive, waving, his heartbeat so strong and fast it was visible on the screen, but not curled up in proper foetus position, rather arched out on his back, clenching his fist against his fate, his legs hanging down, his tiny feet perilously close to a shadow on the screen, one that shouldn't have been there, an opening of the cervix, the edge of his world. I wanted him to keep his feet away, as if he could somehow just avoid making the gap worse. And I knew: so that's what the pain was. Contractions. There were no cysts - that's why the sonographer couldn't find any. It was the cervix opening, to let him out along with the infection that had suddenly and catastrophically edged its way into his perfect, sterile womb-world. But with the opening, the contractions had stopped. Could it close up again? Could he live with that tiny gap? Could he hold on? For five more months? I just didn't know.

But later, when the answer became clear, I found it very hard to accept that my body had expelled him. That he was perfectly fine, perfectly formed, doing his thing, growing and developing, and moving around, and then he died because my body took away his life support from him, and for what seemed like such a trivial and stupid reason: an infection. I kept wondering what the moment of death was like for him. I had to ask the doctor when it would have happened. "Well, at the time of the miscarriage itself, that would be a pretty stressful time for the foetus. That's when he would have died." So as the placenta tore itself from my womb, that's when his oxygen supply ended, that's when he died. A stressful time. But when we saw him, and held his tiny body in our hands, he looked peaceful, one little hand up by his face, his legs curled up. It didn't look like he had suffered at all. There, lying in bed in the hospital with our dead baby in our arms, Adam found a perfect name for him: Philosopher Joe. His expression was so unfathomable, like a baby Mona Lisa, so perfectly balanced between stress and serenity, as if he had borne his fate with an unyielding wisdom that this awful end, so inexplicable, so unrelentingly sad and wrong, could somehow be right, too. Only the wisest philosopher could begin to make sense of such a tragedy, so it seemed right to make it his first name. And, although we were pretty sure we could say he was a boy, the gender-neutral name Joe seemed appropriate too, being the name of one of our favourite horses. He was Philosopher Joe. At least, as Adam pointed out, he would never get teased at school for having such a weird name.

Later at home, lying in Adam's arms, hating my body for

failing my baby, for failing me, for failing all my dear friends and relatives, I cried more. "It didn't fail you," Adam said fiercely. "Your body did the right thing. It was too late for the antibiotics. If your body hadn't rejected the baby, it would have died. You would have got septicaemia and died too. Then where would I be? It did the right thing. You did everything you could. It wasn't your fault. It just wasn't meant to be."

As I took his words in, I could feel the pain subsiding. Was it true? Was this the outcome that was meant to be? Could I have done anything differently?

"I tried really hard," I said. Those months of no alcohol, no blue cheese, no chemicals, no coffee even. All those books I read. I was still in so much shock. I tried really hard, and it still didn't work out. I did everything right, and my baby still died. I went to the doctor as soon as I felt ill. Or at least, as soon as I felt ill in a different way. He wasn't worried about my raised temperature. I had a highly qualified doctor friend staying with me the whole week before. She didn't think there was anything untoward. I racked my brains. What could I have done differently?

"I tried really hard," I said again. "I did my best." Finally the words weren't about trying and failing, and the futility I'd felt. I had conceived and nurtured and grown a little person, and for fifteen weeks, I had loved him for every moment of every day and every night, and he must have known it. Along with the nutrients that had passed through the placenta, which had grown from nothing to support him, he must have felt the flow of my love, and been bathed in it, as he swam and bobbed in his perfect cocoon.

But the loss was formidable. Even having both lost a father, we'd never experienced anything like it. Adam cancelled all his appointments for the following week, and in the process found out that we hadn't heard everyone's miscarriage stories after all: it seemed as if everyone he spoke to had either suffered one, or several, or had a sister or a mother or a friend who had. Everyone was tremendously supportive. But I just couldn't stop crying, and I still feared sleep. I spent hours just paralysed by the grief, and wrapped in Adam's arms, knowing that as bad as things were, it could be even worse, and I could be on my own without Adam, trying to cope without him. And knowing too that there are no guarantees, and that none of us know who or what we may be asked to cope without in our lives, and the only thing we can do is appreciate the people we love while we can.

I cancelled the Mary Wanless Clinic I was due to go on, and the Teacher Training after that. She was immensely understanding. Aside from the fact that I couldn't guarantee more than five minutes at a time without sobbing, the bleeding from the miscarriage was due to go on for up to eight weeks. Eight weeks! Insult to injury. All that lining, built up to sustain the baby, was no longer needed.

Days passed, then weeks, and I'd like to say the pain lessened, but I'm not sure it did - more that I come to an understanding with it, that I'd get on with my life anyway, and it would leave me alone from time to time. I felt genuine gratitude for having had the time I'd had with Philosopher Joe, but that didn't stop the tears welling up every time I thought of him.

We were grateful too that times had changed, and his remains that would once have been disposed of as "hospital waste" were treated with respect, and we were offered a cremation, with a service. Perhaps had we been in less of a state of shock, we might have arranged a rather different send-off, but we went, just the two of us, to see the pathetically small coffin take our child away. It was strange to us that the only person who didn't seem to have anything like the right words to say was the one who had been trained to deal with exactly this kind of situation - the priest who held the funeral. Unable to bring himself to use Philosopher's first name, he constantly referred to him as Joseph, which wasn't his name at all and in fact, a few days later, when we saw another consultant, we discovered PJ had been a girl all along. The service was all about loss and emptiness, when we would have liked it to be more about gratitude and hope, but it was helpful anyway. Afterwards we walked through the graveyard. As we wandered, we found ourselves in the children's section - time and again the epitaphs expressing huge sorrow at the lives that ended so soon, but so often gratitude that the lives happened at all. If we felt such loss over a foetus who had such a short journey, how would it be to lose a child that you'd actually held in your arms, who had smiled at you, and breathed on you, fed from you and grasped your hand? Who you'd felt living and breathing and crying? The sheer courage of people who had lost children and still managed to carry on took our breath away. The knowledge that nothing is permanent, and that anyone can be taken from you at any time left us with a sense that just choosing to be in the world, to make connections and keep an open

150

heart, is an act of bravery and incredible optimism.

A day or so later, we were able to collect PJ's ashes, and headed down to Dartmoor for a few days away. Watching the sun set from the top of a Tor felt like a healing process. The wild beauty of the moor reminded me that wonderful things still exist, even when it felt like the end of the world. We took PJ's ashes in their tiny container as we went for our walks, and somehow felt less loss. And we began to think about where in this suddenly empty world we could leave her to rest, and start to find happiness again.

SEVENTEEN

Paradise Lost
(Adam)

'We are such stuff
As dreams are made on, and our little life
Is rounded with a sleep'
William Shakespeare, The Tempest, Act IV, Sc I

The northernmost tip of the West Maui mountains is like a surreal wilderness at the end of the world. It is only a few miles from some of the most desirable resorts on earth, where every conceivable whim is catered for. The golden, palm-shaded sands lie in sheltered bays fringed with coral, and the manicured golf greens roll from headland to well-groomed headland. But just beyond, as the coastline turns to face the north, to be pummelled by the terrifying waves from Alaska, lies an area almost as wild as the day it was blown and squeezed from the core of the earth. Sandy coves give way to gnarled lava shelves and cliffs. The road leading around the island becomes rougher and eventually loses its tarmac altogether. The trade winds whip in hard from the north-east and the wild waves jostle and beat upon the stark lava which now drops into the sea in vertical plunges. Horizontal marks of red, black, orange and gold running along the cliffs give a lesson in volcanic geology and chemistry. It's a wilderness whose savagery is all the more emphatic given how nearby the pinnacle of leisurely civilisation lies.

We'd been carrying PJ around everywhere with us, her ashes contained inside a small, decorative wooden jar we'd bought for her. We'd take her to the beach or on a hike, frequently checking that she was still there, worried that she'd fall out of the backpack and be left in some unknown place. We knew we needed to let go of her somewhere, but just couldn't bring ourselves to say goodbye.

Eventually, our three week stay, whose sole purpose was to take her on her first and last big excursion, was drawing to a close. We took a day to say goodbye to her and got up early and drove. We headed up the coast, past Ho'okipa beach where the windsurfers and kite surfers skim along the waves, and past fabulous Iao valley, Maui's sacred heart, where immense, sheer walls rise for thousands of feet all around you. Both seemed too much of a tourist trap, too well known to be her spot. We headed out across the saddle between the two volcanoes and then north up the coast that leads to Lahaina, 'The Merciless Sun', former capital of the islands. On our right the mesmerising sight of the chiselled peaks of the West Maui mountains, with their maze of razorback ridges and fearsome gorges, were by now a familiar sight, but no less entrancing for it. To our left, the sea, the surf, and the gorgeous sight of the islands of Lanai, Molokai, and Kahoolawe made their perfect picture. We kept driving, not saying much. There wasn't a lot to say.

Passing the principal resort areas, we found ourselves heading out to the wildest part of the island again. We'd driven here before a couple of times, but when we came around a corner and saw the first stack of stones, we looked at each other and knew we were nearing our destination. For no reason we were aware of, many people had erected small piles of stones on top of each other all over the place, along the cliff edge, as if in offering. We had never seen such a thing before and had not noticed them the previous times we'd been in the area. A place to park invited us in and we pulled up. Something told us it was her spot.

The bay below us was achingly beautiful, although raw and primordial. Below the cliffs, about a hundred feet down, we could see an area where a shelf of lava was broken by numerous rock pools, and then we spotted a tiny island which hung off the shelf and was connected to it by three lava bridges. The ocean, even though the surf was not high, was surging in through holes under the bridges and creating washing machines of turbulent water in the moat between the tiny island and the shore. There seemed no way down but, as we followed the cliff, we discovered a steep path leading to a ladder which had been left fixed to the rough, sheer slope of tormented lava. We climbed down, marvelling at the extraordinary features the eroding cliff had opened up in the rock face. Mouths, faces, fish and animals painted in black, red, purple and orange jostled around each other as crumbling openings, surrounded by stronger veins of lava, left features like an artist's sketch book, nature's graffiti, all over the cliff.

The rock pools were tranquil, their surfaces like mirrors while the sea beat savagely on the rocks just beneath them. Occasionally a violent wave would rage against the rocks sufficiently to cause a splash of foam to arc into the air far enough to break the perfect mirror; within seconds its ripples would be dissipated and tranquility resumed. Gradually the sea was taking its revenge on this upstart land, born in the fury of volcanic eruption, but which, after growing over fourteen thousand feet high, was now almost spent, and every wave was chipping just a little bit more away, to leave eventually nothing more than an atoll, which would finally disappear beneath the waves in a few million more years. The volcano had been angry, the explosions of lava unstoppable; but the sea and the rain are patient, and will win in the end. Already the summit of Haleakala is just ten thousand feet high, and gradually melting under every torrent of rain the trade winds bring. In the few aeons of their mating, the island and the sea have provided a paradise so perfect, its beauty defies man's imagination. This cove, which we named Philosopher's Point, is just another of Maui's wonders.

We chose a bridge and walked the few steps across onto the small ledge of lava. It was the kind of spot that when the surf's up, you can feel the force of the ocean through your feet as it lashes furiously against the land, and you hope that the last bond holding your rock onto the island won't break just now.

A sea turtle suddenly bobbed up from the deep, just below us. Faces soaked in tears, we smiled at each other, and said we hoped he'd look after little PJ, after all she was too small to look after herself. Finally, with a slow turn of the wrist, we opened her wooden bottle, and upturned our little treasure. In an instant the unfeeling wind tore away what had been our greatest hope, and fed her ashes to the ocean.

It wasn't until we were taking off a few days later, beginning the interminable series of flights back home, that we really let out our grief. The pilot announced that he was sorry, that it was always more fun to be taking passengers to, rather than back from, paradise and that we must all be pretty upset to be leaving. But I don't think the crew were expecting such a show of emotion. We sobbed and sobbed, unable to stop ourselves. Our baby, so fragile, so full of potential, now lay scattered to the currents, to be eaten by crabs and fishes. Her beauty and grace, so much possibility, the most precious object in our world, was now represented by only a crude pile of insensible rocks, perched on a cliff looking out over the endless deep. When we finally could weep no longer, we fell asleep, unaware till we were woken that for almost the entire journey back to Chicago, our plane had been bathed in the most brilliant display of the Aurora Borealis the pilot had ever witnessed. A more sentimental person might say it was a farewell from her departing spirit.

Full fathom five thy father lies;
Of his bones are coral made;
These are pearls that were his eyes:
Nothing of him that doth fade,
But doth suffer a sea-change
Into something rich and strange.
Sea-Nymphs hourly ring his knell.
Hark! Now I hear them, ding-dong, bell.
William Shakespeare, The Tempest, Act I, Scene II

EIGHTEEN

Monty's Visit
(Nicole)

If it weren't for Monty, we wouldn't be at Moor Wood, there's no doubt about that. If we hadn't heard of and been inspired by his methods and then met, learned and worked with Kelly, it's hard to see how we could have made a living out of horses, especially in such a wonderful place. The other cottages on the estate are rented by people working in London, who have high-powered city jobs to allow them to cover the rent on a second property, which unfortunately they never seem to get very much time to enjoy. We had opted out of that lifestyle very early on, and have never regretted it, especially when we get to spend all our days in such glorious surroundings without ever having to make the journey to London to earn such a privilege. It feels to us every day as if we are living a manifestation of what they said on the Insight seminars - "If you want something, just ask the Universe". What we're surrounded by is like a heaven on earth, at least until the heavens open and turn the earth into a mudbath!

We always thought it would be lovely if Monty could come and see the place when he was in the country, but it was never possible to find a time. His gruelling schedule doesn't exactly allow for him popping over for afternoon tea, and although Moor Wood was sometimes on his route from one venue or meeting to the next, there was never any spare time. He's a driven man, with a mission so enormous that he doesn't have time for tea, it would seem. But in the early days, before I had plenty of experience of my own to draw on, it felt to me as if Monty were at Moor Wood, almost as if he were sitting on my shoulder reminding me of his concepts. So when Kelly suggested our place as the venue for some filming with Monty in July 2005, we leapt at the chance.

157

I guess it's fair to say that we're quite used to the presence of film crews and the way they tend to work. Not that we're regulars on television, but Moor Wood was a venue for one of the episodes of Barking Mad, a BBC TV series that Kelly did with Philippa Forrester, and many of the Intelligent Horsemanship courses have had film crews along at various points. At Moor Wood, we once had a visit from Jane Goodman (wife of Jonathan Ross, the famous chat show host), who was doing a series on "alternatives", and was looking into the work of Margrit Coates, an author and healer whom we know. We provided the venue and the horse - Sensi on this occasion. Adam spectacularly failed to take advantage of the situation and didn't even hand Mrs J. Ross a SCSI demo CD to give to her husband. It's all very well not being pushy, but I think this could be an example of where the Universe, or God or whatever, would sigh deeply and say "You've got to meet me halfway on this!"

Anyway, this particular crew was from ABC Nightline, the American equivalent of the BBC's Newsnight, and they were doing a feature on Monty's methods and how they had been successfully applied to humans. Some years ago Monty had been contacted by a teacher at Kingshurst Junior School, a primary school in Birmingham. In 1995 the school was condemned by Ofsted, and threatened with closure. This teacher had read Monty's book, *Join-up: Horse Sense For Humans*, and had been to see him give a demonstration, although he had no previous knowledge of horses. He had been trying to put some of Monty's concepts and procedures into practice in the classroom - ideas such as having the kids create and sign 'contracts' - with brilliant results. Monty had worked with the school on several occasions and been very impressed with the dramatic changes this had helped bring about, although he would be the first person to say that the commitment of the staff and pupils was really the root cause of the school's transformation. By 2001, Kingshurst was in the top 100 most improved schools, and has since gained Beacon status. Monty had also been doing some work with a similarly challenged school in California, and the production company thought it would be useful to draw some comparisons between the two. Some of the staff from the American school flew in to visit and find out more about what had been achieved. Fifteen students from Kingshurst would come up for the day, with their teachers, and Monty would start a horse for them, partly as a treat, and partly as a means of explaining his philosophy and approach.

We duly procured a photogenic three-year-old called Brandy, and went about making the place as tidy and beautiful as possible. Moor Wood, probably the most picturesque estate I've ever visited that is not in the National Trust or owned by a member of the royal family, is home to the National Collection of rambler roses, and they were in bloom, so that was a good start, but we knew from experience how stray wisps of hay can spoil a picture. The lawns were mown, the yards were swept, the fields were clear of muck (as usual, of course!). Any dock plants and other weeds that might be in the way of "the establishing shots" were hacked down. The tack was all cleaned and gleaming, the outside loo was spotless. The round pen was harrowed and raked and adjusted to be as round as possible. The hay barn, the feed room, and the tack room were all swept clean. Thinking that our visitors and the film crew might want tea or coffee, we vacuumed, dusted and generally made respectable the whole downstairs of the house. Part of the "making respectable" meant moving junk temporarily (or at least, that's always the plan) upstairs, as we figured no-one would be going up there. It was already somewhat chaotic, with clothes strewn about and dishes needing collecting, so some extra paperwork and odd bits that didn't have homes wouldn't make too much difference. Our housekeeping had definitely improved since our Milton Keynes days, but it still couldn't be described as immaculate.

Which is why it was a little bit mortifying when the first thing Monty did upon arrival was to go upstairs to use the bathroom!

Trying hard not to dwell on this (was there toothpaste in the sink? Just how bad was the cat litter tray? Which bits of unwashed laundry were hanging around?), we soon headed out to the round pen where Monty started the beautiful youngster, brilliantly ridden by Dan Wilson, one of Monty's most talented riders. It was the perfect way to illustrate to the children how much can be achieved in the absence of violence and with respect for the power of communication. Brandy responded very well and was another great success, but anyone could see how spirited and raw he was. He was also incredibly sensitive around his head. Not head-shy exactly, but if you touched his poll area, he would pull back violently, as if in pain. We had already mentioned this to his owner, Janine, and suggested she get it checked out before any more work was done with Brandy.

More than once the kids, looking on very keenly, squealed from the safety of the outside of the pen when they got sprayed with sand and rubber as the horse changed direction abruptly. They were completely silent at the crucial moment of backing Brandy, however, and their awestruck response reminded us of just how extraordinary it is to see a horse go from totally raw to ridden in a few minutes without any major drama. We'd performed this feat ourselves many times by then, in this exact location, but being on the outside of the pen for a change rekindled our sense of wonder. We were due to continue this horse's education with his owner, so we were delighted that the first ride had gone so well.

We had brought all the horses in so that the kids could meet them, and this proved to be a very popular part of the day. I hadn't anticipated that this would all be filmed as well, and in fact had been fully prepared for Monty and the crew to fly in and then fly out again just as rapidly, so I hadn't gone to any great lengths to tidy up the horses. I expected that Misty in particular would hide behind the others and stay out of shot, given that before we had met her, she was completely uncatchable, and so the fact that she was more mud-brown than white, with a decidedly yellow tail, didn't worry me. She, however, decided to use this occasion to demonstrate how much she had progressed, and how much more confident she was feeling. She did a beautiful follow-up with one of the pupils, a quiet and clearly talented boy who was talked through the process by Monty. He had obviously been paying a lot of attention when Monty was doing the starter. He proceeded to pick up all of Misty's feet, paying particular attention to the hinds. She was a bit tickly to start with, but soon relaxed under his careful hands. It was astonishing to think back to what she had been like when we first met her. Letting a child anywhere near her at the time would have been horribly irresponsible, except that there was almost no chance of a child or any other person getting within a hundred feet. Seeing her respond to this young boy so calmly was very moving. Hearing that he had a previously troubled start in life as well made it particularly poignant.

Finn, not to be outdone, excelled himself by being exemplarily well-behaved and giving a bareback pony ride to anyone who wanted one. He is very used to giving bareback rides, because Adam frequently hops on him in the yard or practises bombing around uncontrollably in the school. The lightest touch of a stick on any part of his rump or flank, and Finn goes off like a rocket sideways across the school in some kind of random lateral movement yet to be described by the dressage manuals. Adam claims that Finn is his riding instructor, and that riding him bareback (which is like sitting on a banana skin on top of a very round and lively barrel) is good training, although personally I think he's just too lazy to put on some tack.

I'd just about got used to him doing this when one morning I found myself looking out of the window after he had gone out to get the herd in from the winter field, to find him cantering bareback on his pony amidst a throng of charging, kicking horses. They are supposed to come when we call, guided and sometimes driven into a frenzy by our over-enthusiastic border collie sheepdog, Scrabble, who seems to think that sheep range in height from about 11 to 17 hands and have hooves, manes and long, flowing tails. Those small fluffy white things he sees around the countryside clearly are not sheep since we do not pay any attention to them. But in high winds, when they can't hear us (perhaps the grass in their winter field is so long it muffles their ears), and on days when they can't be bothered, the horses sometimes just kick the dog away and hang around until we go out with a head collar. At this point they generally high-tail it back to the yard like a wild herd pursued by a pack of wolves. It never ceases to impress how fast they can cover the quarter-mile or so to their stables, but it is also somewhat irritating, given that what can take them about twenty seconds takes us about five minutes of struggling through the mud. Adam had decided that morning, when he got out into the field to get them, that it was too much hassle and humiliation to walk back, so he had vaulted on Finn, bareback without a head collar, and hitched a ride home. In between nearly getting bucked off, having his knee bashed into a gatepost, and being kicked by the other ponies, he managed to stay on, which was a good thing given that he wasn't wearing a helmet. When I challenged him as to what on earth he thought he was doing, he told me he had just invented a new extreme sport, inspired by what we had seen at Jaws, and which he called Pony Surfing. Given that he had recently stopped drinking coffee, on the grounds that it was bad for his health and that he didn't need a kick in the morning, I could scarcely believe my eyes.

Finn, whose full name (so he tells us) is Finimus Minimus, Dudus Maximus, Exmoorus Superbus, ex Equis Imperator, never seems to forget that, as an Exmoor, he's the closest relative to the only wild horses left in the world (the Przewalski), and that humans have eyes on the front of their faces and are therefore potential predators, so he can occasionally be a little challenging. But he behaved as though he had been giving seaside-style bareback rides to small children all his life. He didn't even try to eat any of them. It was clearly a massive thrill for the kids, who kept coming back for more.

The weather was gorgeous and we got some charming pictures of the kids with Monty and Finn, on the lawn in front of the magnificent three hundred year old Cedar tree. Monty and Kelly came into the house for a snack, and it was very pleasant just to get the chance to sit and chat for a while before they were dragged out for more interviews.

It had been a perfect midsummer's day, and a real treat to be able to show our place off to Monty. He had been suitably impressed, too. There's no escaping the fact that the Cotswolds are just stunning, and our particular corner is decidedly gorgeous. As he came down the drive with Kelly, seeing Henry's house and the immaculate lawns and roses, Monty apparently raised an eyebrow and said to Kelly, "They've certainly done well for themselves!" Even though our house is somewhat more modest than Henry's, and we do not own it, there's no way we would disagree with him. Meeting Monty was the start of the journey that took us to Moor Wood, and his visit completed the circle. Seeing the whole thing on screen, and knowing approximately twenty-two million Americans had done so as well, was a bonus.

However, not everything went quite according to plan. Brandy stayed overnight and the next day Janine came along with her trailer to take him back home. He was young and inexperienced, and we were not surprised to see that he was more than a little hesitant to load. Coming to Moor Wood had been his first outing, and on the last part of the journey the roads are steep, winding, and narrow. Our driveway also has a particularly nasty speed ramp on it, and no matter how slowly and carefully one drives, it isn't possible to give a horse an optimal experience.

Janine was an experienced owner, however, and we had no particular reason to anticipate doing a session with her and her horse. In fact, we were looking forward to a day off, and were just keeping a casual eye on her should she need any help. It soon became clear, though, that her horse was getting more and more agitated, and that some sort of assistance would be necessary if she were ever to get her horse loaded to go home. Soon we were both involved, and had accumulated our helmets, long-line, dually halter, and poll guard. We'd even deployed sections of our round pen to make it safer and easier, and we loaded and unloaded him a few times until he was walking in and out smoothly. As it turned out, however, getting him in was only the start of our troubles.

Having loaded him one last time, we carefully moved the partition across and closed up the ramp. We would have very much preferred that he travel without the partitions in, as this would have given him more space to load and then balance himself, but removing the partitions would have meant him having to travel without a breast bar, which is illegal and dangerous. The bar prevents the horse from bashing into the front of the trailer in the case of an emergency stop. Also, should the horse's weight come in front of the wheels, the front of the trailer would be very overloaded, possibly causing the tow bar to hit the road, with potentially disastrous consequences. A full length single breast bar would have prevented these issues, and allowed him to travel with more space, but Janine wasn't aware of the benefits of giving her horse more space to travel, even thinking that being confined in one half of the trailer might make her horse feel more secure.

Anyway, Brandy was loaded and Janine was just slowly setting off, when a terrible banging broke out from within the trailer, which suddenly began to lurch forwards and backwards. Signalling for her to stop, we opened the jockey door and were greeted with a truly heart-stopping sight. Brandy was shaking uncontrollably and, nearly sitting on his quarters, pawing frantically with his forelegs. As we watched, he started to throw himself around, rearing and thrashing, and bashing his head against the ceiling. Before we could do anything about it, he launched himself forward in a desperate attempt to escape, and landed on the breast bar, with his front feet suspended in the air. Snorting and scrambling, he tried again and again to free himself, but there was no way he could lift his body over the bar. For a moment he stopped, helpless, his flanks heaving as he tried to breathe with almost his whole weight on the padded bar under his sternum. It was one of those moments when you pray for something to break, to give way, just so long as it isn't his leg[2]. To go in and try to lift him off the bar would not only require superhuman strength, but also an almost suicidal bravery.

So that was exactly what Adam did. He ran his hand quietly down Brandy's leg, hooked his palm under it and pushed up on his foot. That seemed to give him the right idea, and with a monumental effort Brandy lifted his whole body onto his hind legs and took a step backwards, his forelegs slithering back over the bar. I immediately ran around to the back of the trailer, to let down the ramp and carefully undo the breaching straps to release him.

Brandy flew out backwards and stood trembling, sweat dripping down his body. Still shaking with adrenaline ourselves, we checked him over carefully. He had a few cuts and bruises, but appeared otherwise unscathed. After a few minutes, Brandy began to show an interest in the lawn, and we noticed that he was moving a little stiffly. To attempt to load up again and travel him that day was out of the question.

Janine was clearly unsettled by the incident, but rather less taken by surprise than we were. "He did something rather similar when he was a foal," she said. "He put his head through his field gate, and got it stuck. When he pulled back, he managed to pull it off its hinges. He dragged it around the field for quite a long way before it finally fell off."

Adam and I looked at each other in astonishment. That explained why Brandy was so touchy around his poll.

"What did they say when you got it checked out?" I asked, wondering what sort of effects had occurred.

"They?"

"Well, you know, the chiropractor, or physiotherapist - the vet?"

"I've never had it checked out," she said, suddenly realising it might have been a good idea to have done so.

Our equine chiropractor duly came out the next morning, and confirmed that Brandy had previously sustained some injury to his poll, but that with treatment the pain would be alleviated. A few

---

[2] We recently discovered that the Rice Richardson trailer company have developed a device which enables one to release the breast bar from the brackets holding to the wall of the trailer without lifting them. Better still, it is operated from outside the vehicle.

164

days of rest was prescribed to make him more comfortable after his recent trauma, giving Janine time to arrange a lorry. Although he was understandably hesitant to load, he bravely went in with just a little encouragement, and travelled home safely, without partitions, in as much space as the lorry could offer.

NINETEEN

Opposites Attract
(Adam)

Perry, who was no longer behaving anything like Piglet, had been living at Moor Wood with us for more than a year and we had become firm friends with Jo and Derek. Among the many teachers various 'horsey' friends had told me about, the name Craig Stevens had often cropped up. Annabelle had been to see him several times and was very interested in his work, which is based on French school classical dressage, a world seemingly unconnected to our training methods. Now that Perry had got functional feet, was no longer violent about being caught or groomed, could be hacked out and loaded and generally seemed much more confident in himself, Jo decided to take him on a clinic which Craig was doing in the UK. Afterwards, she informed us in the kindest possible way that although she wasn't even thinking of moving Perry elsewhere, she didn't want any more lessons from us. She explained that Craig had a very different approach that she didn't think was compatible with our style of riding, and that she thought his approach was the one she wanted to follow exclusively.

It could have come as a massive blow to me, but it came around the time of my Insight seminar and, as a result, I was able to take it instead simply as feedback. I guess the universe was telling me I had better look at how other people worked. So I decided to take a chance and booked a clinic, taking along Sensi, while Nicole was away on her own Insight seminar.

It would have been a challenge to me already, just to shut up and listen to another person's version of events, but the clinic was attended by several of my own clients and even a couple of my working pupils. I had, however, come with an attitude that was very much more open than it could have been - whatever I might dislike about this way of doing things, I felt I had nothing to lose by having an unbiased look at it, from which I might take or leave whatever I chose. Previously, I would have found this a difficult position to adopt. It's easy to be open-minded if that means "Open to any ideas that are compatible with the views I already hold"; it's far harder to be open-minded about anything that appears fundamentally to contradict what you hold to be true. There was something else, too. In our early days, a lot of the trainers (and their ideas) that we were coming across were essentially new - at least to us - and the amount of information and differing approaches out there seemed overwhelming. The easiest way to deal with this was to operate a strict "One strike and you're out" policy. So if someone said or did something objectionable enough, it was easiest to discount everything they said, even if it risked throwing the baby out with the bath water. Later on, even though I think it would still be true to say we learnt something from every trainer's clinic or demonstration we attended, the amount of new information inevitably dwindled, so that if we came away with just one useful nugget that we could add to our skill set, it would make the ticket price worthwhile.

Applying the "One strike and you're out" approach to Craig would have meant never even attending a clinic, since we had been warned by more than one person that we would probably find some of what he did objectionable. In particular, we had heard that on occasion he would strike a horse with a whip, but that most of the time what he did was extremely gentle. Using the Insight mantra of "Use everything for your learning, upliftment and growth" meant that I would be in a better place to see if there was anything useful we could incorporate from his approach.

Up until that point, the biggest influence on our riding and instruction had come from Mary Wanless, and although we didn't agree with absolutely everything she said and did, we were very happy with the results we were getting through using and adapting her techniques. Judging by the feedback we got from the evaluation forms we handed out on clinics, so were our students. Perhaps this helped, too: we could be open to new ideas because we already had effective strategies in place for helping people to improve their riding. We could look for techniques which might help us expand our repertoire, but we weren't coming from that defensive place of having run out of answers. And even though we had effectively been sacked by Jo, a favourite client, who later cited a lack of progress as her reason, we could also see that she might be measuring progress using different criteria, and that it was perfectly possible neither of us were right, or wrong, and that it could just come down to preferences. I was looking forward to a challenging and thought-provoking clinic.

Arriving at the clinic the afternoon before it was due to begin, I was greeted by a very informally dressed man who resembled a walrus in everything from his whiskers to his enormous size, except he had no tusks. With his baseball cap, jeans and sporting a pony tail, a more different person than diminutive, super-fit Mary could not be imagined, and he looked nothing like I would have expected as a French Classical Dressage master. Craig was very friendly and relaxed in conversation, and I was struck during the lecture he gave the first evening by how, like Mary, he was acutely intelligent and knowledgeable on many diverse subjects, ranging from philosophy to martial arts, but especially the history of riding. He lectured without notes for several hours, beginning with a detailed history of the origins of classical horsemanship, followed by a discourse on the aids, described in a completely different way than Mary. It was all a world away from what I was familiar with - I felt intrigued and ignorant, and completely out of my depth, all at the same time.

Which just about sums up my first ride. I came out and did things the way I knew, and immediately heard muttering from the public gallery, as Craig went out of his way to say that the way I rode was how he used to ride too. He encouraged me to "relax" (almost a taboo word in Mary's work, as it doesn't usually help), and so I did, but I found that Sensi went all over the place. At one point I remember not being able to steer at all, which was mildly disconcerting since I had been through that many years before when I had first learned to ride on this very same horse. As we approached the wall I would try, deliberately weakly and exclusively by use of the rein, to steer her one way, and about half the time she went completely the other way. I knew how I could have fixed this using internal strength through my legs and torso, but to do so would have simply been a way to avoid discovering whether there was any truth in Craig's way of doing things, to save face, to save myself from being embarrassed in front of my peers and students - in short, to avoid learning.

The clinic seemed to revolve around everything being

'opposite day'. Not only was I being asked to use my body in a completely different way from the toned control I had been trying to develop, but I was required to carry a whip. For over seven years, since the first time I had seen Monty, I had not even held a stick in my hands, yet this was something Craig insisted upon. Not that he was advocating that it be used with violence. Indeed, it became clear to me that the stick was so crucial to him because it was the means by which he was able to avoid violence, although that might sound strange. Every effort was made to prevent any type of 'denting' - pressure moving into and changing the shape of the horse's body, via the bit or the legs, with the result that the horse's body changed shape. Without hurting Sensi in the slightest, by very gentle use of the whip I was able to get her much more attentive and responsive to this rein aid, without tying myself up in knots either.

Not surprisingly, to my eye, most of the riders were displaying faults in their position, and moving far too much. No attention was being paid in the clinic to asymmetry or bad posture, causing what I saw as serious side effects. A lesson with Mary would have focused almost exclusively on these aspects. But Craig simply stated that, although it is impossible to deliver perfect aids without a perfect seat, curing these problems took too long to be practical in a weekend clinic. This sounded to me like he was avoiding the issue, but there were some wonderful moments, and I began to see that his way had a lot of advantages. Certainly, I could see that combinations of schooling movements led to the horse taking up a more collected position. And for the first time I understood what true collection could do. I witnessed a rider prompting her young horse to do his first flying change under saddle without even knowing that was what she was attempting, and the aid was nothing more than a slight raising, followed by a lowering, of one hand.

There were areas where, although we were coming from different worlds, we had so much in common, and I found this most interesting. For example, Craig detests gadgets, such as side and draw reins, martingales and the use of tight nosebands or strong bits, all things we rejected many years ago. Although there were areas where he appeared to be advocating the exact polar opposite to Mary, there were also areas of overlap and compatibility. Refreshingly, he also abhorred the practise of severely overbending the horse, which seems to me to be the overwhelming preoccupation of most modern dressage, in spite of being against the rules. Along with Monty, and unlike Mary, he put great emphasis on the importance of rein back in ridden work, something we had long incorporated too. One of his main inspirations, the Frenchman Baucher, was said to spend almost as much time going backwards as forwards. Having said all that, once in a while I'd see Craig do or encourage the rider to do something I thought was utterly unacceptable, generally involving the whip. It all left me thoroughly confused, but very stimulated.

Perhaps the biggest lesson for me was about myself, and I hope it has stuck, for I know I am inclined towards certainties and rules, in spite of myself, which can lead to overstatement and egotism. It's dangerous not just because it can result in mistakes, but also because the consequences of those mistakes can be broken bones, and dead riders as well as dead horses. As Mary says, an ounce of correctness is worth a ton of strength, and being a kinaesthetic, feeling-based activity, it's very difficult to describe that correctness. In the end, the only reliable way to describe things in the sensory world is by experience - one teaspoon of strawberry jam will do more to inform you of its taste than a book full of descriptions of strawberry jam written by the greatest poet. Ironically, there were times when as a result of doing what Craig told me - often the exact opposite of what Mary seemed to be after I'd experience something which felt exactly like what she had described. It was as if I was undertaking exactly the same journey she had been on many years ago, when in frustration at her lack of progress, she tried doing the exact opposite of what she was being told, and found this worked better for her. I seemed to be experiencing the same thing, only in reverse. For me, the taste of being able to influence the horse through absurdly weak actions, whilst making no effort to do anything internally, was one that I found immensely appealing.

The clinic was very challenging mentally and emotionally, because I was having to question what I had been teaching. Much of it went right over my head. So it was interesting to me when the contents of one lesson, with an exceptionally elegant and organised rider who was by far the most accomplished member of the group, suddenly began to cross over to ground in which I was experienced. All the other students, most of whom were far more familiar with Craig's work than I was, were as confused as I had been the rest of the weekend. The rider asked him about her seat bones and how they moved in the walk as the horse went in a circle. What followed was one of the most brilliant lessons I've ever witnessed.

He began by getting her to concentrate on one seat bone - the outside one - as she went in a circle, and getting her to describe in detail how it was moving, how to imitate and go with the movement of the saddle and the horse's back underneath it, how she had to let it move in all sorts of directions. It was a very detailed description and whenever she seemed to settle on one dimension of the movement, Craig would bring her awareness to another, until she finally realised that it was moving in every direction, upwards and down, right and left, forward and backwards, though obviously not all at once! After several minutes of this, Craig hinted, without any of us recognising how devious he was being, "...and do you notice how it's moving a little bit more than the other seat bone?"

"Gosh", she replied, "I'd never noticed that before! Wow, it really is! That's amazing! Right, now I've got it!"

But clearly she hadn't, because, as she continued to circle in the same direction, Craig began to talk about her inside seat bone, and get her to describe what was going on with that one. After dwelling on it for some moments, he said, without the least irony in his voice, "...and do you notice how it's moving just a little bit more than the other one?"

"Yes!" she answered, but then she lapsed into an unsure silence. "But hang on, just a minute ago, I'm sure the other one was moving more! What's going on? How can they both be moving more!" A look of confusion and consternation came over her face.

The same was true for those of us who had been following this from the viewing gallery, all as bewildered as the rider. But Craig had a wider point to make. By getting her to concentrate exclusively, almost obsessively on one thing, especially something new that she had never noticed before, all other parts of the picture faded into the background. It's easy to assign too much importance to any discovery, particularly when, as in this case, the teacher is "leading the witness" - whether deliberately or not - by suggesting to the student what she is or isn't feeling.

This incident brought home to me how all of us see what we want to see. It's also known as "confirmation bias", meaning that one particularly notices anything that confirms our world view, and effectively "deletes" from our attention anything that doesn't fit in. It's why proofreading is so hard to do - the brain knows that writing 'the the horse' is wrong, and reads it as 'the horse', to make sense of it. The consequences are rather more serious when it comes to behaviours and beliefs, however. It's why many theoretical discussions or arguments, although they may be lively and interesting, prove fruitless, as it usually becomes clear that no-one is going to change their minds. Cliques and "clubs" also make it easier to keep your mind firmly closed and not be bothered to examine alternative approaches. It's illuminating to attend, say, a Craig clinic and hear all the devotees criticising everyone else, and being so sure that they hold all the answers, and are the only riders who are doing it properly, and then attend a Mary clinic and hear exactly the same thing! Having a foot in more than one camp makes it a lot harder to be certain that any one group really does have all the answers. Many times the people teaching the clinics are more open-minded than their followers.

In the end, as with so many horsemen's opinions, the horses are the only ones who know all the answers, but in general they keep them to themselves (apart from Sensi, who was kind enough to write the introduction to this book, although it doesn't make particularly flattering reading for me!). As they are unable for the most part to tell us their thoughts directly, we attempt to interpret their actions, filling the void with our observations, based as they are on prejudice, loyalty, wishful thinking, ideology and only a sprinkling of facts.

As for me, I've found myself adapting some of what I had learned from Monty, not least because, unlike him, I don't usually have a round pen to work in. I'm also not as good at keeping my adrenaline down, or knowing what a horse is going to do before, apparently, he even knows himself. It follows that to stay safe I should take things slower, adding interim steps which Monty might not feel the need to include. I've had a few pretty hectic moments especially when young or abused horses felt their first long line around the back of their legs. Various incidents (none of which worked out as badly as they might have done), have led to me being taught a type of single-line groundwork by the horses I have worked with. In spite of Monty's abhorrence of all lunging (he describes it as one of the very worst acts of horsemanship), I found this type of line work useful in training both horses and humans, sometimes as a step between loose work like join-up, and long reining with two lines. I feel that the problems Monty ascribes to single-line lunging

- all of which are serious and about which I agree completely - are avoided, and can even be cured, by this type of work, which I sometimes refer to as line dancing, because it is like dancing with the horse, but you have a line. It doesn't resemble the traditional way of lunging much at all - for example, I don't stand still or ask the horse to perform a circle, and don't use a whip or my voice. Still, I was blown away when ultra-classical Craig showed me 'his' way of lunging, which was almost exactly the same as the way I had learned from horses I'd worked with.

I'm immensely grateful to Jo and Perry for putting me on the path to learning with Craig. We've spent a lot of time over several years watching, talking and riding with him and have incorporated a lot of the work we have seen into our own teaching and riding. He's also become a really close friend. Learning with him has helped us to have a much more rounded attitude, even if it has also led to a lot of sleepless nights and heated discussions between us about where his ideas might diverge from Mary's, Monty's, or whatever else we might know. It's been an endless conversation, which has brought about many new insights into our understanding of equitation. I'm unbelievably lucky to have someone so balanced, rational, intelligent, and knowledgeable as Nicole, with whom I can have this conversation and exploration. Amalgamating such apparently different approaches has made the learning we've received from each of these Master Teachers even more powerful. It's a never-ending quest to deepen our understanding and perfect our techniques, and sharing this journey with so many enthusiastic horse lovers and students has been one of the most fulfilling areas of our work.

TWENTY

A Grand Day Out
(Nicole)

It was shortly after Monty's visit to Moor Wood that I found myself volunteering to take a horse to Kingshurst Junior School to meet the kids there. Kelly's amazing horse Pie usually did the honours, but as his social schedule and tour commitments escalated, Kelly didn't feel she could prevail upon him once more. I felt sure that somewhere in our herd of eight, there ought to be someone who would be a suitable candidate. Finn had been an absolute gentleman when the kids had come to visit, so he was one obvious choice. On the other hand, Misty with her flowing white (well, yellow) mane and tail and pretty features had been extremely popular. It suddenly dawned on me that taking them both might actually be easier than taking just one of them.

By this time, we had got rid of the Big Green Monster. 'Unreliable' didn't even describe it; it wasn't even reliably unreliable, and for the sake of everyone's sanity it just had to go. It appeared to require some very precise conditions in order to start, but since we succeeded so seldom in getting it going, we never really worked out what these were. Something to do with planetary alignments, leap years, and months with a 'g' in them, we suspected. It also required a rather simpler condition to be met - specifically, turning the immobiliser off.

Adam's relationship with the Big Green Monster had never been good. In fact, "Monster" would be a term of endearment compared with what he usually called it. I don't think he had ever really wanted the lorry, and although he predicted that running one would incur a lot of expense, I think he expected to get some use out of it in exchange for the vast sums of money we had sunk into it. To add insult to injury, my success rate with cajoling it into life

175

was marginally better than his, but offers to have a go were usually met with an uncharacteristically surly, "No, I'll do it!"

In fact, Adam's usually calm and patient nature was transformed whenever he got anywhere near the lorry. I noticed our working pupils would scatter like frightened chickens whenever they saw Adam approaching it, keys in hand, a look of grim determination darkening his features. Even Scrabble, our ever-vigilant sheep dog, would abandon his horse-herding duties and slink off into the kitchen.

Perhaps if we'd got the BGM after Adam had attended Insight, he might have found himself reacting differently. I was certainly surprised when he came back from his first seminar eager to tell me about an "amusing" parking incident. This involved a ticket, clamping, towing, and a release fee, totalling around £200, but he was completely serene in the face of this extortion and keen to explain about the learning he had experienced as a result. It was something to do with having the choice about how you respond in any given situation. I hoped some of the learning would help him to focus more around noticing parking restrictions in future. Anyway, before his seminar, in his outlook towards the lorry he was not in a place to see its refusal to go anywhere as an opportunity for "learning, upliftment, and growth". In fact, even attempts to point out how his frustrations with the lorry might be similar to an owner's frustration with their reluctant loader were unwelcome. Their horses had many legitimate reasons to be unhappy with loading. The lorry, according to him, was just being bolshy and stubborn. It was clearly 'taking the Mickey'.

So one day as Adam was heading outside to take the lorry to an appointment, I made myself scarce. I was just settling down to some accounts when I heard the usual curses coming from the car park, accompanied by an unpromising whirring of the Big Green Monster's starter motor. After a few minutes the swearing abated and Adam stomped into the house muttering expletives and something about "not messing around this time." Moments later he was on the phone to John, our trusty local mechanic, describing how yet again the Monster had let him down, wasn't starting, and that he'd tried *everything* he could think of. John kindly agreed to come out, and arrived within ten minutes. I went out to see what he thought the problem was. John tried the ignition, and was also greeted by the sound of an engine turning over but seemingly not catching. He was just about to have a look under the bonnet when he noticed something. "What's that flashing red light on the dashboard?" he asked.

Adam's face drained white and then flushed red as he mumbled, "Ah. That'll be the immobiliser. Perhaps that's the problem then?"

I don't know why we ever even bothered putting the immobiliser on. If anyone had actually succeeded in stealing the lorry, we would have been overjoyed. The worry would have been that they might have brought it back again once they realised it was so untrustworthy. Perhaps it's just that it was about the only thing on the lorry that actually worked reliably; any other part of the Monster, as Adam put it, was inclined to "Go Microsoft".

He turned the immobiliser off, and turned the key in the ignition. The Big Green Monster, as if deliberately to add to Adam's embarrassment, roared confidently into life. As the engine settled down to a healthy sounding purr, Adam slunk off to find a bottle of whisky for John, for his trouble, since he would accept no payment for his extraordinary mechanical skills. Perhaps Adam was hoping that, if he got blind drunk, John might forget about the whole incident. Somehow this episode did nothing to endear the lorry to Adam, and shortly afterwards we sold it. Not just to anyone, though - I think he wanted to make sure it went a very long way away, and in fact it was sold for a measly sum to someone who was planning to take it to Africa. Perhaps skilled African mechanics could keep it on the road, and it would certainly prefer the weather.

We were surprised, therefore, to be contacted a couple of years later by someone enquiring about our past involvement with a green horsebox with a registration number that sounded very familiar. It was an individual who was interested in buying it but something fishy was going on. Apparently, it was registered as scrapped but was now being driven around Ireland. Needless to say, Adam gave the prospective purchaser some explicit and heartfelt advice about how much happiness it was likely to bring.

In time, we found ourselves a much more suitable arrangement, borrowing a lorry from a livery client. Sadly, we never managed to secure a livery client with a really posh lorry, but I guess we would have been worried about borrowing one of those. Instead, on this occasion, we had use of an old Mercedes - very reliable, if somewhat slow. It made attending clinics so much easier, and it was very reassuring to have transport on site should a horse need to go to the vets in an emergency. Best of all, any breakdowns or failures to start were not our problem, and we were doing the owner a favour too, as the occasional long trip was helpful in keeping the lorry running well.

Adam had a prior commitment on the day of the school trip, and although he would have loved to come along, he felt duty bound to honour it, so it was just going to be the two ponies and me. Learning from my previous mistake, I remembered to wash and whiten Misty's otherwise nicotine yellow tail, and to comb out her beautiful mane. Nothing could be done to improve Finn's appearance, however. Unlike Misty, he never rolls in the mud, and he has fantastic colouring, particularly on his mane, where his highlights would cost a fortune if he had to have them done professionally. We were soon ready to load up.

Luckily, we had a space in the diary the day before the trip, so we had been able to do some loading practise with the ponies, neither of whom had been in a lorry, or a trailer, or gone further away from Moor Wood than they could travel on their own feet, since their arrival several years previously. I wasn't too worried about loading them to come home again - Monty, Kelly and her assistant tutor Linda would all the there, so if between us we couldn't get them in, we would all have to seriously reconsider our professions. It didn't seem worth trying to turn them into seasoned travellers in a couple of days, since that isn't at all what they were, and I wasn't worried about Monty being unimpressed if they were reluctant to go back in, as he knew that they were being called upon to do something that for them was quite out of the ordinary. So the day before their Grand Day Out, I loaded them both up and just took them for a short ride, taking the opportunity to refuel the lorry, and left it at that.

On the day, Misty and Finn, looking particularly glamourous, loaded into the lorry like pros, and proceeded to munch their hay nets calmly throughout the entire journey. The school is in Solihull, Birmingham, and by some miracle, I found it easily and parked up temporarily on the road outside the school gates, until Monty and Kelly arrived. Monty guided us expertly through to the playground at the back - pointing out low cables and turns that needed to be made wide, in a way that most people just wouldn't think of. The ponies both neighed when they arrived, and looked interested as the ramp came down, but otherwise were perfectly happy to stay where they were - which was just as well. It was nearly break time, and within five minutes the playground was swarming with excited children, who seemed particularly delighted to find a couple of ponies in a lorry at their school.

Children were soon climbing on the ramp to get a better look, but those playing with footballs, as soon as they were asked, kept a respectful distance, for which I was immensely grateful - I couldn't imagine that Misty and Finn would cope with the noise of one of those thudding against the sides of the lorry. The ponies just kept munching their hay, taking the occasional slurp from the water buckets I put down for them, as if absolutely nothing was out of the ordinary from their usual routine of hanging out at Moor Wood.

They were coping so well, that when the break was over, we closed up the ramp and went off for a short assembly in which the Deputy and the Head and Monty all talked to the kids, who sat on the floor with rapt attention. It was hard to believe this was a school in which indiscipline and disrespect had been so rife just a few years previously that the government's education watchdog had been on the brink of having it shut down. The same children who had previously been known for their bad behaviour, were now so obviously proud of themselves and the institution they were part of. Whilst they were singing a couple of songs to finish off their assembly, Linda and I went to unload the ponies and lead them around a bit, before the students all came out, class by class, to meet them.

The children lined up in single file queues, and Misty and Finn received them like the hosts of a wedding party. As the children had been given strict instructions not to go behind the ponies, or even to approach them from the side, Misty and Finn never felt crowded and hemmed in, and aside from Misty's aversion to small hands appearing too suddenly in her face, they rather seemed to enjoy their celebrity status. They stood incredibly patiently, meeting and greeting literally hundreds of pupils. I think they thought that such recognition of their greatness was well overdue. For the kids, it was clearly a real treat to come so close to such majestic animals. Many of them could hardly contain themselves and their enthusiasm made it all the more clear just how positive the presence of horses can be in one's life, even in such a brief encounter. It's so much more meaningful than that staple diet of TV and Playstation.

When every single last child had said hello, with a few of the keener ones even sneaking around to the back of the queue for another go, Misty and Finn hopped back into the lorry and resumed munching their hay nets. I'm not quite sure exactly why, but the lorry had to be moved, and so I took it around to the car park to get it out of the way before grabbing a quick bite to eat in the canteen.

I was in two minds about staying for lunch. The ponies had behaved so brilliantly it seemed a bit unfair not to take them straight home. On the other hand, it's always nice, and rare, to get a chance to sit down with Monty and Kelly. What really swung it for me was realising that I was suddenly starving, and literally shaking with low blood sugar. It didn't seem sensible to attempt the long journey home in such a light-headed state, so I gratefully accepted the offer of lunch in the school canteen and set about moving the ponies.

The car park was fairly small and crowded, but there was a perfect spot for the lorry, alongside a pavement, just big enough for us. There were about three cars parked behind it, on a slight incline, and all I had to do was to manoeuvre the lorry around a bit of a corner and back it into place. Although I didn't have anyone helping me, I got it in pretty well on the first attempt. I don't know what perfectionist streak in me decided it could do with being a little closer to the kerb, but having hopped out to have a look, I decided to tidy up my parking a little bit. There wasn't much room, though, and I'm not especially skilled at parking a car, never mind a lorry, so not surprisingly the second attempt was hardly an improvement on the first. I got back into the lorry, and tried again. Getting out once more to have a look, I could see I was getting closer, and gave it what I hoped was one last try. I put on the hand brake again, and jumped out to check my progress. I was greeted by the heart-stopping sight of the lorry rolling towards the cars behind it. Perhaps it was more of a hill than I had thought, because the door slammed shut as the momentum picked up. Trying to stay as calm as I possibly could, I wrenched open the door with trembling hands, and leapt into the cab, slamming on the brakes and hauling on the handbrake. I managed to force the lorry to an abrupt stop, and was greeted with a stamping of feet as Misty and Finn rebalanced themselves after this uncharacteristically un-smooth driving. Misty even gave an indignant neigh. I turned the engine off, left the lorry in gear, and went to check on them. They were already back to eating their hay, so I walked around to the back of the lorry to see how close I had come to a collision. There was less than an inch between me and the car behind. Feeling decidedly shaky, I turned the engine back on, and pulled the lorry forward again, before turning it off, leaving it in gear and heaving as hard as I could on the handbrake, for good measure. Now I definitely needed lunch.

At this point in time, it had been nearly 18 months since we had lost PJ, and although we had been trying for a while, we were still not pregnant and had begun fertility investigations. I think I was hoping that a visit to what had once been a failing junior school would make the prospect of remaining childless easier to bear, and that I might even be able to see my situation, as I had many for years previously, as "child-free". But nothing of the sort. Even in the canteen, which was not exactly fine dining, I saw nothing but polite if occasionally boisterous behaviour, and was charmed as each child carefully put their dinner tray away and cleared up their things before the dinner staff stacked all the tables and chairs away. Of course, there was careful supervision, and occasional reminders about the agreed appropriate behaviour were needed, but it was clear that there was an air of co-operation and respect that wasn't just put on to impress Monty. I even felt optimistic that if we were lucky enough to have a child, we might be able to find an acceptable school where s/he could be nurtured and cherished, rather than processed. All in all, it was quite an uplifting day.

Misty and Finn travelled home beautifully and I didn't have any more adventures with the lorry, arriving back just as dusk was settling. The surreal beauty of Moor Wood seemed more appealing than ever, and all the more special for the contrast with the urban environment I had just come from. Thanking them for being such wonderful companions, I let the ponies out to the field and they cantered off excitedly to join the herd and, I liked to imagine, to tell the others of their great adventure. In the fading light I could just see Misty finding the muddiest corner of the field to restore her colour to the usual brown.

TWENTY ONE

Making Common Sense Common Practice
(Adam)

'Hand without legs, legs without hand.'
Attr. François Baucher

For a long time after I became a professional trainer, I was put off doing anything which could be described as dressage. Indeed, I hardly thought of myself as a professional horseman at all. Although I had started many youngsters, and worked with severe remedial cases suffering from a huge variety of problems, I had never taught a horse to do the high school movements, so I couldn't argue against the prevailing methods from a position of authority. I just felt an instinctive disquiet about the competitive world, but especially so of dressage. Now, fifteen years into my career and with at least a thousand horses under my belt, I'm in a much better position to have an opinion. Given that I know much more about horses, you might expect that I'd have changed my mind and accepted the rationale behind much of what's done. It seemed to me back then as if many of these riders were imposing indignities on the horse, strapping its mouth shut with a tight dropped noseband, kicking almost continually with spurs and forcing submission into a posture that is described as classical, relaxed and correct. I now know that it is neither classical, nor relaxed, nor in the least necessary to ride like that. Whether or not it's correct is a subjective judgement.

If anything, I feel more strongly than ever that horses and their admirers are being badly let down by the teaching establishment, and that there are very few horses being trained for competition who are not ridden in a way which is restrictive, forceful, illogical and uncomfortable. This is as true or even more so for horses in advanced competitive dressage. So it was like a breath of fresh air to meet Craig. He has trained many horses to upper levels, but his description of modern riding made me burst into laughter, tinged with sadness that it should be so. "This is dressage!" he said, putting his chin right down on his chest, mimicking a horse trotting. Speaking as if he were the horse, although hardly able to draw breath in this stifling posture, he added, "This sucks!"

I suppose the first time I noticed a discrepancy between received wisdom and what I think is the truth, was when Sensi was becoming a bit more developed and Nicole said it was time to start riding her "properly". We'd been told we shouldn't have reins like "washing lines", and to keep up a contact. Sensi made it really clear that pulling her head down in an attempt to bring her 'onto the bit', wasn't working for her, and she hated being continually kicked. It didn't make her easier to ride and it undermined the understanding she had of the aids. I don't think it had any beneficial effect, such as allowing her back to come up and carry our weight better, as is so widely believed. In fact, I reckon it confused her even more than me, and made her resentful.

In the photo section in the middle of this book, there is a great picture of Monty riding a horse in a sliding stop, with reins so loose you wouldn't be able to hang your washing on them, because your clothes would be on the floor! His horse is so well engaged behind that he is almost sitting like a dog, going from a full gallop to a complete halt. Interestingly, the horse's poll is the highest point, a feature consistently advocated in classical manuals, and also very much visible in four pictures of Monty performing championship-winning sliding stops with different horses in another of his books, *The Horses in My Life*.[3] It's also clear that Monty's legs are not doing anything to collect the horse and engage his hind legs. His feet are well forward in the stirrups and a long way from the horse's flanks. He's doing this partly as a signal, but also as a means to stay

---

[3] The sliding stop, initiated by the hind legs, with a raised poll, may, depending on how much traction is produced by the surface the horse is on, involve the front legs walking forward, accompanied by a lowering of the head as his momentum takes some time to slow in this extreme form of halt - all the more reason to allow freedom of movement to the head.

on, without getting impaled on the pommel, because the horse is going from full speed to halt in one stride. But surely these cowboys are wrong. After all, it's the rider who collects the horse, isn't it?

In May 2004 Cavallo magazine published the results of a very interesting experiment. A Western rider (Grisha Ludwig, who has studied with Monty) was compared objectively with some dressage riders, using an electronic sensor that measured and recorded the amount of tension in the reins. The Western rider used a snaffle bit with no noseband and achieved his halt from canter by applying a pressure of 2.7 kg per rein, once. As most classical texts would have him do, the rider has lifted his hands and the horse's poll is moderately open, and distinctly the highest point. His legs, like Monty's, are nowhere near the horse's sides. This, by the way, is a lot more pressure than we have seen Monty use himself, because we've seen him ride in demonstrations with a very fragile fishing leader attached between the rein and the bit, which would break if anything more than a few ounces of pressure was put on it.

The dressage riders, who used snaffle bits but with dropped nosebands that were as tight as possible, used repeated "half" halts varying from 8 to 10 kilos in weight per rein, before they stopped their horses by pulling with between 10 and 12.5 kg per rein. In other words, instead of a single pressure of 5.4 kg on the corners of the horse's mouth, as the Western rider used, these riders were exerting pressures of 16 to 20 kg multiple times without even stopping. Additionally, due to the significantly lower height at which the hands were held, the pressure used by the dressage riders was applied to the tongue and bars of the horses' mouths. To stop, the heaviest rider used 25 kilos of weight, almost five times more than the Western rider. That's about as much as I can carry, more than the baggage allowance on a typical passenger airline. Imagine repeatedly lifting a sack of feed on the gums of your mouth via a thin metal rod. It can't be good for the horse.

Something is rotten in the state of Denmark. Can it be correct that so many horses have marks on their flanks, where all the fur has been rubbed off, grooves in their noses where the bone has been dented by tight nose bands, and dead nerves and bone spurs in their mouths where bits have destroyed the sensory function? But at least they know to keep their noses (behind) vertical at all times! They are moving in a 'correct' outline! It's bad for their backs otherwise!

So what about 'collection', balance, the famous 'engagement' of the hind quarters which the rider must do to stop the horse from hollowing his back? In popular European dressage wisdom, this is achieved by keeping the horse's nose on the vertical by means of continuous contact, and pushing him forward from the leg into the bit.

Let's start at the beginning, without a rider. Collection (if defined as the action of bringing the front and back feet closer together) is something the horse does naturally whenever it is in danger. But in bringing its feet together, resembling an elephant on a drum, it becomes less stable, not more balanced. It does this, whether consciously or not, when it, or a member of the herd, has smelled or heard a predator but does not know where the danger is coming from. It's not the time to take a position like it does to have a pee, and put its hind legs out half a mile behind it, although in this position it is very stable indeed. It might, at any moment, have to leap forward, or rear and spin to either side.

The horse at rest relaxes all the muscles in its neck, dropping its head down on the nuchal ligament, which supports the neck in a roughly horizontal position. For the horse to graze, it does not relax, but actually pulls its head downwards. This additional weighting of the forehand, which the natural horse does most of the day, accounts for the fact that the horse's forelegs are structured exactly like a pillar, which is useful to hold weight. But the hind legs are built like springs. They aren't good for holding up weight because it costs the horse calories to hold weight on them; he has to use his muscles to do so, just like you do if you stand with your knees bent. But like a spring, there is more potential energy when the spring is compressed. Putting the hind legs under him weights the spring and will therefore give the horse a better start if a lion does leap out of the bushes. But if we think of this picture, there is something else blindingly obvious about how the horse moves in this crucial situation. The horse was grazing, head down, then he smelled a lion. His head goes right up, as far as it possibly can, making his poll the highest point. It is also open; his chin is not on his throat. This is the natural posture of collection/engagement. Should it be significantly different when he has a rider on his back?

I'd never really thought much about this, nor what dressage aspires to be, until the day that Major met Joe. Major is a shire cross thoroughbred, so not the most light-footed horse I've ever come across. He was bumbling around in his field the way he usually does, until Joe, the big ex-racehorse whose sad tale is described in *Whispering Back*, was put in with him and his mates. All of a sudden Major disappeared, to be replaced by the most magnificent horse I had ever seen. He picked his head up and produced the most astounding transformation. His poll was right up, so much so that his neck was almost vertical. His nose was pointing out. He was showing off, trying to impress, but he was also putting himself into an optimal position to move out of the way fast if he needed to. The movements he and Joe produced as they met included passage (a very elevated trot with suspension between the strides); pesade (or rearing), which by definition requires the weight to be on the hind legs; canter pirouettes; halt to canter and canter to halt transitions, and striking with the forelegs (not a million miles from being a Spanish walk). All these were performed with flamboyance and, although it clearly took a lot of calories, and would not have looked useful to anyone who wanted to use these horses to get a herd of cattle across the midwest to a railhead, they made it look easy.

I was struck simultaneously with the thought of how incredible it must feel to ride a horse working like that, and with the knowledge that I had never produced anything like that degree of brilliance in any horse I had ever ridden. Not only that, but I had never seen any rider get near it either. At the time, I had not noticed that the things I was seeing Major do - elevation, collection, impulsion - are made so much harder when the horse is in a state of physical and mental bondage, so that even the fittest, strongest, most perfectly conformed horses can't do it as well as Major, pot-bellied with grass and unfit though he was. And I was not aware that the world of official dressage, which pays lip service to the classical masters, does not actually practise what they preached. If you don't believe me, find me a picture of a modern dressage rider whose horse has his poll at the highest point, as the manual tells you it should. Many horses are trained to keep their poll no higher than their withers, making their poll the lowest point of their neck. The FEI (Fédération Equestre Internationale), which make the rules of competitive dressage, might say overbending is not desirable. As the manual states, "The head should remain in a steady position, as a rule slightly in front of the vertical, with a supple poll as the highest point of the neck, and no resistance should be offered to the athlete." (By "athlete" the manual refers to the rider! I'd be in agreement if they said no resistance should be offered to the real athlete - the horse!)

The fact is, although this statement ("The head...should remain slightly in front of the vertical") could not be clearer, overbent horses (with the head behind vertical) are not only accepted in competition, but overbending is promoted. Although they are breaking the FEI's own rules, overbent horses are often scored very highly, frequently - one might argue always - above the horse with a raised poll and a nose in front of the vertical. But if the FEI itself is not going to defend the horse against those who contradict their own ideals, who will? We should remember what the FEI was, in its own words, founded to do:

The FEI instituted an International Dressage Event in 1929 in order to preserve the Equestrian Art from the abuses to which it can be exposed and to preserve it in the purity of its principles, so that it could be handed on intact to generations of athletes to come.

It seems to me that in many ways, competitive dressage is producing the opposite effect to what was intended. I can certainly understand the idea that to ride with spurs and a double bridle gives the rider tools so powerful that it is a mark of their skill that they can ride without upsetting the horse. This is a legitimate justification for the compulsory use of FEI-approved equipment. But if a rider could produce the movements that are desired, to the standard required, using a head collar or for that matter without any reins, surely that would be a desirable achievement? Unfortunately, you would be disqualified, even though the rules talk about 'achieving perfect understanding with the rider' and the horse giving 'the impression of doing, of its own accord, what is required' - something that is hard to square with the image I have of a horse moving at liberty, because he won't have his nose vertical, let alone on his chest.

Western riding is coming from a completely different tradition (cattle herding as opposed to combat), and practises movements (such as spins) that are not described in "classical" dressage. Yet it seems to me in many ways closer to classical principles than modern dressage is. True classical work focuses on lightness, and the Cavallo magazine experiment is just one example that proves Western riding cultivates greater lightness than modern dressage does. Lightness is impossible without eliminating conflicting aids, as Western as well as classical masters propose. For example, the classical master Baucher advocated "Hands without legs, legs without hands", which is certainly closer to Western riding than modern European dressage. As for 'natural horsemanship', if there is any such thing, it seems the natural movement of the horse was the real inspiration for the most important classical authority, the Frenchman de la Guérinière, author of 'Ecole de Cavalerie' (1733). Interestingly, he did not advocate fixed hands, crank nosebands or training aids like side reins, and he often advocated the raising of the horse's head and neck, just as a horse does when it comes into collection ready to flee a predator. He also clearly describes inwards use of the outside rein to turn, just like neck reining which is so closely associated with Western riding.

It won't come as a surprise to those who have read this far, that the way we ride and coach others to ride avoids some of the most obvious contradictions that are found in many riding manuals. From the start, we have been teaching people not to use their legs when slowing the horse down, halting and reining back; and not to apply pressure with the hand when you are asking him to go forward.

But what does a horse prefer, you might ask? And what if the horse in question has had years of being taught differently? It seems reasonable to assume that any horse would prefer light signals delivered quietly and one at a time. One thing that modern horsemen are unquestionably brilliant at is breeding and selecting horses with appropriate characteristics for the work they want them to do. It's my belief that some horses appear able to cope with more forceful riding because they are so incredibly well-bred and perfectly conformed, selected by breeders for their particularly malleable temperament. It still doesn't make it right. The backup of professional equine masseurs and chiropractors enables them to stay sound. A more average horse would probably break down and be of no competitive usefulness very quickly.

We have often found ourselves asked to pick up the pieces after a horse has been physically or mentally trashed, or both. One such horse is Asterix, and his story is interesting to me on many levels.

I was originally called by his owner to help sort out his napping, which sounded fairly pathological. Even in company, he couldn't be ridden out of the driveway. His standard way to express his negative feelings was to rear. But in the school he was a real gent. He would jump anything and, being a nice-looking ten-year-old Belgian warmblood, he had the pedigree to move with a great deal of panache. No problems there.

The day before I was due to go down to meet him, I was shocked to hear my client had decided to have him slaughtered. She told me her husband, who actually owned Asterix, but who was away working abroad most of the time, had decided he didn't want to have to deal with his behaviour any more. Evidently he did not have faith in my capacity to change things. Given how dangerous Asterix was when he 'lost it', they had decided not to risk someone else's health by trying to sell him, and as they also could not guarantee that he would not then be sold on to someone unsuitable, they had decided the best thing would be to have him put down.

I could hardly believe my ears, because apart from being a bit nippy about his girth being done up, he was not problematic in any other context except hacking out. I fully agree that there are some fates worse than death, and that for a horse to be passed from pillar to post in an ever declining spiral would be horrendous. I think sometimes it is the more responsible decision to have a dangerous horse put down rather than passing them on to someone else and hoping that it all works out - at least, it is if you've actually tried to get help from a competent trainer to see if the problem can be worked out. But this horse was not dangerous except in the most specific of circumstances. They were killing him simply because he was not "fit for purpose". I found it hard to justify such precipitous action, especially when I was prepared to guarantee that I could provide solutions for them. Furthermore, the property he lived at was large and plush, with quite a lot of land, and a very nice school. I guess the money which could have been used to retrain or keep him in grass for the rest of his days had all been spent on the school, or the expensive cars in the driveway. All this was particularly hard to swallow, because sitting on our dresser at home was a little jar containing a few grams of ashes, which we were due to take to Maui in one week's time.

I made an offer to go and see him anyway and save his life if I thought I could, and then, thinking further about it, I gave Jo a call. By this stage she and Derek had made a massive life change. They had rented a house and small yard not far from us, where there was an indoor school, and had begun to move towards becoming professional horsemen. Derek was still coaching Oxford, who had gone on to win the Boat Race with almost monotonous regularity. But he had also been learning a lot with Craig and had bought his own horse. Craig was now visiting the UK regularly, staying with Jo and Derek who were hosting his clinics in this country. As well as supplementing their income by computer programming, Jo had been busy learning as much about feet as possible, and had become one of Gloucestershire's first Applied Equine Podiatrists. They were keen to have access to more horses to improve their skills and it seemed to me that if I couldn't find a place for Asterix at Moor Wood, they might be interested.

Jo, typically, was distraught at the idea that this horse would be killed for behaving exactly as Perry might have done in his previous porcine incarnation. So we made the trip down to meet Asterix together. On the way, we talked a bit about what we might offer if he were not a complete basket case. It was clear that the owner was not an unfeeling person, for she had spent a huge amount of money on vet's bills, repairing a severe injury he had suffered. Another horse had attacked him as he was going through a gateway and he had been impaled on a protruding gate-hook, which had ripped a huge hole in his shoulder and flank as he ran away. The bill had come to several thousand pounds, and he had supposedly made a good recovery, but it remained to be seen whether the damage to his shoulder was such that taking him on would be crazy. I wanted to see whether the owner's version of 'safe to ride in the school' was the same as mine. His feet also had to be assessed.

Jo sounded very keen. "Well, if he's OK, I suppose we should offer her something, even if it isn't much. I was thinking a thousand pounds, he must be worth at least that."

I surveyed Jo's face as I considered her suggestion. "No." I paused, more to collect my thoughts than for emphasis.

"The most I'm prepared to pay for him is one pound. If she's prepared to kill him just to get the meat money, then let her live with that. If one of us takes him on, by the time he's had a single trim, he'll have begun to cost us money neither of us has to spare. We're not running a rescue centre or a charity. It'll require hard work to keep him." Jo was shocked, and so was I, to see how hard a bargain I was prepared to drive. We agreed that I should do the talking when it came to the negotiations.

We arrived at the house, and were greeted by a very attractive, cordial lady. She took us to meet Asterix, and both Jo and I immediately liked him. His big, bright eyes and smiley, engaging disposition made it doubly hard to accept that he was booked in to be turned into cat food the day after tomorrow. A chestnut with a big white blaze running down his nose, he was a sturdy horse with a solid look about him, sixteen hands in height. If I hadn't seen so many lovely horses displaying a huge range of severe behavioural problems, it would have been almost impossible to believe that a horse with such a pleasant temperament could behave the way she had described.

She tacked him up, which he allowed her to do, although he did make a small move to nip her as she did up the girth. Explaining that he had got a lot better about that since he had been bought a new saddle, she took him out to the arena, where a number of jumps had been set up. She duly rode him, not inelegantly, but in what I would say was a conventional fashion. Fiddling with her hands, she continually squeezed his sides with her legs, for example each time she sat when doing rising trot. He duly 'came round'; in other words, he put his head down until it was almost between his knees. It was clear he had a willingness about him and that he was good-natured enough to accept this was the way she wanted him to go. In spite of the obvious contradiction between her hand and leg, he worked out what she wanted, and halted, trotted and cantered upon her request. She popped him over the fences a couple of times, and I was convinced straight away that this was a horse who certainly did not deserve to die and who could be of use to someone. He was big, and capable of carrying a reasonable weight, although his hocks did not flex well, which would make him of limited use as a weight carrier. Too many years of too much jumping with shoes on had made a mess of those joints, and stiffness or arthritis had already begun to set in.

We took him back to his stable and his future was decided very quickly. I insisted on actually handing over the pound, and on having a receipt. Jo and I left, and his now previous owner agreed to bring him up to Moor Wood the next day.

The first time I rode him, I was immediately struck by the way he "offered a contact." That is to say, he immediately bent his head down and forward, and leaned on my hand in a steady way. He wasn't trying to pull the reins out of my hands, nor to take control; it was obvious that he thought this was the thing to do. I immediately vibrated the reins as if I were shaking a tambourine, and he came up, slackening the rein completely. I then shortened the rein until I could feel the very lightest connection possible. At which he began to lean on the bit again, and the cycle repeated itself.

This was the entire basis of our first ride. It was as if he were saying, "Should I lean on your hand? Just a bit? What about when we walk? What about when we halt?" My answer to all these questions was to vibrate the rein, but he took a lot of convincing. Nicole rode him the next day, and that was the only thing she did as well. A few days later we were off to Hawai'i with PJ for three weeks, so he had some time off, and when we got back, I think he was surprised to find that we still didn't want to have any part in holding his very large head up, but in fact wanted him to be responsible for that.

We began to tackle some of his other issues. Saddling up was made completely non-confrontational with the use of distraction. I bought a molasses-rich salt lick, which came in a tub, and found that Asterix was obsessed by it. When given that to occupy him, he didn't seem to notice the saddle going on or girth being tightened. The only drawback was that the stuff got all over his nose, and then when you put the bit in, it tended to get all over you. Put the bit in first, and the next thing you knew, the bridle leather was all covered in slime and sticky brown molasses, so that wasn't much better. Nowadays, I sometimes just let him loose on the lawn when tacking up.

As usual, we removed his shoes and, as usual, we found that after a period of transition, his feet changed shape and strengthened, becoming capable of carrying us out for hacks cross-country, on the road or gravel tracks. Except that he probably wouldn't allow us to ride him out without rearing. It was time to start work on this issue. I was sure this was related to his early weaning, as Perry's napping had been. It was really separation anxiety.

I was careful to take this training at a pace that would suit him, so I only rode him in the school when the horses were all nearby in the yard. Even so, he spent much of his time fretting about where they were, and trying to get to the part of the school where he could see the yard.

When they were all out in the field, with Asterix mingling in the herd, he had a lot of interesting characteristics. You could catch him with complete ease, although he would always put the head collar in his mouth. Clearly he had been fed treats when the head collar went on. But then, when haltered, he was very easy to lead, as long as I didn't try to take him away from the gang. He would willingly follow me anywhere, until I was about twenty yards out from the edge of the group, when he would plant. With a pressure halter and by use of angles, circling and backing up, I could get him to go further, but he would often throw his head up, and then all of a sudden you could see the side of him that had brought him so close to the knacker. His normal exceptionally placid demeanour could flip when his adrenaline came up, and there was nothing valuable to be gained from continuing to work after that, until his calm had been restored.

So I worked on improving his leading, and getting him over his separation anxiety at the same time. I would take him out of the group, but before he got to the stage where he began to worry, I would turn around and lead him back into the middle of the herd. Then I'd do it again, just asking for a little bit more. In the early days, I took him back into the group before I let him go, so he wouldn't have a surge of adrenaline as I left, and go charging back. After a while, he was able to cope with it really well. I could take him out of the group, and let him go, and as long as he was not miles away from the others, he would simply graze where I left him, a useful indicator of his progress.

Within a few weeks it was easy to bring him in from the winter field, which is several hundred metres from the yard, by himself without incident. He could even be led in company with another horse around the village, a critical opportunity to condition his feet and strengthen their walls by walking him on smooth tarmac.

I had by then ridden him in the school numerous times, and done a lot of work on his rein-back, which was something he had never done before. Tamsin, our working pupil, and I had led him out with Amber, the reformed nightmare Arab described in *Whispering Back* who has now become so reliable that she can be used as a schoolmistress for a horse like Asterix. He was familiar with the route I chose, which went across the set aside fields seen in the background of the cover photo, and meant we wouldn't encounter any traffic.

So on a day with suitable weather, Tamsin tacked up Amber and I got Asterix ready, carefully wiping the molasses off his face with a towel before I put his bit in. As usual I did not put a nose-band on, not even a cavesson, but I left a head collar on under the bridle, and took reins with clips on the ends, providing me with a ten-foot lead rope if I decided the best option was to dismount and lead him. Tamsin took a mobile phone and I emptied my pockets in case of a fall. We led the horses down the first bit of the bridleway, because it is steep and particularly stony. A short distance later, we mounted and as Tamsin and Amber moved off, I turned Asterix to follow, which he willingly did.

For several hundred metres we lounged along in a most relaxed fashion. I was really enjoying my ride, and it looked like Asterix was too. When we turned the corner of the wood, putting the yard and all the other horses out of sight, I was expecting to feel his adrenaline rise, but could not notice any change in him. A hundred metres on, we crossed some water, and a really boggy patch, again with no difficulty. I began to think that I had driven too hard a bargain over Asterix. He didn't really have too big an issue, he just required his needs to be taken into consideration a bit more, and not to be beaten with a whip, as his previous owner had witnessed before she bought him. If she had only done the gradual and progressive foundation groundwork that I had put in place, I reflected, he would not have reared with them and they would never have felt the need to sell, let alone shoot, him. As if to confound my hypothesis, he suddenly stopped and reared.

When he came back to the ground, I quietly stroked his mane and took a few deep breaths, trying to keep my adrenaline down. I called to Tamsin, riding ahead on Amber, and asked her to wait for us, but Asterix reared again and turned towards home. I gently picked up the rein to indicate that I wanted him to look at Amber, and go to follow her, but he reared again and again. Looking to guide him on without any hint of forcing him with my legs, I opened a rein to invite him to step forwards, but not directly away from the yard. He turned for home and before I had even closed one hand to turn him away he was already going up once more. Although I did not hold his mouth, kick him, get remotely angry or try to force him forward in any way, and wasn't even carrying a stick, he repeatedly reared.

I asked Tamsin to bring Amber back, but this seemed to make no difference at all. Trying to get him to hook up with her, I asked Tamsin to circle us, and Amber, seemingly oblivious to the stress eating up her companion, did exactly as she was asked. Asterix, after another brief protest, followed her as she circled a couple of times, and it looked as though we were getting somewhere, but when Amber then went off down the track again, he went back to rearing. Amber came back but by now Asterix was in such a state, his flanks heaving with the effort of his antics, his mouth gripping the bit, that I didn't really expect him to follow, and indeed he did not. Instead he reared another dozen times or so. He was so experienced and proficient at 'standing up' that it felt comparatively safe to stay on him. He meant it, it wasn't a half-hearted protest, but he knew how high he could go without losing his balance and it felt most unlikely that he would fall over backwards. All the same, he was not a happy bunny, and neither was I. It was time for another approach.

Taking a light touch on the rein, and turning him towards home, with my legs relaxed by his sides, I brought my hands up and back, asking him to reverse. He wasn't expecting this, and when he stepped back, after a momentary release of the rein, I asked again. We backed up about thirty feet along the track towards Amber, and when we got to her, since we were by now well past the place where he had got stuck, I turned him back in the direction of travel. He immediately stopped, although Amber continued walking away. Within a moment he was rearing, so I simply turned him round, and backed him up again.

We went backwards for about a quarter of a mile before I could detect him making an effort to turn and follow Amber. I have no idea what she was thinking about her new stable mate, and why he had such an unusual way of going. But every time he stopped, he would meet the contact of the bit, which would only release when he moved backwards. To remain comfortable in his mouth he had to keep moving his feet. Leaving some slack in the reins, I bridged them, holding each one in both hands across his neck, so that when he threw his head down in an attempt to evade, I didn't have to try to hold against a horse who has far more muscle in his neck than I do in my whole body, let alone my puny arms. But every time he stepped backwards, he met a release of pressure of the bit.

Still in reverse, we crossed an open field (the one shown in the middle background of the cover photo) and got to the bottom of a dip leading to the last, steep field. Suddenly, he reared and, as he did so, performed a fine pirouette, turning to face the same direction as Amber. He then settled down to walking the whole of the rest of the hack without incident. He has never reared with me since.

The most interesting thing about his story, though, was yet to come. Although I am sure he would be much happier if he were consistently ridden by one person, and preferably in an indoor school because he really hates flies, nevertheless, to pay for his keep he is one of the horses we use for clinics. It's not ideal, but I think it's preferable from his point of view to being in a can, or quietly growing old, fatter and stiff, and *some* of the horses we look after have to earn their grass! So the next summer, I began to let relatively experienced riders use him, and for the first couple of clinics, he coped pretty well. Then he met a young rider who I will call Michelle.

Michelle was only sixteen, but she had been riding for many years. Although English, she was living with her parents in France, and instead of a regular school, had been attending a riding academy for some time. Given that I had been so impressed by what I think of as French classical riding, I was delighted to have her come on a clinic. It could only benefit Asterix to be ridden well. He was sure to improve. I was a little less sure that Michelle would get as much out of the clinic, because I expected her to have such excellent instructors at the academy, from whom I could have learned a thing or two as well.

So when she mounted, and immediately began to kick persistently, whilst maintaining a low, fixed hand and short, tight reins, I was pretty dumbfounded. Clearly the French have suffered, at least to some extent, the same disconnection from classical principles as the English have. At any rate, the way she was riding was exactly the same as one typically comes across in this country, and whatever I said, she did not find it easy either to stop cramming her boots into his side on every step, nor to stop pulling him constantly in an attempt to force him into 'an outline', 'onto the bit', or whatever you wish to call it. It was exactly the kind of thing Asterix had been so used to before I met him. But now, to my surprise, he attempted to free himself from this bondage; he threw his head down, snatched at the rein, stopped frequently, backed up, and occasionally appeared to acquiesce, or perhaps the word would be 'submit', by overbending and putting his chin between his knees. I could tell he was not delighted to be ridden this way again.

I tried to be as tactful as I could, because Michelle was so young, and also because I'd try to be tactful with anybody, but also because she genuinely seemed to be here to try to change. At least, she gave the impression of listening very intently to everything I had to say. I could not fault her commitment to the welfare of horses nor her love of them. She made all the right noises, just like the theory sections of most manuals do. It was just that the actions she took, like those of so many competitive riders, were completely at odds with the theory, or with her core values - respect for the horse while pursuing the achievement of light and responsive co-operation in a communicative athletic partnership. Searching for something positive to build on, knowing that I needed to keep her from feeling I was down on her, I complimented her on how well she was handling the emotional side of this situation. Indeed, she gave no hint of being stressed herself. But, whatever the theory says about the horse being a mirror, and that if you keep yourself calm he will come and join you in that state, he was getting more and more worked up. In fact, I wish she had got more stressed. It might have helped her notice how unhappy the horse was becoming. Remaining like a beacon of serenity atop a frustrated horse, it was as though she were deliberately ignoring how he was feeling. Her lack of empathy was only making it worse.

Asterix got more and more emotional and then, to my surprise, he reared. Since the day of our first hack, I had not seen him do so except very occasionally when playing with his mates in the field. He had never reared in the school. I endeavoured to point out to her how he was trying to do what she wanted, but couldn't work out what to do because her hands were contradicting her legs so profoundly. But I could not find the right words to get her to change her habits. Fortunately, Asterix only had to rear one more time, before I finally got it through to her, though not as bluntly as this: I don't care how important you think it is to get the horse's nose vertical. He has to understand what you want, and pulling and kicking at the same time serves only to confuse, handicap and irritate this horse, at the same time as dulling his response to both the hand and the leg.

What is most interesting to me is that this was a horse who only a few months earlier had been routinely ridden in this fashion, and who had accepted it without appearing to be upset. On my first ride, he had seemed content to spend the whole time overbent, leaning on my hand in the way Michelle was now asking him to do. His flanks had been rubbed by the boots of his owner so much that he had bald patches on both sides. For just a few dozen rides, he had been shown a different way - hand without legs, or legs without hand, and both as gentle and brief as possible, with the emphasis on letting him feel free. I believe the reaction he had to being ridden the old way is testament to how profoundly wrong it is.

Many horses submit to the authority of this method. Some do not. I believe no horse performs to the best of his ability under these confusing restraints, although many do work out what is being asked of them and do their best to produce it. Those horses who accept it are labelled as having the best temperaments, when it could be argued that actually they have the worst, for in their acquiescence they prevent the rider from noticing the errors of this way. Some become dull and withdrawn. Only occasionally will a horse show the rider as clearly as Asterix did that day, that such force is a form of abuse.

TWENTY TWO

Peace On Earth Begins With Birth
(Nicole)

**'We're searching for truth, we're holding the darkness back.
Not making the past the future.'**
Tim Hills / Adam Goodfellow, You Are Not Alone

It seemed to take forever to get pregnant again.

If we had known it would take so long, it would still have been a difficult wait, but not knowing if it would ever happen again was the hardest thing to bear. Time was ticking inexorably away, and I didn't know what to do. We went through some very painful medical investigations that revealed our "secondary subfertility" to be "unexplained". We followed sensible measures to increase our odds (eat well, don't drink much alcohol and, not surprisingly, have lots of sex), but if there was nothing wrong, then why wasn't it happening? Was it me? Did I want it too much, or did I subconsciously not want it at all? Did I need to "get over" PJ first? And if so, how was I meant to do that?

I tried a few things. "Thought Field Therapy" was a technique I had seen work with nervous riders. It involves tapping various points on the body, on the meridians defined by traditional Chinese medicine, whilst thinking about the relevant issues. I found it helped somewhat - after the first session I could see pregnant women and babies without bursting into tears, so that was a helpful start. I had a session of hypnotherapy, which made it really clear to me that I needed more help, and in the end I gave counselling a go. I was embarrassed to need it, although I wouldn't have thought badly of anyone else receiving it. I knew I needed to talk about what had happened with PJ, and my hopes and fears for the future. The thought of being emotional in front of anyone, even a stranger, was excruciating, but Insight had at least given me some practice, and allowed me to recognise these inhibitions for what they were. It seemed to do the trick, because I got pregnant during the counselling (not in an actual session, I hasten to add).

This time when I found out, I was on my own. Adam had gone to see Mark Rashid, popular author and horseman, who was teaching a clinic some distance away, and he had left in the early morning before I was even awake. I had decided against going on this occasion, favouring staying home to "get things done". It was November 11th, Remembrance Day. I knew Adam would observe the two minutes silence, so I rang him with my monumental news while he was still on his way there. I would have preferred to tell him face to face, but the idea of waiting was impossible. I was ecstatic, but the joy I felt was tempered with the sadness of all that loss, suffered by so many people in so many parts of the world. All the soldiers who've died in wars were someone's son, someone's child. Some were even underage when they signed up, very much still children, and some were fathers. The loss to their families must have been terrible. It is truly beyond imagining.

There's a war memorial in the village just down the hill from us, and I can never ride past it without thinking about all those who lost their sons, their fathers, their husbands, their brothers. In the First World War, it was common practice for men from the same area to join the same regiment, so one day of "action" could wipe out almost all of the fit, healthy men in a village. The view across the valley from the memorial can hardly have changed in the years since then. The bereaved must have looked out over the same fields, trying to make sense of such an incomprehensible tragedy. They say a parent's job is to worry. My baby was barely a cluster of cells, and already I was imagining him or her dying fighting a war in Iraq or Afghanistan. Yet, even if this were to be their fate, I knew that I wanted them to come into existence, for however long, and that I would do my best to cherish the time we had together, never knowing when it might end.

There was no reason why we should lose this baby in the way we lost PJ, the doctor said. On the other hand, we could miscarry again for any number of reasons. It was impossible not to dwell obsessively on every twinge I felt. All we could do was wait, and "try not to worry too much". The days passed, slowly, but they still passed without incident, and eventually we got to the twelve-week scan. PJ had met her untimely demise at fifteen weeks, so we were relieved when we got through that and to the twenty-week scan. Finally, we reached the twenty-four-week "might just survive if born now" milestone, and I felt I could relax, and enjoy the last weeks of pregnancy. Except that it suddenly dawned on me that now I'd better start worrying about the birth.

"Oh, you're a rider? Hmmm, you might well find that a real disadvantage when you give birth. All those tight abdominal muscles can really get in the way. You'll be working against yourself when you try to push the baby out. My sister is a keen horsewoman. When she went into labour, Margaret Thatcher was in power. The baby wasn't born until Tony Blair was elected. She completely missed the Major years, although she says it's probably just as well. Of course, the baby was just getting bigger and bigger in there. By the time he eventually came out, he was more or less fully-grown. Had to have a C-section in the end. She puts it all down to the riding. Wishes she'd stopped years before she got pregnant…still, you might be alright…"

Perhaps this is a slight exaggeration of what people said, but the stories of long, drawn-out, complicated and painful births abounded. Everyone seemed to have a horror story, and to relish telling me all about it. The idea that being fit was actually a disadvantage was a popular one, but as I had continued riding and mucking out throughout the pregnancy, there wasn't much I could do about this.

Very early on, before we even got pregnant for the first time, Adam tentatively suggested that although he realised this was a big thing to ask, and that he wouldn't remotely judge me for it if I didn't feel I could go ahead with it, he would love it if I gave birth naturally, without drugs. I remember snorting, and proposing that he should at least be having his legs waxed at the same time: I had images of the wax strips already in place, and me pulling them off with each contraction. It seemed only fair. This was before I'd heard about "back, sack and crack" waxes, obviously; otherwise I'd have been suggesting all of the above being done simultaneously. But much as I thought it was a bit unfair that a labouring woman should have anything less than the very best in pain relief, I also didn't want to drug a little baby before it was even born, and the idea of an epidural (in which drugs are injected directly into the mother's spine to block the pain) just filled me with dread. I know that they are a lot safer than they used to be, but I feel very protective of the integrity of my spine, and the idea of a needle going into it just wasn't appealing to me.

The more I read up on it, the clearer it became that there really wasn't an ideal option for pain relief in labour, and also that women had widely differing birth experiences, from the truly horrible (even leading to post traumatic stress disorder) to the truly joyous, although stories about the latter were extremely rare. I began to wonder if there was anything that could be done to influence the type of birth I would have.

When I miscarried PJ, the pain was outrageous, and nothing really touched it. The morphine I had when I first went into hospital distanced me from the agony a little, but it certainly didn't make it go away, even with two doses, and I hated the feeling of being "out of it". The gas and air that I had the following night also didn't really do much for me, and I remember wondering whether cracking the mouthpiece against my head might actually work better for obliterating the racking pains. To me, this didn't bode well for pain relief during a future labour, especially given that PJ was a tiny fraction of the size that a full-term baby would be. But there were a couple of slightly more positive things to focus on: even though it had been incredibly painful, I had actually survived the experience and, also, a considerable part of the pain was wrapped up in the fact that I was losing our wonderful little baby. I didn't want to be opening and letting go, I wanted nothing more than to hang on. The shock and outrage of my body expelling this little being against my will, causing her to die, and there being nothing I could do to stop it, was agonising in and of itself. If I were giving birth to a full term baby, there would be the joy of meeting a new, living little person at the end of it, not the loss of a life ending before it had even begun. I began to consider birthing as possibly the biggest challenge of my life, with the opportunity to develop enormous mental courage if I withstood the pain without relief.

Since that positive pregnancy test result, I had found myself skipping over the horse monthlies I usually bought, in favour of pregnancy magazines which I read compulsively. There was an article about "hypnobirthing" in one of them, and I thought it might be worth a try. It promised a labour that if not painless, was at least easier and usually quicker than normal. There were even statistics from independent trials that confirmed this.

By a strange twist of fate, someone emailed asking for help with her horse, and the initials after her name looked familiar, with "hyp" in there somewhere. It turned out that Tara Economakis was a qualified hypnotherapist specialising in fertility issues and birthing. By another curious coincidence, an Intelligent Horsemanship colleague of ours, Sam, was also pregnant. I explained to her what little I understood about the approach. Not surprisingly, the prospect of an easier birth was appealing to her too, so we arranged to attend a course with Tara together.

Appropriately enough, Tara's house was located on a stud, near Lambourn, and Adam and I enjoyed a pleasant drive through the countryside to get there. We were planning to go on to a demo of Kelly's in Hampshire afterwards, and the whole venture had the feeling of a fun day out. Sam was there with her lovely husband, Nick, and after being introduced to another person who was doing the course, we got down to business. The first exercise was to write a list of five things that we associated with childbirth. I think mine were pain, blood, screaming, drugs and loss of control. Adam's were at least as negative; in fact, out of the total of twenty-five things which the group came up with, only one was anything but dreadful, and that was "Meeting my baby", which the rest of us seemed to have forgotten about. We realised we were actually planning, subconsciously, to have a traumatic, nightmarish marathon of a birth. It wasn't that we wanted to have an awful experience, exactly, it's just that the possibility of anything else had not entered our minds. That was the scenario we were projecting into the future. The feeling of being on a pleasant outing was quickly evaporating.

The tension was relieved somewhat when Tara showed us a clip from Monty Python's *The Meaning of Life*. It depicted a high-tech, hospital birth, in which the delivery suite (or "foetus frightening room") was crammed with instruments, including "The machine that goes 'Ping!'" The mother, or "patient" is nearly left outside, hardly missed with all the paraphernalia in the room. At one point she asks, "Doctor, what do I do?" Dr John Cleese replies irritably, "Nothing, Dear. You're not qualified."

Much as we laughed, the sobering reality struck us all that

many births are still conducted like that, particularly in the States. It wasn't so much the amount of medical intervention available, which could be life-saving for both baby and mother, it was the lack of compassion. The little baby being roughly cleaned, shown briefly to the mother, and then being whipped away to some nursery. In the scene, she doesn't even know whether she's had a girl or a boy, and is told off for enquiring. "It's a little early for imposing stereotypes, don't you think?" another doctor scolds. Almost kindly, he then goes on to say, "You may find over the coming weeks you experience completely irrational feelings of depression and hopelessness," and suggests pre-emptive anti-depressants.

Before moving on to the videos of the hypnobirths, Tara asked if we had any questions or concerns we wanted to share. I mentioned the oft-repeated suggestion that riders were at a disadvantage because of ending up pushing against themselves. I was as much confused as reassured by her response. "Being fit will only work to your advantage," she assured me, "although you *will* need to be able to let the muscles go." Then she said something which made me wonder if she really did know what she was talking about: "There's no need to push, anyhow. In fact, we actively discourage it. It's usually counter-productive."

Could that possibly be true, I wondered? Every birth scene I had ever witnessed involved long, strenuous bouts of pushing. Admittedly, I had never seen one in real life, but everyone I had talked to about giving birth had all claimed to have pushed. What about animals, surely they did what was natural? But didn't James Herriott spend half his life with his arm up a cow, helping her as she pushed the calf out? What had Sensi done? When I cast my mind back, I remembered that although there was an action that expelled the foal, it didn't seem to be Sensi doing it herself, using her abdominal muscles. Could it be like that for humans?

Tara then showed us videos of several 'hypnobirths', and the contrast with my mental image of what a birthing mother looked like could not have been greater. She was right, it seemed. There was no screaming, no pushing, seemingly no real effort, and the women smiled or were calm throughout, having gone off to some other, inner place. Yet they were clearly not drugged. It was amazing, and instantly re-defined for us what birth could be. I suddenly realised it wasn't going to be about enduring great pain, it was about relaxing and letting go in such a way that there wasn't nearly as much pain, and it wasn't experienced as such. The challenge was going to be in learning to relax that much, and undoing years and years of cultural programming about the nature of giving birth. In my own life and so often in my work I had seen expectations, both positive and negative, creating realities. Now more than ever, I needed to change my mind about what was going to happen when the time came for me to birth.

To round off the session, Tara guided us through some deep relaxation exercises that were so effective we spent the rest of the day in a complete daze. We could barely concentrate when she gave us directions to a pub for lunch, and got hopelessly lost trying to find it. Sam and Nick, who were also going to the Kelly demo, were similarly spaced out, and we travelled in convoy for what seemed like hours trying to get a vegetarian Sunday lunch in or around Lambourn. Everywhere was either full or didn't have a veggie option. The latter made us feel as if we had travelled back in time. We were getting increasingly light-headed through hunger, and eventually found somewhere to eat in Marlborough, but I still don't remember much about the demonstration.

I was about thirty weeks pregnant when we started the course with Tara. After each session, we were given exercises to practise, particularly breathing, relaxing, visualisation, and affirmations. Having the impending deadline of the birth helped me to be unusually conscientious about doing them. The idea is that being in a deeply relaxed state makes the mind open to hypnotic suggestions, so that statements like, "I am preparing my body for a smooth, comfortable, easy birthing" can become reality. I felt I had to do the affirmations a lot, just to counteract the vast amount of conditioning about birth I had already received. The wording was also very important. Contractions became "surges", and were described as being "intense" rather than painful. I particularly liked that "complications" became "special circumstances", so that if it didn't all go according to plan and you ended up with an emergency C-section, you could feel your situation had been special rather than that you had failed.

At around the same time, we were doing classes run by the National Childbirth Trust, and found them very enjoyable and informative. Not wishing to leave anything to chance, we also attended the antenatal classes offered by the NHS and were suitably impressed. The relaxation techniques and the emphasis on breathing were very similar to the work we were doing with the hypnobirthing. The main difference was the amount that was offered, it just wasn't anything like enough. Near the end of the NCT course we had half an hour on relaxation techniques; the other half of the session had been spent telling us about epidurals, pethedine, and gas and air. The techniques were helpful, but you would have to have picked them up very easily, remembered them well, and practised them conscientiously to have them make any appreciable difference during birth. If you weren't really familiar with the breathing, being in the throes of labour was probably not the best time to start trying it out.

We toured our local hospital in Cheltenham, and were cheered by the visit. I could almost forget that this was where I had lost PJ. The rooms were pleasant, if extremely warm, and the atmosphere was calm and welcoming. The midwives we met all seemed friendly, and amenable to the hypnobirthing approach. There was a birth pool, too, although of course there was no guarantee that someone else wouldn't be using it when we needed it. There was also the reassurance that should anything go wrong, the theater was just there, and an emergency Caesarian could be performed within minutes if necessary. We felt very fortunate to have such a good facility so near to us.

They even seemed happy to not do internal examinations if we didn't want them. This was another key point for me, which I had learned from the hypnobirthing and NCT classes: an internal exam can be the start of many women's difficulties in labour. They are done to find out how dilated the cervix is, and thus, theoretically, to give some idea of how far along the labour is progressing. But it may be normal for labour to slow down, and even stop. Many midwives consider this natural and not a sign of anything going wrong, but the more common view is that the labour is "failing to progress", and should be speeded up with interventions, such as hormone drips. This can make the contractions harder to deal with, and lead to more pain relief being needed and then a "cascade" of interventions, possibly ending with surgery. Without the internal exam, there's less chance of a timescale being imposed, and no chance, as happened to a friend recently, that an inexperienced midwife will tell you that you are fully dilated and get you to start pushing when you aren't ready. This incompetence resulted in a great deal of stress and pain, a forceps delivery and an episiotomy (a cut to enlarge the birth canal). The only difficulty with the hypnobirthing approach is that birthing women can be in an advanced state of labour without giving any of the "normal" signs, so it can be hard for the birth attendants to know where they're at. But since labouring women aren't usually left alone in this country, it doesn't really matter. Whenever the baby arrives, there'll be someone there to 'catch' it.

But however pleased we were with Cheltenham General Hospital, it was still very much a hospital, and not exactly a romantic place to give birth. By now, all our fear and dread about having the baby had been replaced with a calm anticipation, and I questioned whether the hospital was the setting we wanted to be in.

The big issue that kept coming up for me again and again was that I didn't want to have to negotiate for the birth I wanted. I didn't want to have to be on guard against some undesired intervention, to have to explain why I didn't want pain relief, or an internal examination, or to remind people not to mention pain scales, or even anything that would have negative connotations. I didn't want to be trying to do my calm breathing on a ticking clock, under deadlines, with the dreaded "Failure To Progress" assessment hanging over my head, the precursor to intervention, possibly eventually surgery. I didn't want to be an awkward patient, to make anyone's life, or at least, their shift, difficult. I just wanted to be a good birther, doing it in my own time, in my own way, with a supportive team of people there for, well, support. I also didn't want Adam to have to be my advocate, to have to stand up, as diplomatically as he was able to, for my rights. I wanted him to be able to relax into the process too, to give himself over to our experience, not to be some sort of shield between me and the medics. I didn't want to take the risk of a clash of personalities, or having to cope with the almost inevitable change of shift among the medical staff.

Time and again we meet clients whose daily experience on their livery yards is like that. They often want to do things differently, and find the pressure from those who are doing it more conventionally to be intrusive. Having to explain that they don't want their horse hit, or shouted at, or even to be fed treats by hand, becomes wearing after a while. They may find that they elicit a surprising amount of interest and criticism when they go into the school to work their horse. Sometimes, they're just trying out an approach that they've seen at a demonstration, and are bound to make mistakes, but feel judged. They don't want to feel they are a representative of an approach they're not familiar with, nor to have to defend their preferences and beliefs. We usually encourage people in this situation to find a more sympathetic yard, even if the facilities are less good. They have always reported being happier as a result, and often say that they just didn't think they really had a choice. There are, of course, always choices, and this is what we were reminding ourselves of when we were trying to decide on our birth options.

Adam was also worried that the birth might be speedy, and that the whole decision about when to go to the hospital would be almost impossible to judge. Much as all the advice points to leaving it for as long as possible, he was concerned that we would risk having the baby on the way if we left it too long. My mum had given birth to both me and my brother very quickly (although she had been induced by hormone injections) and he was aware that I might follow her lead. But, of course, if my labour followed the more usual pattern for first-timers, it could mean a long spell in hospital or the maternity unit, or the prospect of being sent home, and making more than one trip in. To cap it all we were about an equal distance from all the various different hospitals and birthing units in the area. None was very close. At least the baby was due in July, so the weather conditions, which often make our driveway impossible to negotiate in winter, wouldn't be a problem.

I had originally been adamant that I didn't want a home birth. Believing birth to be inevitably and invariably traumatic, I couldn't think why I would want to have that experience at home, and remember that awful nightmare every time I went into a certain room. I recalled a particularly agonizing night with toothache, and the relief I felt when I was able, the next day, to go into the dental surgery to get it sorted out. I wouldn't have particularly welcomed the dentist coming around with her drill to fix my tooth in my own home, nor did I feel that the familiarity of the environment would help reduce the pain and anxiety. It hadn't while I'd suffered all night.

Even with our shift in attitude about birthing, having the baby at home still felt like quite an extreme step, and we didn't know anybody who had done it. We visited a maternity unit in Stroud as a potential middle ground option. This was run exclusively by midwives, and did indeed have a more homely feel than the hospital. Any "special circumstances" and you could be transferred immediately to the nearest hospital, although this wasn't Cheltenham, and it was half an hour's drive to get there. Adam would have to follow in the car, which would be pretty miserable for us both. The problem was, the risk posed by the long journey meant that they were not keen on the non-examination approach, as they felt they needed to know more about what was going on in the labour to decide whether a transfer was necessary. About a third of all birthing mothers would be transferred. That felt like quite a high risk to us.

As we continued to discuss all our various options, part of me was growing aware that I just didn't want to leave home to have the baby. Now that I wasn't anticipating the birth with fear and dread, I wanted to have him where we live. It's beautiful and peaceful, and would be such a lovely place to be born. We were just getting our heads around the fact that actually, giving birth at home could also be the safest way. After all, this was something my body was designed to do, not a medical event. Nothing was wrong which required the attention of a doctor, so why was I thinking I needed to go to hospital to do it? When someone at a National Childbirth Trust antenatal class asked about what would happen in an accidental, rapid home birth, I leaned over and whispered to Adam, "That's what I want!" I guess I didn't quite want to stick my neck out by actually committing to this option, but in my heart of hearts I knew it was what I wanted. He leaned back and whispered that if that was what I wanted, would I mind if we could actually plan for a home birth rather than having it 'accidentally' at home without any preparation?

We had, however, left it rather late, week 36 to be precise. I wasn't at all sure that I could negotiate a home birth with the NHS at this stage. Also, although the pregnancy had been very straightforward, because we had lost our first, and were so old (38!), I had been "under" a consultant throughout. I didn't mind this at all, and didn't see it as intrusive or unnecessarily cautious, and in fact was grateful for the extra care. The difficulty was that we didn't know what had really caused the problem with PJ. By the time they had done tests, I had been on antibiotics for a while, so although they knew it was an infection, they couldn't tell what it was caused by. The most statistically likely culprit was Group B streptococcus, but there was no actual evidence of it. Tests throughout this pregnancy had all been negative, although it's a notoriously difficult bug to nail down. So, on our last meeting, the consultant had been talking about a massive, intravenous, entirely precautionary dose of antibiotics. This ruled out not only a home birth, but also going to the local midwife-led birthing unit. Going down this route, it would have to be a hospital birth.

One of the other Hypnobirthers was going to hire an Independent Midwife. She had previously negotiated a home birth with the NHS, but the midwife she had ended up with was not particularly positive about this, so she had ended up in hospital. On this, her second birth, as well as preparing with hypnobirthing, she was determined to have the right person for support. Her decision to follow the hypnobirthing route really paid off, when a few days before the birth it was discovered that her baby was in the breach position. With some extra help from Tara, she managed to 'persuade' the baby to turn over, head down again, before she birthed at home. It turned out not to be a straightforward birth, and she felt sure that her previous midwife would have insisted on a transfer to hospital. She firmly believed that having such an experienced, confident midwife, and the hypnobirthing work she had done, had allowed her to achieve her dream.

Looking the Independent Midwife option up on the Internet, I was initially a bit put off by the cost. Not that it seemed an unreasonable amount, it was just a sizable sum, about three thousand pounds, and I wasn't sure it was the best use of funds; put into an account for the baby, it would make a great nest egg. It would cost a lot more than our car was worth, but then our car wasn't worth a lot. We'd been talking about replacing it for a while, but the cost of the independent midwife would definitely mean we'd have to shelve those plans. Not that either of us cared - how could a car be compared in value to what this could mean to us all? Sitting in the warm June sunshine, beside our newly created vegetable patch (the result of some pretty manic nest building on Adam's part), we decided it was worth it for the chance of being able to have the birth we wanted. No amount of money later on could compensate if we didn't go for it. I could live with a transfer to hospital if events required it, but not through a lack of resources, or potentially a midwife who didn't really support home births. I wanted to be able to engage someone's services, to know them beforehand, to be confident that barring the most extreme circumstances, it would be that person attending. Going independent seemed the only way.

Once we had made the decision, I felt incredibly empowered. Understanding that we didn't have to go for the options offered to us, but could choose another approach, even if we had to borrow money to do so, was liberating. Now all we had to do was find an Independent Midwife. Oh, and find somewhere for the birth pool to go.

Of the dozen or so people I emailed, only one person, called Liz Nightingale, was able to consider taking me on. Luckily, I had rather liked the look of her from her website, and one of the other people I had been drawn to, Sarah Ifill, turned out to be her backup, her working partner, so that was all good. We immediately felt a connection of purpose on many levels - personal, emotional, political. It all seemed meant to be, however close we were getting to the due date. Meeting Liz and Sarah, they immediately felt like old friends, and I felt completely safe in their care. Finding a suitable spot to give birth in was rather more tricky.

We had painters due, or should I say overdue, to decorate the baby's room, although by now we had decided he would be sleeping with us, at least to start with. That made that whole section of the house unsuitable, and not just because decorators sanding and glossing away might not be conducive to the best birth atmosphere. There were also the paint fumes to consider. The annexe, the part of Moor Wood we had originally lived in, before we became sole tenants, might have worked even though it was so small, but we weren't at all confident that the floor would sustain the weight of more than a tonne of water. We also had my brother, his wife and their two boys, as well as my mum staying, so finding a private spot somewhere in the house would be a bit of a challenge.

Also, as we anticipated our baby's arrival on that lovely June day, the birds were singing, the sun was shining, and giving birth somewhere nearer to nature felt very appealing. If only we had a suitable piece of flat land, some sort of marquee might have worked. We were still pondering the options when Adam suggested the foaling box in our barn.

I wasn't at all sure. For a start, Misty was using it as a stable at the time, and quite a lot of it was bedded down. Swallows had been using it to nest in for years. There was a fair bit of accumulated dust and cobwebs, and it wasn't exactly a sterile environment. But as he described his vision for it, with drapes and cushions and candles, and a thorough cleaning out beforehand, it began to seem possible. It would be nice and dry if the weather were at all inclement. Pushing aside the religious connotations of having our first-born son in a barn, I tentatively agreed. What clinched it was that the midwives seemed to think this was an entirely suitable option.

Adam, who had been in a frenzy of activity for weeks, building projects in the garden and woods, trying to make the place safe for a child, now set to the task of clearing it out, decorating the walls and ceiling with cloths and coverings, installing candle holders and fairy lights, and a sound system on which to play the birthing compilations we had been preparing. Best of all, if she wanted to check on me, Sensi could simply poke her head through the open window between her part of the barn and mine, if the curtain was opened. Accommodating though Cheltenham Hospital appeared, they probably had some sort of regulation about not having horses in the delivery rooms. I wondered what she would make of me, wallowing in the birthing pool we had bought, which could be filled with lovely hot water from the house. It seemed exactly how it should be - instead of me having to travel to the unknown staff at the hospital, I would have my best friends, family and trusted supporters around me.

In the event, the weather was more than "inclement". It was July 2007, and the worst floods in decades hit Gloucestershire. I hadn't seen the news for a few days, which was probably just as well, but I had noticed it was raining quite a bit - four inches in one day, I later discovered. There was even standing water in our school, which had never happened before. But, oblivious to all the implications of flooded roads and the long journey faced by the midwives, I was awoken early one morning by a strange sensation. It was like a pulse of energy travelling through me, followed shortly by another, then another. I realised I was definitely in labour.

I woke Adam up, and he phoned the midwives and made tea before going about filling up the pool. I began to feel a bit lonely in the bedroom, so I relocated to the birthing room, formerly known as the foaling box. As I stepped inside I immediately felt cocooned in an environment of complete safety and harmony. A light air of incense and soothing music drifted around me, while patterns of

214

every hue lulled my eyes. I snuggled up in the nest of duvets there and concentrated on slowly, fully, breathing.

I felt sort of calm and excited at the same time. Any anxieties or fears I'd retained just melted away. "I'm doing this," I thought. "Finally, I'm doing this, and it's all going to be fine". The prospect of giving birth without pain relief was thrilling instead of daunting. I was full of confidence and felt strong and powerful and although not exactly in control, I was up for any challenges that might lie ahead.

I took off my watch and threw it onto a straw bale. Adam made porridge and tea, and although I had to pause for the surges (contractions), both went down very well. Then I snuggled back down, noticing that the feelings were getting stronger and more intense, and that the gaps between them seemed very short.

I didn't notice what time Liz arrived, only that she parked on the hose pipe, which made me smile, especially when Sarah did exactly the same thing several hours later. It was very reassuring to have her there, although I hadn't been worried, as I knew we were still some way off the "critical" phase. I got the sense that she was perhaps expecting a slightly different scene, but when she felt the surges and timed them, she seemed happy that it really was all happening. She said wonderfully encouraging things and checked the baby's heartbeat, which was strong, and had good variability, and also my blood pressure and pulse. I decided to get into the pool for a while.

I was vaguely aware of her sorting things out - she'd brought down the equipment that had been stored in the studio, ready and waiting for this moment. I had meant to say, "Don't bother with the entonox" (the gas and air dispenser) because I knew I wasn't going to use it, but it was one of the first things to be brought down. I gathered she was probably preparing the resuscitation station for the baby should he need it, and various other things. Adam had arranged a screen to keep those things out of sight and I had taken great care not to look too closely at the very medical looking stuff in the boxes, just in case it put me off at all.

It seemed like things continued smoothly and progressively for quite some time, with the surges getting stronger and closer together, quite a few of them back-to-back. I could feel a tightening, rippling sensation course through my body, like a wave, and I had to hit it with my breathing at exactly the right moment. If I didn't breathe deeply and fully, the pain was intense. If I was a little late, the pain would start and then melt away. Getting it exactly right meant it was simply a sensation, with no discomfort at all. Physically, it was almost effortless, but mentally I had to give myself over to the process, and focus in a dreamy kind of way.

The music we played really helped, too. Adam had put together a compilation of our favourite artists. I had originally thought I would need it all to be very quiet music, of the sort played on relaxation tapes, perhaps with a little whale-song thrown in, but in fact quite a lot of the music was properly rousing, energetic stuff, like Muse's *Invincible*, and some of my favourite SCSI songs. It was music to get lost in, and to this day I feel a deep emotional connection to those tracks.

The baby's heartbeat was checked frequently, by means of a little microphone placed on my belly, but it never disturbed my concentration, and could be done wherever I was in the pool. After a while, Liz, who although being a very experienced midwife, had only witnessed one hypnobirthing before, suggested that if I were happy to do so, a quick internal exam might be a good idea, just to see where we were at. Although she could feel the contractions clearly, and they seemed very efficient, she was concerned that, since I was so calm and not in any apparent discomfort, I might not actually be in active labour.

I was pretty sure that he was making his way down, and that we were getting quite close, but I also wanted to know where we were at. I did let some doubts creep in, "What if I haven't dilated at all? How long could I continue this for?" and for a fleeting moment thought I would ask them to ring up the hospital to arrange the anaesthetist for the epidural. As my mind began to go down this track, I stopped concentrating on the careful breathing. Suddenly I felt a serious, stabbing pain and began to panic. Adam, seeing what was happening, leaned over and, in a quiet but firm, calming voice, reminded me how to breathe and kept me focused on it. It was more helpful than any drug could have been. Within seconds I was back in that curious state, a focused absence of awareness, and the sensation had receded to being easily manageable. By the time Liz did the internal I had got my thinking back on track and knew it was right to stay at home even if we were a ways off. In any case, I was thrilled when Liz, surprised and delighted at the state of progress, announced that he was actually well on his way down. She had thought it unlikely that I was more than half way dilated. I slid gratefully back into the pool for the next stage.

The hours upon hours of preparation all paid off. I was so grateful we had found and followed a structured plan to make this process as easy as possible, instead of just hoping for the best. Although he was posterior (facing my belly button instead of my spine), our little baby made his way almost effortlessly out into the birth pool. A small amount of tearing occurred as I rushed it and got a bit enthusiastic at the prospect of meeting him. Adam immediately scooped him up into my arms, and he cried lustily, though briefly. I knew he was alright.

We couldn't stay in the pool for long for fear of chilling him, so I was helped out soon after. Adam, our son and I curled up in the duvets, and were all immediately warm and comfortable. Once it stopped beating, Adam cut the cord, and we could snuggle more easily. It felt so normal and yet so miraculous to finally be holding him in our arms.

With Marley latched on, and feeding well, I had an amazingly delicious and restorative cup of tea. We went into the house and I showered, while he was weighed in at 8lbs 10oz, and then we had toast and more tea and cuddled up in bed. Our visitors, who had made themselves scarce when they knew we were in labour, arrived back from town, bearing flowers and gifts. A couple of hours later I had dinner with the family, with Marley in my arms, and a small glass of champagne to celebrate, while learning how to eat one handed! Shortly afterwards, we went to bed. It had been a long day, after a short night, and I was tired, but now we faced one of our biggest hurdles - our first sleepless night, the first, I assumed, of many. What should we do to get him to sleep, I wondered. He seemed a bit young for a bedtime story.

Adam stopped me worrying about it by simply saying, "Let's try this." He reached over and turned out the light, at which he and Marley promptly fell asleep. With nothing else to do, I followed suit. Marley slept in my arms all night, and when he awoke, hungry, I could just feed him and we would both fall back to sleep again. Those anticipated sleepless nights have never materialised.

I'm sure co-sleeping doesn't suit everyone, but for us it felt the most natural thing in the world. Anything else seems to harbour the potential to create all sorts of problems. Carefully studying the statistics and recommendations for safe sleeping reassured us, as did the fact that in countries where co-sleeping is the norm, cot death is unheard of. There isn't even a word for it. It turns out that when people from those countries live in the UK and continue their normal sleeping practices, the incidence of Sudden Infant Death Syndrome is also zero amongst their communities. There are people who would like to share a bed with their babies, but who don't because they have been told it's unsafe. It might be, if there are special circumstances present, such as drug or alcohol abuse. But being separated at such a vulnerable time seems to me like yet another symptom of how disconnected we can be from our own children, and not a good start. Perhaps this is why children are scared of the dark, and why parents spend so much of their time reassuring frightened children at night.

I look back over the last weeks of my pregnancy and the birth itself as a magical time. From the moment I met Liz and Sarah I felt they completely shared our understanding of how special this time was, and throughout I felt empowered and totally cared for - almost revered, although it sounds strange to say so. I got the strong impression they felt like this about every birthing woman. They had the utmost respect and awe for the everyday but totally miraculous experience of birth.

But the more I think about it, the sadder I feel that our experience isn't more commonplace. Really positive birth stories are rare, to the point of being almost unheard of. There's a campaign called One Mother One Midwife, which is appealing for exactly that - being able to choose a midwife who will see you through the pregnancy and also attend the birth, wherever that might be. Having Marley at home with such fantastic midwives was wonderful, but I'm certain the hypnobirthing preparation made a huge difference, and indeed most hypnobirths are also hospital births. Looking at the provision made by the NHS for birth preparation, I'm sure hypnobirthing techniques could be included quite easily. It would also be extremely cost-effective, as there are very convincing statistics for how it speeds up labour and reduces interventions and the need for pain relief - and surely epidurals, caesarians, and other procedures are expensive?

I was on a high for months afterwards. Far from suffering from postnatal depression, I experienced postnatal euphoria. Looking after Marley felt so normal, and, as I said to Adam, he's no trouble, just the twenty-four hours a day care and attention. I loved (almost) every moment. Aside from minor complications with the tear I'd sustained, physically I felt back to normal very quickly, and although I had three weeks off mucking out, I didn't feel I particularly needed it. I was back riding almost immediately, with Marley sleeping peacefully in his pram in the corner of the school. Yet the world felt like a completely different place. More intense, more magical. Nothing would ever be the same again. It didn't feel like we'd "settled down" to have children. It felt like we'd embarked on the biggest adventure of our lives.

TWENTY THREE

What's It All About?
(Adam)

'Equitation and music are the same art.'
Craig P. Stevens

It'll change your life forever.

Every parent who's ever said these words - which is nearly every parent there ever was - knows how impossible it is to describe, and like most clichés, it's deeply true but often unheeded. For us, as for almost any parent, it's been amazing to discover we never really understood the meaning of the word love, never knew how strong it could be. Sure, we'd loved our parents and each other, and many other people and animals, but there's something about your own child that goes beyond putting yourself in harm's way to save them. You suddenly have to become responsible for looking after yourself in ways you never thought you would. Having fun in the 'sex, drugs and rock 'n' roll' sense' just doesn't feel right any more, and makes you wonder if it ever did. You immediately start thinking all the same things your parents did, and find yourself saying them. Suddenly, especially if you know how devastating the death of a parent is, you become aware and horrified of your own mortality. It's bad enough that you've got to die some day, and maybe leave your partner alone. But to leave your child, it doesn't bear thinking about. Everything becomes focused more on the long term and is suddenly serious. World events such as climate change or the unendable wars we have embarked on against terror and drugs, leave you unable to pretend it doesn't matter or won't affect

221

you. You find yourself building a nest and trying to protect yourself and your family. At the same time, because you want to provide them with everything they might want, the waste you create bringing up a baby is staggering.

The thing some people fail to mention when they say it'll change your life forever, is that you may be surprised by how much you'll welcome it. Nothing else will help you understand yourself better. Your baby reflects you, so you'll learn more about yourself than you may have wanted to know. You'll certainly learn more about bacteria than you ever wanted to, because they'll pick up everything and bring it home. You'll inevitably teach, and since you do so mostly by example, you'd better start setting a good one. Anything you approach with enthusiasm, whether it be mucking out, cleaning your teeth or vacuuming, will be seen in the same way by your child. Marley loves all these activities, even though I don't, but so far I've fooled him by making it seem like I do. You might say he thinks vacuuming is it's own reward.

I still don't believe in fate, but I also don't know what to think about all the uncanny coincidences. One of them happened at the time of PJ's death. On the same day that Nicole was admitted to hospital when our miscarriage began, my sister had her first baby. I got back from the hospital after our disaster to receive a call from Venetia, probably the most difficult phone call I've ever had in my life. She had been rushed in for an emergency Caesarian after she'd been unable to deliver because the cord was wrapped twice around the baby's neck. It seemed as though fate was pointing out to us, in spite of it all, how lucky we were. Although it was almost unbearable to hear the good news, knowing what I was just about to tell her, nonetheless it was so welcome. At a time like that you really need a boost, and there's nothing like a new member of the family to give you that. It was much worse for her to hear our difficult news. Despite the agony we'd just begun to go through, I preferred it to be me delivering the bad news and hearing the good, rather than the other way around, if it had to happen to one of us. By the way, Venetia is the most wonderful mother. It suits her so well, although I didn't really think it would. I've never heard her yell at her children, although I did have premonitions that she'd take to mothering as she did to coxing Caius' first eight.

For me one of the biggest coincidences was to do with the band. The coincidences started early, like the way Tim Hills happened to be the cashier at the bank we used. Like most bands, SCSI agonised about the name (SCSI is a bit of a computer that talks to other computers, and also the way you feel the morning after a big night out). Then we discovered it was Hebrew for 'rock'. That seems like an uncanny coincidence. For years we'd been very gradually, imperceptibly, scaling down our dream of world domination, even if we never really settled for just being the greatest rock band in Woodmancote. There had been some changes in personnel and a few unlucky breaks. I am still kicking myself for not taking my first (and so far, only) opportunity to give Jonathan Ross the chance to hear SCSI. I know he would love it. But musically we had gone from strength to strength. It didn't feel like an opportunity when our incredibly talented singer, Andy, who is also a brilliant drummer, decided to move to Spain. But that's how we ended up with Murdoc on vocals.

They don't come more authentic than Murdoc. You don't get more rock 'n' roll than him. An alcoholic and former drug addict, he's certainly had his fair share of brushes with the law. Practically born down the pub, he lives and breathes the rock. He may not be the world's greatest guitarist, but then neither was Kurt Cobain. He's the kind of guy who consistently surprises me with his depth of character, and the stuff he's done and knows about is diverse in the extreme. He left school at 16 but didn't go to it much before that, so you might think I wouldn't have much in common with him, having gone to Cambridge. But apart from Nicole I can hardly think of anyone I have more desire to listen or talk to than him.

He was in a band who supported Green Day. He tells me SCSI knocks the socks off them, but we've never had a gig as good as that. Just when you think you know him you'll find out he's read books about Egyptology or is a really good cook. Once, when we were jamming some weird tune we'd made up, he started reciting some long prayer in Arabic. As likely as drinking or taking drugs all day, you'll find he has been down the gym or practising the martial art Wing Chun. Or writing another great song. Or caring for his grandparents, one of whom he and his mum looked after at home until the advanced stages of Alzheimer's finally defeated even them.

The pain and pleasure of living such a full life leaches out into his voice the way it did with Janis Joplin. When most singers are asked to do a sound check, they lean into the mike and say,

"Testing, one, two. One, two." Murdoc screws up his face and lets rip a strangled scream so hoarse and painful, it's as if he's gargling boiling nails. You're expecting to see him collapse, frothing at the mouth. Rock needs people like him, not plastic pop idols doing choreographed dances while they mouth lyrics about nothing at all, written by someone they haven't even met, over chord sequences that have been hashed out a million times. Joplin, Hendrix, Lennon - they're turning in their graves. Cobain was turning well before he landed in his.

We'd had one thing after another, though. A burst of song-writing genius had followed Murdoc's arrival in the band, rejuvenating the artistic flow of myself and Tim, the other creative mainstay. With Murdoc's song writing to add to ours, we felt unstoppable. We recorded a lot of stuff but, as so often happens, a kind of stagnation set in. We wanted to produce recordings worthy of the music we had composed, but the production of perfectly manicured, flawless recordings stilted the creativity. We had met someone who loved our sound and ethos, and had a load of top quality digital recording gear, and all the time in the world. But nothing kills rock like having all the time in the world. The studio, above the birthing room at Moor Wood, was all decked out with mikes and recording consoles, but after take 150, the soul was draining out of it.

What really killed it, though, was the drummers. Andy had been unbelievable, completely reliable in every way. One take was all he needed, even with really complex drum parts. When Andy was drafted into being lead vocalist, we got another drummer, who was unreliable and overcommitted even before he went AWOL. The replacement for him wasn't quite as good and, being only eighteen, had no idea how unlikely it was that he'd ever be in such a good band again. One night he dropped a bombshell. "By the way, I'm going to University in a couple of weeks." I thought Murdoc would probably hit him, especially when he missed the last gig we would have done together, because he'd crashed his car, again. He was lucky he was in hospital, where Murdoc couldn't easily get to him, and where he had a reasonable excuse. Not a good one, mind you, as he had only mangled one of his hands. Murdoc once played a benefit gig whilst suffering from organ failure, without thinking twice about it.

We got another drummer, but it was tedious to teach him all

the songs again and, worst of all, he wasn't even as good as the last one. It was all becoming a compromise, something rock 'n' roll should never be. Still, we got it all up to scratch and did a gig that went down well. It was the last time I ever saw the guy. He had moved down to this area to be with a girl who dumped him, he lost his job, some bad news came from his family, and he went back up north where he had come from.

We couldn't face getting another drummer and going through it all again for the third time in a year. Besides, by now, Nicole was pregnant, and with a baby due in a few months I was finding myself gradually conscious of how my priorities were changing. I knew Nicole wouldn't pressurise me to be at home if I didn't want to be, but the idea of spending hours practising the same old stuff so a new drummer could learn it all before disappearing, exploding or moving away, didn't appeal. Besides, having done so many gigs in near-empty venues, we were finding our enthusiasm sapped. Only on a couple of occasions had we seen a decent audience, of kids who lapped it up, moshed and head-banged. They caught me when I stage-dived, and carted me off to buy me drinks. Knowing we were really good made it all the more frustrating when we'd find ourselves performing in an empty pub. When we discovered that with virtually no practice, Murdoc, Tim and I could scratch together an acoustic set that seemed to go down as well as our rock versions, it was the logical way to go.

But we all knew that world domination was probably not going to come like that. And then Murdoc had an opportunity to do something really worthwhile, adventurous and even lucrative. A friend who worked as a contractor for the UN - travelling to the earth's most troubled hotspots to see if it was too dangerous for the UN to operate in parts of countries like Afghanistan, Sierra Leone and Cambodia - offered him a job. There was no way I was going to object.

So Murdoc booked a flight, and left the country. If there was a day you'd say my dream of being a rock star died, it was then. No prizes for guessing what else happened on the same day. Nicole went into labour and Marley was born, probably at the exact moment Murdoc touched down in his first Godforsaken war zone. It felt as though one door was closing and another one was opening. Just like they'd said on the Insight seminars. Somehow, although it wasn't what I thought I wanted, or what I thought was right, the demise of SCSI as a force of rock ended up being right on some level. Several years on, it's a shock to find I feel much the same about the death of little PJ. Anyhow, Murdoc's back now, and we still play. Forget Jonathan Ross. Marley is our number one fan.

Learning a musical instrument is much like learning to ride, possibly because both involve the need to develop a sense of rhythm as well as bringing a harmony to life. A kind of magical synthesis occurs, a sublime beauty is created through the mundane, tedious mastery of a technical skill. The way I learned to play has taught me a lot, mostly about how not to do it. It being rock 'n' roll, strictly for fun, I didn't want any lessons. Like so many kids I started to play by learning some of the classic songs that originally inspired me to pick up the instrument. Led Zep's 'Stairway to Heaven' was one of the first, followed by numerous Hendrix numbers. Twenty-five years later I can play stuff by almost anyone, but I still can't play a single Hendrix song properly all the way through. Anyway, I don't recommend that way of learning any more than I recommend getting on a starter, a bucking horse or trying to go round Badminton the first time you ride. At least on the guitar the worst you'll get is a blister, cramp in your fingers and perhaps a bit dispirited, where if you take that approach to learning to ride, the consequences might be a bit more serious.

For the first seven years I played, I learned stuff from friends, and song books, but mostly by sitting there and listening to tapes and working it out. I could play loads of songs relatively well, strumming the chords and singing along, but I couldn't play lead guitar. I struggled to imitate good solos, had to learn each one phrase by phrase, and couldn't go fast enough. Then I met Ivan.

I'm sure if Ivan had been around in the sixties, and if there were any justice in the world of rock (which is unlikely), you'd hear about the legendary guitarists Hendrix, Clapton, Santana and Chaudhari, or Johnny Rams as he called himself. I met him when I found his lost cat and took her home, leaving a note up in the local shop. The next day I got a call and he came round to pick her up. Noticing my guitar in the corner, he offered to teach me. To my prejudiced eye, he looked too small and much too Indian to be any good at rock guitar but when I went to his house and heard him play, he blew me away. Although I was broke, I agreed to pay for lessons.

At the start of my first one, he played a simple twelve bar

blues riff and asked me to ad-lib a solo over the top of it. I bumbled along, struggling to get the music in my head to come out of the strings. I was completely unaware that the way I had learned had handicapped my future progress so much. Lots of practice of bad habits had made them permanent, for practice does not make perfect, practice makes permanent. Only perfect practice makes perfect. My little finger was always drawn right back and screwed up, because I had initially found it weak and difficult to use. Not surprisingly, it didn't get stronger or easier to use as a result of not being involved. And every stroke of the pick I made was downwards. As Ivan pointed out, if I wanted to be any good, I'd need to be faster. Using more fingers and doubling the number of strokes might help.

He showed me some exercises. It wasn't music. It wasn't even really scales, not ones that make any musical sense, although major and minor scales were the next thing he got me to do. Critically, his brilliance had impressed upon me the need to do this foundation work. I was really motivated, not - as had often been the case at school - by threats or from outside. It came from within. I knew this was how Ivan had learned to be so good.

For six months I played that stuff every day for more than an hour, sometimes as much as five hours, till my hands and arms were knotted in cramps. I'd sit in front of the TV all night going up and down the fret board, repeating those abominable exercises. Somehow, Nicole managed to tolerate it, although she probably spent more time mucking out the field than usual. To avoid being kicked out of home, I almost never played it through my amp. I didn't even try to learn another song.

Then suddenly I could play along with anything I heard on the radio. I wouldn't pretend I was on a par with Clapton, but I could listen to a tune and immediately come up with a half-decent solo. I knew what people were playing most of the time (with the exception, as always, of Hendrix), just by hearing it once and could often copy it immediately without any effort. When I played a gig with the covers band I was in at the time, I could batter out riffs that had always seemed impossible before. People would even come up to me afterwards to tell me I was great. I never got to bed any groupies, but Ivan hadn't given me any useful tips on that score.

When I think about riding, and meet people who have tried to learn to ride using the same method I did for learning the guitar, I realise why they have so many problems with it. Most brilliant riders have spent a lot of time practising their 'scales' (like Hendrix, who used to virtually live with a guitar round his neck and who, by the way, was also a keen rider). There's a form of these scales called seat training. These are exercises, generally performed as the horse is lunged, a sophisticated version of which has been taught to us by Craig. As well as showing you how to balance your torso above your seat bones, you'll get more supple, especially in the hips, and more confident. The most difficult exercise I have done is to clap my feet together above Sensi's mane as she cantered. Juggling three balls as you lift your legs up and down on a cantering horse is pretty hard, too - particularly when the horse is familiar with the sound of an apple landing on the arena, and stops like she's hit a brick wall before throwing her head down to investigate. After doing exercises like these, you'll never fear a horse spooking or spinning again, for the very good reason that you've done something much more difficult, and are going to stay on. Like musical scales, which can hardly be described as music, the exercises are not exactly 'riding'. It's understandable that most people won't put in the hours of work required to master them.

But the difference they can make is unbelievable. Time and again, we have seen them transform the confidence and capability of average riders who've come on our clinics. I used to fall off fairly regularly before I practised them. Since then, I have only fallen off twice in over five years, and both of those times the horse started bucking before I had really got on. On one occasion, a horse moved off when I was getting on from a fence, and my backside didn't even touch the saddle - I landed on his rump. When he bucked I was projected over his head like a stone from a catapult, which was probably just as well as being thrown off any other way would probably have meant I got kicked at the same time.

Interestingly, the other horse was our very own Karma, Sensi's foal. Had I been working with someone else's horse I would never have been so careless and haphazard. But when it's your own horse, whom you picked up in your own arms and carried in from the field before she fell asleep with her head on your lap, and who never seems the least bit fazed by anything you do, it's easy to get complacent, which suddenly and surreptitiously makes everything extremely dangerous. It was another classic case of ignoring the obvious, of doing something that I knew was risky, but I chose not to heed my inner voice. This was telling me, unsurprisingly enough, that hacking out down the valley where there were hordes of biting horseflies on a horse I was riding for only the second time, was not such a great idea. When I went to get on, I did so in a real hurry while Nicole held both her and Sensi, and tried vainly to swat the flies. In a rush to take advantage of what seemed like the best moment I was going to get, I clunked down carelessly in the saddle as though she were an experienced horse (Nicole had ridden her quite a few times, but she was still a long way from being a school master). Of course, when she erupted in a long series of bucks and rears, Nicole could do nothing to help, as she was trying to hold Sensi. In spite of having no stirrups I sat on at least ten bucks and ten rears, and a couple of spins, and then I baled out as much as being dumped. She wasn't going to stop and it was best to give up before something worse happened. It was a bit humiliating to fall off my own horse and watch her canter off back to the yard, but it was all I deserved. As well as feeling humbled, and not a little stupid, I was also quite impressed with myself. I'd never thought of myself as much of a rider - from the beginning I had always felt a bit of a fraud. After all, I never had a pony as a child, and many a horse-mad kid has spent more time in the saddle than I have. A lot of them have ridden bigger jumps than I ever have, too. But I had finally learned to ride almost well enough to be in a rodeo. Not that I'll be intending to practise that again.

This incident makes it all too clear that we are nothing like perfect horsemen. We hope that this story, and this fact, will give heart to all those who train horses - which is everyone who has any contact with them - for there is no such thing as a perfect horseman. You don't get an easy ride just because you raise and care for a horse. You get what you deserve, often at the very moment that you deserve it most. You can train a thousand horses and write a book with an introduction by Monty Roberts, but if you stray from being thorough, listening to your horse and staying in touch with your intuitions, you'll find you regret it.

If anyone in horsemanship pays attention to detail, listens and acts with intuition, it's Monty, and he's got what he deserves time and time again - tens of thousands of horses whose behaviour has been transformed for the better. For all our successes, often with dangerous and difficult horses, we are far from perfect, and our clients are probably even further from it than us, but that doesn't mean we and they can't help a horse or train them effectively. Keeping us on track, in tune with our core values, is potentially their most valuable gift to us. To be with a horse is a commitment to listen, trying to hear their every whisper and to speak softly and clearly, staying true both to them and to ourselves. Maybe that's why finding the right path for a horse has led so many people to find the right paths for themselves. Perhaps we all were born to whisper.

Epilogue

Marley And We
(Nicole and Adam)

It seems so long and so short a time since we made our first journey down the drive here, yet we have now marked a decade since we took over the tenancy here at Moor Wood Stables in September 1999. We've had a lot of other celebrations recently, too. It's twenty years since we met and (thanks to Nicole's dad working for an airline), visited my parents at their Ambassadorial Residence in Gabon, in what turned out to be an African honeymoon. We also both turned forty in 2009, while Marley has reached the very grown up age of two.

It hardly seems like yesterday that we were celebrating the publication of *Whispering Back* in our landlord's magnificent home back in 2003. Our story seems to move much faster than we are managing to keep up with. That's our excuse for not finishing this instalment of it earlier!

The horses are all fine, if a little plump. Misty is actually trimmer than most since she spends a lot of her time running away from our sheep dog, who herds her up incessantly in the yard and field. Sensi continues to make spectacular faces at most of the horses that come along, as well as Finn, who remains her nemesis. Amber, who has come such a long way from the frightened, angry horse she used to be, was given to us this summer. This brought our livery vs. freeloader ratio to a yet more ridiculous imbalance at 2:9, prompting us to make bold statements that we are going to do something about it by putting some out on loan or selling them. As a first move towards that we recently got Karma back up and running, without incident so far. The pressures of life being what they are, we have to take decisive action to reduce the number of heads in the field whose main role is to be decorative.

Our clinics are still thriving, and if anything are busier than ever. It is such a privilege to be able to impart the skills and knowledge that we've accumulated over the years, and helping people overcome problems with their horses is still a humbling and emotional experience. Just as fulfilling is working with people without particular problems, who simply want to improve their knowledge, capability and understanding, particularly if caught in the minefield of modern riding. Those 'A-ha!' moments, when years of confusion and frustration fall away and a seemingly unattainable achievement is suddenly within reach, are priceless to us. It's not unusual to hear that someone has learned more in a weekend than they did in years of lessons, but this must reflect as much on their previous instruction as it is a credit to our teaching! We know that the real reason for the popularity of the work we do is the same as why Monty's approach has been so welcome. It's because the world is sick of violence, and because people yearn to be better at communication. It's the only way forward that has any chance of saving us, no matter how advanced our law enforcement or military technology might become.

In 2009 we began to offer Equine Facilitated courses for team building and personal development, in conjunction with an associate with both experience and qualifications in that field. It felt like a leap into the dark, but in a sense, everything we have ever done has been team-building, given that any horse and human who we have ever worked with have been trying to build a better team, and personal development has always been a strong feature of what we do. In fact, it's almost unavoidable in any encounter with horses.

In the depths of the worst recession of modern times it might seem unlikely that businesses would jump at the chance to spend any money they could possibly save. But those who wish to survive the cull know that they must galvanise the team around them, and face new challenges with the same resourcefulness and determination that can be built through exposure to the kind of stimulus horses can provide. The recession is creating great opportunities as well as generating casualties. Companies like Microsoft, T Mobile and the Manchester Business School have been previous clients of corporate courses run by Intelligent Horsemanship, and they know how powerful a vehicle the horse can be as a catalyst for change, both personal and institutional. The parallels between communicating with horses and with humans are fascinating, and the equine mirror provides opportunities to reveal much about the behaviour and psychology of both individuals and organisations.

Monty and Kelly have gone from strength to strength. In 2008 the new head of the BHS was introduced to Kelly and a number of constructive initiatives have been set up, beginning with Kelly visiting every BHS regional group in the country. At the same time, we await the results of a set of independent scientific trials that have been investigating and evaluating Monty's procedure for starting young horses, alongside that of a respected conventional trainer. Demonstrations of Monty and Kelly's work are still extremely popular and well attended. The Intelligent Horsemanship Association now boasts 32 Recommended Associates and 4300 members, and continues on its quest to educate and support horses and their owners. Monty, at the age of 74, is finally talking about travelling less - that's as close as he's likely to get to retiring - and has set up an online University at www.montyroberts.com to enable him to reach more people through the Internet, rather than being on the road around 310 days of every year. He remains in close contact with the Queen, who continues to follow and support his efforts to make the world a better place for horses and people.

Jo and Derek have continued their development in dramatic style. They have accumulated more horses as well as skills and knowledge. Jo became one of the first Equine Podiatrists in Gloucestershire. Derek, as well as continuing to assist in the coaching of generally triumphant Oxford boat race teams, became a master practitioner of Neuro-Linguistic Programming (NLP), and a fully qualified hypnotherapist. In September 2009 they leased a major equestrian facility near Daventry in the centre of England. Craig is intending to sell his place in Seattle and move to Europe. Annabelle fluctuates between teaching clinics, having adventures and taking time out to recover from them.

Chris is still tanned, fit and surfing in Maui, and we do our best to see him as often as possible. In 2008 he nearly died after impaling himself on the back end of a tandem surfboard whose nose got caught in a wave and hit a reef. His ruptured intestine was not diagnosed until his girlfriend insisted he be scanned, by which time it was almost too late. After a year out of the water he has now made a full recovery, and has another tale to add to his collection of stories and scars. It's going to be a while until he is good enough to try surfing Jaws. He still comes to England, to visit friends and family, so it would be impolite not to make the effort to go and see him in Maui occasionally.

We carry PJ forever in our hearts, and the pain of losing her is still incredibly raw, particularly for Nicole. We know we are not alone in this loss, and that countless others have experienced it, too. Writing down her story was one of the hardest things we've done. We hope that sharing our experience will help others in similar circumstances come to terms with their grief.

The joy of having Marley in our lives is indescribable (although we'll probably try in our next book!), and as we watch him learning to dance, play the guitar and ride a horse, we know how lucky we are to have him, and how lucky he is to be in such a wonderful environment. But our cup floweth over, as they say, and there's another little person who's brought yet more happiness into our lives. A beautiful daughter named Layla Rose was born to us on 15/06/09, again at home in our foaling box, in the most peaceful of circumstances. At the time of writing, she's five months old, and immense fun, already giving her brother a run for his money. Marley seems extremely pleased to have her around.

Around the time of Marley's birth, I put my guitars away, and didn't pick one up for ages. There hardly seemed any point. Murdoc was in Afghanistan or Cambodia, and the prospect of ever playing another gig seemed so remote as to be as far away as he was. Tim and Si from SCSI formed another band called the Shining Lies with an old friend of Simon's called Dave. They asked me to join. Check them out on www.myspace.com/theshininglies - they're brilliant, but I just didn't have the enthusiasm for it, and the idea of going down to London to perform in front of a (probably) empty room just didn't appeal as much as staying at home cuddling my wonderful new friend. Then, after a few months, I brought an acoustic guitar back down from the studio, at around the time that Marley learned to 'cruise' - walking and standing while holding onto the furniture.

I'll never forget the moment when he noticed the guitar, and I picked it up and played just a two-note C major chord. His eyes lit up in an expression of complete rapture. The way two notes can rhyme together and make such a sweet union is utterly miraculous, expressing as it does the joy and wonder of life, like birdsong. I'd forgotten how special it is. One of the most amazing things about having children is the way that they help us to notice just how wondrous so many things are, things that we take for granted because they surround us all the time - the moon, a light bulb, trees, cars, birds, helicopters, the water coming out of a tap - and horses. So it was with music, for Marley helped me notice what had faded into the background of my consciousness.

We started going up to the studio when they were using it to practise, and Dave's incredible guitar playing, expressive singing, and the way he just can't keep himself in check and simply has to let the music flow into his feet and arms was immediately picked up by Marley. Wearing ear defenders to protect him from the volume - he has never once complained about having them put on - he would stare at Dave and within minutes, he was copying his moves. We got Marley some footage of the first concert he ever went to - he heard Muse play Wembley stadium's first ever sell-out gig in June 2007, one month before he was born - and soon Marley was picking up my ridiculously big guitar and copying Matt Bellamy's jumping, kicking, cavorting dances. He'd go on and on about Dave, who has no idea what he's done to deserve such adoration. Then Murdoc came back.

Before we knew it, we'd reformed SCSI to do a charity gig. Next thing we knew, that one-off reunion had attracted a new drummer, Martin, and we're about to relaunch the band. The first gig is at Martin's birthday party next week. He's going to be nineteen.

Marley's had such a profound and beneficial effect on Nicole and myself, but it hasn't escaped my attention how much he's helped other people too. Murdoc loves him, and until now he's really hated children. Now, he gives Marley a hug and a high five and says, "How's it going, Marley?" You can see the hardness of Murdoc's life, and the things he's seen on his travels, evaporate in the smile Marley brings to his face when he dances and rocks out - and he's a great mover. Meanwhile I'm learning 'Dad-dancing'. We sometimes go round to Dave's for tea, where Marley sits reverently, silently taking in the wonders of the shrine of his great rock God. I think we are all grateful for the way he has rekindled our love and appreciation of music, of life, and of each other.

The heir apparent of rock 'n' roll.

IF...

Could I but glimpse through the eyes of a horse

Any horse

Breathe through his, her nose, to smell as strongly as they!

Any horse, even old Cobweb, with his rather poor sense of smell -

Just for a moment, to hear what they can hear...

Swivel my ears around like that - like eyes towards the sound I

Follow a mouse as it scurries across the stable behind me.

To chew sweet meadow herbs in the cool dew

But O to feel the things they feel

The hair - the skin,

To feel the fly and know it is not a horse-fly.

The muscle, the beating heart. To feel! Move as a horse!

The effort as my shoulders lift me up over the jump.

The rider bumps my back as I trot...

Ah, but most of all to know what things they think.

Could I be a horse, just for a day?

I should learn more in each moment than man can teach me in a lifetime.

A.G.

240

Information

To purchase further copies of this and our other books, in the UK and worldwide, and to find out more about attending our Integrated Equitation courses, private intensives and other services that we offer, please visit our new website via either of these links:

www.whisperingback.co.uk
www.integratedequitation.co.uk

Our email is us@whisperingback.co.uk. We love to hear from people who have read our books and we always reply. However we are a little anxious that we may be deluged with letters and emails from people who have suffered the same misfortune we did with PJ, and who are really seeking counselling which we cannot readily provide. We hope those in that position will understand if we are not able to make adequate responses. We recommend contacting the following helpful websites - The Miscarriage Association: www.miscarriageassociation.org.uk or the Stillborn and Neonatal Death Charity: www.uk-sands.org

Our postal address is: Moor Wood Stables, Woodmancote, Cirencester, Glos GL7 7EB.

For information on Intelligent Horsemanship courses, products, demonstrations, and for Recommended Associates in your area, please visit www.intelligenthorsemanship.co.uk.

There are details of more instructors, based in many countries and trained at Monty's home in California, as well as further courses, products, and demonstrations, at www.montyroberts.com.

Monty's new online University can be reached from that website, where a wealth of information is available on subscription.

You can listen to many SCSI tracks at www.worldofscsi.com, or www.myspace.com/worldofscsi. Tell Jonathan if you know him.

Contact Simon Palmer www.into-the-lens.com for a range of great photographic services, including prints of some of the pictures found in this book.